REBUILDING

CHILDREN'S
LIVES

Also from the Boys Town Press

Books

Common Sense Parenting®, English and Spanish
The Well-Managed Classroom
Teaching Social Skills to Youth
Basic Social Skills for Youth
Effective Skills for Child-Care Workers
Building Skills in High-Risk Families: Strategies for the Home-Based Practitioner
The Ongoing Journey: Awakening Spiritual Life in At-Risk Youth
Working with Aggressive Youth
Caring for Youth in Shelters
Unmasking Sexual Con Games, Leader's Guide, Student Guide, Parent Guide
Treating Youth with DSM-IV Disorders: The Role of Social Skill Instruction

Audio/Videotapes

Common Sense Parenting®, Audio Tapes
Helping Your Child Succeed
Teaching Responsible Behavior
Videos for Parents Series
One to One: Personal Listening Tapes for Teens
Sign With Me: A Family Sign Language Curriculum
Read With Me: Sharing the Joy of Storytelling with Your Deaf Toddler

For a free Boys Town Press catalog, call 1-800-282-6657.

Parents or children in trouble or having problems can call the
Boys Town National Hotline anytime, toll-free, at 1-800-448-3000.

REBUILDING CHILDREN'S LIVES

A Blueprint For Treatment Foster Parents

BY
CHRISTENA B. BAKER, LCSW
RAY V. BURKE, Ph.D.
RON W. HERRON
MARIAM A. MOTT, Ph.D.

BOYS TOWN PRESS

BOYS TOWN, NEBRASKA

Rebuilding Children's Lives

Published by The Boys Town Press
Father Flanagan's Boys' Home
Boys Town, Nebraska 68010

Publisher's Cataloging in Publication
(Prepared by Quality Books Inc.)

Baker, Christena B.
     Rebuilding children's lives : a blueprint for Treatment Foster Parents / by Christena B. Baker [... et al.].
     p.cm.
     Includes bibliographical references and index.
     ISBN 0-938510-76-2

     1. Foster home care – Handbooks, manuals, etc. 2. Foster parents – Handbooks, manuals, etc. 3. Father Flanagan's Boys' Home. I. Father Flanagan's Boys' Home. II. Title.

HQ759.B35 1996   362.7'33
                                    QBI96 – 20158

6   7   8   9   10

ACKNOWLEDGMENTS

Many talented people contributed to this writing and we want to take this opportunity to thank them for their generous help. We would like to thank Father Val Peter and Dr. David Coughlin for their leadership and commitment to developing Boys Town's Treatment Foster Family Services. They have inspired us to provide the very highest level of services to our children and their families. Karen Authier, who directed Family-Based Programs at Boys Town, not only provided very helpful suggestions regarding the content of this manual, but also gave us much encouragement and support. We are grateful to her for her guidance in developing Treatment Foster Family Services and for her warm friendship. Andrea Criste wrote the original Boys Town Preservice manual and we appreciate the important foundation she provided for us. Lana Temple-Plotz also contributed significantly to this manual by preparing the drafts of the chapters on Motivation Systems and treatment planning. She also patiently read through many drafts of other chapters. We want to thank her for her tireless work and support.

A special thanks to Jayne Arneil for her thorough work in preparing the glossary and to Kelly Shannon and Craig Ferguson for their suggestions. We also would like to thank Dr. Patrick Friman for the "Time-Out" appendix, and Terry Hyland of the Boys Town Press for his expert editing. The Family Preservation Services staff gave us many helpful suggestions for the chapter entitled "Respecting Cultural Differences in Children and Families." We want to thank them for their willingness to share their expertise with us. Barbara Lonnborg and Lisa Pelto were very helpful in developing the front cover and helping other professionals in the foster care field learn about this new training. This writing could not have been completed without Phyllis Gabbert, who patiently typed and formatted many drafts and sent them to numerous individuals for review. We appreciate her perseverance, her humor, and her professionalism.

Most importantly, we would like to thank the many generous Treatment Parents who exemplified the commitment, thoughtfulness, and tremendous ability that are the most important hallmarks of the program. In addition, we would like to thank the Treatment Foster Family Services staff in all our locations across the country for their creative ideas and tireless work.

Book Credits

Editing	Terry L. Hyland
Cover and Page Design	Rick Schuster
Page Composition	Michael Bourg
Cover Photograph	John Melingagio

PREFACE

This book describes a treatment approach that Boys Town uses to help children and youth who are cared for in Treatment Foster Family Services. Boys Town is a nonprofit, nonsectarian organization dedicated to changing the way America cares for her at-risk children and families. This training material is based on more than 75 years of caring for children who have complex problems and unique needs. Boys Town has many cutting-edge child-care programs to help children, families, and other child-care providers. In 1994, Boys Town provided direct care for more than 24,000 children, directly assisted more than 575,000 children and families through the Boys Town Hotline, and indirectly assisted more than 550,000 children and families through other outreach and training programs.

This book is written for Treatment Parents who want to or have already begun to provide care for foster children. Most Treatment Parents believe they have a lot to give to foster children. Some who already have begun their own families feel they are good parents and are up to the challenge of caring for foster children who have been abused and neglected. Some Treatment Parents do a very good job with little outside assistance. But some become discouraged, because in spite of

their best efforts, the foster child does not respond or, in the beginning, becomes even more difficult to parent. In these situations, some Treatment Parents begin to wonder if they were such good parents in the first place. This training manual is written to assure these Treatment Parents that they are contributing a great deal to the foster child in their care and to offer additional skills to help them be even more successful.

If you are not a Boys Town Treatment Parent, some of this training may not apply directly to how you provide foster care. But we do believe that the basic elements of the training are very appropriate and helpful in providing care to a variety of children in many different types of homes. So as you read the manual, even though the title "Treatment Parent" may not apply to you, we hope that you and your organization can benefit from the information that is presented.

In addition to caring for foster children, many of you also have your own children. We would like to make a suggestion about how this training can be used with the children of Treatment Parents. It has been our experience that having significantly different consequences for biological and foster children who are about the same age is not very successful. For example, it is not helpful to spank your own children as a form of discipline while you cannot use spanking with foster children. When this occurs, it creates tension between the children, appears to create two sets of rules in your home, and generally undermines your position as the authority figure in the home. We suggest that you find ways to use the Boys Town Family Home Model with your own children as much as possible. While we do not have the right to tell you how to parent your children, we do believe that our program is a highly effective way to parent any child. On the whole, if children see that they are treated similarly, conflict will be reduced, your home will run more smoothly, and you will feel more successful.

So although foster children are the focus of this training, we sincerely hope you will use this parenting method with all the children in your home. We know that this method is successful for children who live with their own parents, as well as with those who are in another type of home or in substitute care.

In addition to training its own Treatment Parents, Boys Town provides full Treatment Foster Family Services through contracts with outside agencies and organizations that offer foster care for children. Public or private organizations that are interested in receiving assistance in training, evaluation, supervision, consultation, and administration of Boys Town's program should write or call:

Boys Town National Resource and Training Center

Treatment Foster Family Services
Boys Town Center
14100 Crawford
Boys Town, NE 68010
(402) 498-1556

TABLE OF CONTENTS

Understanding the Child and the Family

Appendices

Glossary

CHAPTER 1

Introduction to Boys Town's Treatment Foster Family Services

From the time he took in five boys from the street in 1917 until his untimely death 31 years later, Father Edward Flanagan sought to provide the best care possible for homeless, troubled children. Starting in a small house in downtown Omaha, Nebraska, the Irish priest eventually moved his "family" of boys to a farm west of the city that would eventually be known as Boys Town.

For years, the boys lived in dormitory-style cottages, the norm for the time. But Father Flanagan dreamed of a village of family homes where children could learn and grow in a family atmosphere. This dream was kept alive through the 1950s and 1960s by Father Flanagan's successor, Father Nicholas Wegner. In 1973, Father Flanagan's vision became reality when then-executive director Father Robert Hupp initiated the Boys Town Family Home Model.

Since that time, Boys Town has extended its reach to help more children and families, establishing itself as a national leader in child care. Under the direction of current executive director, Father Val Peter, Boys Town has created new programs and developed 16 new sites in 14 states and the District of Columbia.

At the core of all of Boys Town's programs is the Family Home Model, which is used to teach children the social, academic, and behavioral skills they need to be successful in life. Although Boys Town has changed as the needs of children have changed, its goals have remained consistent – to instill in children the values of love of God, respect for self and others, hard work, and a good education.

In 1994, more than 24,000 children received direct treatment and care through the many programs Boys Town offers. These include the Boys Town Residential Family Services, the National Resource and Training Center, the Boys Town National Research Hospital, Father Flanagan High School in north Omaha, the Boys Town National Hotline, Boys Town USA Sites, and Boys Town Family-Based Programs.

Residential Family Services is the foundation and source of all training and technology. It is based at the Boys Town Home Campus, the place where more than 550 boys and girls live in 76 family-style homes.

National Resource and Training Center provides training and technical assistance to other child-care organizations around the country.

Boys Town USA® develops wholly-owned and operated Boys Town Sites (both Residential and Family-Based) around the country.

Family-Based Programs, established in the late 1980s, consists of four separate programs: Common Sense Parenting®, Emergency Shelter Services, Family Preservation Services, and the focus of this manual, Treatment Foster Family Services.

The Boys Town Treatment Foster Family Services (TFFS) program is currently operating in 11 cities from Florida to California, New York to New Orleans. Since 1989, Boys Town has provided care for more than 500 children in our Treatment Foster Homes. More than 100 Treatment Parents currently are implementing this program at Boys Town Sites or through other affiliated programs.

The unique strength of this program is that it teaches parents how to encourage positive behavior from their foster children and respond specifically to problematic behaviors by teaching appropriate social skills. The training also shows Treatment Parents how to create an environment that is safe for a child, and gives parents the many tools they need to help children accept responsibility for their behaviors and learn more appropriate ways to get their needs met. The training helps Treatment Parents learn how to motivate a child to change, how to include the child's family in the treatment process, how to parent a sexually abused child, and much more. As a result, children learn how to be successful in foster care, in school, and ultimately, in their own families.

TFFS Hallmarks

Boys Town Treatment Foster Family Services can be summarized in the following five hallmarks, which are standards that describe our mission and commitment to children.

Hallmark 1

Treatment Foster Family Services uses a core of data-based treatment technology as the basis for the design and implementation of the program. This means that the Boys Town Family Home Model is based on 25 years of development, research, and proven effectiveness. Initial development, which took place at the University of Kansas, was funded by the National Institute of Mental Health (NIMH) in the early 1970s. Since that time, the Model has been adapted for Treatment Foster Family Services. As with all Boys Town programs, TFFS:

- Is safe and humane.
- Is behaviorally based.
- Focuses on skill development.
- Can be replicated in other cities or towns.
- Satisfies the people receiving our services.

Treatment is the key service we provide. Treatment Foster Family Services is not simply a foster care program to care for more difficult children, but a treatment program defined by a set of treatment principles and technology.

Research has shown that the Boys Town teaching method is effective in helping each child develop skills, as well as in promoting strong positive relationships between the child and the foster family. Over the course of treatment (average of about one year), about three-fourths of all presenting problems improve, and most children successfully achieve treatment goals prior to discharge. Nearly two-thirds of children leave Treatment Foster Family Services to live in a less-structured setting, such as with a family member, an adoptive family, or another foster care program. Three months after a child leaves our program, about three-fourths of the families rate their overall relationship with the child as "somewhat" or "much" better than when the child was initially placed in Treatment Foster Family Services (Mott, Authier, Shannon, Arneil, & Daly, 1995).

Hallmark 2

Treatment Foster Family Services provides intensive consultation and support for Treatment Parents. Boys Town believes that Treatment Parents are the most important treatment providers for the children in their care. They spend more time with the children than anyone else, and teach the skills that each child needs to develop.

Although Treatment Parents are the primary treatment providers, they cannot be expected to take on such a task alone. That's why our staff includes Consultants, highly-trained professionals who work with Treatment Parents to design and review Treatment Plans, ensure that the program is used correctly, and coordinate the child's treatment with the rest of the treatment team. (The responsibilities of the Consultant and other administrative staff members are described later in this chapter.)

Consultants initially meet with Treatment Parents in their homes every week to discuss the various aspects of the placement and treatment issues, and to provide encouragement and support. The number of visits may eventually be reduced to no less than two a month once the child stabilizes and the Treatment Parents have developed strategies to effectively manage the child's behavior. Each Consultant typically works with six to eight children in six families, but caseloads may vary depending upon the seriousness of the child's problems, the Treatment Parents' skill and experience, whether siblings are placed together, and travel requirements. Consultants also carry pagers, making them available 24 hours a day, seven days a week, for crisis situations.

In addition to regular consultation meetings, a Consultant observes how the Treatment Parents and the children interact on a regular basis (twice a month initially), then talks with the Treatment Parents about what was observed. This includes reinforcing or praising the things the Treatment Parents are doing well and making suggestions about how they can improve their skills.

During the first portion of the child's placement, a Consultant probably will have daily phone contact with the Treatment Parents. As the placement progresses, telephone contact decreases to an as-needed basis. Throughout the placement, however, Treatment Parents are required each day to report any significant events involving the child that occurred during the previous 24 hours.

In addition to Consultants, another valuable source of support for Treatment Parents is other Treatment Parents. Treatment Parents are encouraged from the beginning of Preservice Training to get to know one another. This networking is encouraged on an ongoing basis during monthly or bimonthly inservice meetings, social events, and informal contact.

Hallmark 3

Individualized Treatment Plans are developed on the basis of referral information; assessments are conducted in the Treatment Home and are formally reviewed monthly by the treatment team. It is standard procedure in the Boys Town program to develop and review Treatment Plans for each child in placement. These plans then can be revised to correspond to the child's changing treatment needs. The Treatment Parents

and Consultant first identify the behaviors that are most important to change; these are called "target behaviors." Target behaviors are described very clearly, treatment strategies are selected and defined, and goals are established. Every 30 days after this, the Treatment Plan for each target behavior is formally reviewed and updated if necessary. Chapter 18 reviews the treatment planning process in detail.

Hallmark 4

Staff and Treatment Parents are trained before beginning their work using a skill-based and competency-based approach.

Staff Training: Professional staff hired for Treatment Foster Family Services are required to complete a comprehensive training program prior to working with families and children. In this training, Consultants learn how to use the Boys Town treatment approach. Consultants practice and become competent in the skills they will train Treatment Parents to use. Following this training, Consultants further develop their skills by observing experienced Consultants as they work with Treatment Parents and other professionals. Boys Town also offers a variety of other advanced workshops as Consultants gain experience in the field.

Treatment Parent Training: Treatment Parents complete approximately 35 hours of Preservice Training, during which they practice the skills they will use to provide treatment to foster children. They must demonstrate an ability to use these skills in order to graduate from Preservice. This manual contains the topics (e.g. teaching social skills and problem-solving, preventing confrontations, child rights) that are taught in Preservice Training.

Boys Town's services are provided in an environment that advocates strong child-care technology, and respects Treatment Parents, recognizing their role as an integral part of the professional treatment team. Our teaching methods are used not only in Boys Town's Treatment Foster Family Services around the country, but also are being successfully used in therapeutic foster care programs operated by other private and public agencies.

Hallmark 5

Consultants and Treatment Parents are expected to achieve and maintain a specified level of competence and performance.

Consultants: Consultants are expected to meet Boys Town's standards for delivering services to foster families and children in placement. These services include technical assistance, training, support, etc. To ensure quality, a certification process is conducted annually for all Consultants. The process includes directly observing the Consultant's skills, reviewing files to assess quality of treatment, and soliciting input from other members of the team (e.g. Treatment Parents, caseworkers, supervisors, etc.) to determine their satisfaction with services provided by the Consultant.

Treatment Parents: Treatment Parents are expected to have a basic understanding of and ability to implement Boys Town's program when they complete Preservice Training. Consultants meet with Treatment Parents at least once a week for several months to continue developing the Treatment Parents' skills. After six months of service, program staff evaluate the Treatment Parents' progress to determine if they are acquiring and developing the skills they need to deliver effective treatment and to become certified. Treatment Parents are evaluated again after providing treatment foster care for one year. Certification depends upon satisfactory ratings on "consumer" surveys answered by caseworkers, biological parents, school personnel, program staff, etc. All evaluations also include in-home observation visits conducted by two trained evaluators. These evaluators look at Treatment Parents' and youth skills, conduct a youth consumer questionnaire, and inspect specific licensing requirements. Certification evaluations are completed annually, and passing certification may be linked to an increase in the "per diem" (daily) stipend for the Treatment Parents.

Program: To assist Treatment Parents with their responsibilities, Boys Town has developed clearly defined support services which fall under the categories of administration, training, consultation, and evaluation. Each Treatment Foster Family Services Site undergoes a regular review of each part of the program. This helps us make sure that all of our programs across the country provide a high level of quality and consistency.

TFFS Staffing

Each Site where Boys Town provides TFFS and other programs is staffed by an administrative team of professionals, experienced in the Family Home Model, who are there to help the Treatment Parents and foster children. These professionals are the Site Director, the Treatment Foster Family Services Coordinator, and the Consultant. (The chart on Page 5 is an example of the administrative organization of a Boys Town Treatment Foster Family Services program. The numbers of Consultants, Treatment Parents, and foster children may vary from program to program.)

The Site Director is responsible for making sure that all of the Boys Town programs at the Site are running smoothly and working together to help the children and families being served. In other programs, this position may be the Agency Director.

The Treatment Foster Family Services Coordinator has the specific responsibility of ensuring that the children in foster care are receiving appropriate treatment. The Coordinator supervises the Consultants (see organizational chart), works closely with state agencies that refer children, and generally watches over every aspect of the program to ensure that children are getting better. In other programs, the person with these responsibilities is often referred to as the Supervisor.

The Consultant works with the Treatment Parents to design and review Treatment Plans, and to ensure that the program is being implemented appropriately. The Consultant also works with other people on the child's treatment team (e.g. the child's family, state caseworkers, courts, schools, and therapists) to make sure the child is getting the help he or she needs. The number of Consultants hired by each Site is determined by the number of the children that are placed in the program. Each Consultant is responsible for six to eight foster children. In other agencies, this person frequently is referred to as the caseworker or social worker.

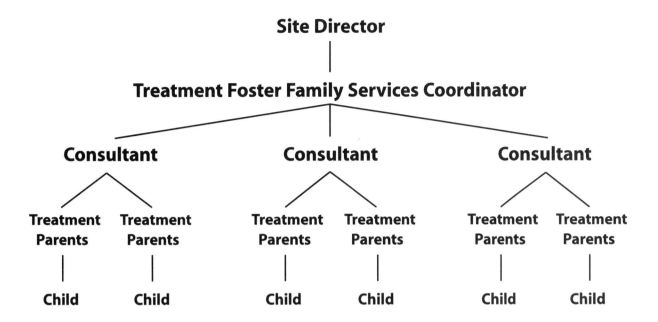

Treatment Parenting

The responsibilities of Treatment Parents are numerous and varied. They must meet state licensing standards and be willing and able to use the skills taught in Preservice Training while a foster child lives in their home. They serve one, and occasionally two, children who have emotional and behavioral problems. (The role of the Treatment Parent is described in detail in Chapter 3, "The Professional Treatment Parent.")

Children in treatment foster care bring with them histories of instability in their own families created by such factors as alcoholism, various kinds of abuse, mental health problems, abandonment, death, etc. This instability is seen in the children through a variety of problems such as delayed academic progress, delinquent behavior, substance abuse, social skill deficits, and/or emotional disturbance. Typically, the child will have experienced multiple failed placements in traditional foster care homes and may have been placed in more-restrictive settings, such as group homes or psychiatric hospitals. Treatment Parents must be prepared to treat the child's problems and then to promote normal emotional and social development.

Before Treatment Parents make a commitment to begin the placement process with a specific child, they are strongly encouraged to answer the following questions:

1. Are we willing to work with a child who has a lot to learn and may be a slow learner?
2. How will this new child in our home affect members of our family, relatives, friends?
3. What changes in our lifestyle will occur as a result of providing a home to a troubled child?
4. Are we willing to take the time to implement the child's Treatment Plan and complete the daily paperwork and reporting?
5. Are we willing to work cooperatively with the parents of the foster child living in our home?
6. Are we willing to have the Consultant meet with us in our home on a frequent basis?
7. Are we willing to attend periodic staff meetings/conferences which involve the child (e.g. court hearings, school conferences, case reviews, etc.)?
8. Are we willing to accept the temporary nature of providing Treatment Foster Family Services?
9. What qualities do we possess that would make us good Treatment Parents?

Summary

Parents who are considering the challenges and rewards of becoming Treatment Parents are encouraged to make a thoughtful decision based on a realistic understanding of the program, the demands of parenting a treatment child, and their individual and family strengths and resources. Treatment Parents are encouraged to be active participants in the training, ask questions, and take some risks in developing new skills and knowledge. We thank you for your interest and desire to help children and to become our partners in caring for some of America's most valuable and vulnerable citizens.

CHAPTER 2

Creating a Safe Environment

You may have read in the paper about children who have been neglected or physically or sexually abused in detention facilities, group homes, or foster homes. It is completely unacceptable for a child to be mistreated, but sometimes it is hard to know exactly how to care for children with behavior difficulties in a way that doesn't harm them in some way. For instance:

- Is it okay to restrain a child who is trying to bite other children and who hits you when you try to guide him into a time-out chair?
- Is it okay to withhold a meal from a child when she throws her food or repeatedly disobeys your instructions to use table manners?
- Is it okay to deny a child a home visit because he refuses to follow most of your family's house rules when he returns?

We live in the real world and know that it is somewhat difficult to decide what is and what is not acceptable when the child's unique personality and a specific situation are taken into consideration. As an organization, we have developed a list of Child Rights to help us ensure that the care and treatment a child receives is safe and promotes growth. Some of these rights are the result of laws or court decisions. Some grew out of our own experience of caring for thousands of children for more than 75 years. All of these rights are built around caring for children in the least-restrictive environment possible.

Boys Town believes that children have the right to live in an environment that is safe and promotes spiritual, emotional, intellectual, and physical growth. The Boys Town approach to promote safe environments is built into our entire program. The following list includes the components we use to create and promote a safe environment for the children in our care:

1. Policies and Procedures
2. Training in Positive Interaction Styles
3. Ongoing Program Evaluation
4. Regular Foster Child Interviews
5. Feedback from Outside Consumers
6. Training in the Rights of Foster Children
7. Child Rights Violation Inquiries

Information from these various components is constantly used to update and modify the program as it becomes necessary to ensure safe, humane care.

Policies and Procedures

Each Treatment Parent is given a copy of the written policies and procedures, which include a description of the rights of foster children. These policies and procedures not only emphasize the intent of the program, but also outline the steps followed when potential policy violations occur. Policies and procedures are discussed in Preservice Training, and each Treatment Parent receives a Policy and Procedure Manual to read and study. Treatment Parents are responsible for asking their trainer or Consultant about anything in the manual they don't understand.

Training in Positive Interaction Styles

All Treatment Parents are trained in positive ways to interact with or help foster children change their behaviors, while respecting their basic dignity and freedom. Also, Treatment Parents are trained in promoting positive relationships with foster children by using Effective Praise® and other skills. This training is covered in more detail later in this manual.

Ongoing Program Evaluation

Supervisors, Consultants/case managers, and Treatment Parents should receive systematic feedback through regular evaluation reports. These reports give staff and Treatment Parents insight into the quality of care they are providing for foster children. (Your Consultant will teach you more about the evaluation process used in Treatment Foster Family Services.) Routine updates on important behaviors like school attendance and progress, runaways, and changes in referral behaviors also help to maintain overall program quality and ensure that treatment goals are achieved as quickly as possible. One way Boys Town does this is by regularly looking to see whether a foster child's Treatment Plan is helping to accomplish his or her treatment goals. In addition, the quality of treatment that Treatment Parents provide for a foster child is evaluated through the "Certification" process, which will be described in more detail later.

Regular Foster Child Interviews

In addition to routine conversations with the child during consultation, each foster child is formally interviewed at least twice a year. During these interviews (Youth Consumers), the foster child is asked if he or she has been mistreated by the Treatment Parents or others. The foster child also is asked to express his or her opinion about the pleasantness and support of the Treatment Parents and others. These questions provide important information regarding the atmosphere in the home. Information taken from these questions can be used to improve the Treatment Parents' interaction and communication skills or to confirm that they are using the program well.

Feedback from Outside Consumers

"Consumers" – interested and involved persons from outside the treatment foster care program (teachers, probation officers, the foster child's family, etc.) – are another important source of information about the quality of care provided. Consumers are asked their opinion about the care and treatment the foster child is receiving at least once a year. Again, this helps to confirm that the foster child is receiving appropriate services, and indicates where changes may be necessary.

Training in the Rights of Foster Children

All Boys Town Treatment Parents receive training to increase their awareness of the rights of foster children. Typically, this training will occur before they work with foster children. Following Preservice Training, Treatment Parents are updated about foster child rights issues during consultation and through the program's materials and inservice training.

Fifteen major child rights are introduced in this chapter. These are not all-inclusive, but give a good overview of the training content. For each of these 15 areas there are both rules and guidelines. Certain priorities are called rules because they are rarely modified. In the very few circumstances when rules might be modified, the Consultant/case manager/ program supervisor must grant permission in advance. Guidelines are less absolute. They serve as guiding principles around which Treatment Parents must exercise discretion and sound judgment. Guidelines are considered to be good practices under most situations.

Right to Nourishment

Treatment Parents must provide each foster child with healthy food and proper nutrition.

Rules:
1. Treatment Parents must provide three nutritionally sound meals to the foster child each and every day.

2. The three main meals (breakfast, lunch, and dinner) should never be withheld as punishment or sold as a privilege. A foster child has a right to these because he or she is a person.
3. Meals should never be made intentionally less adequate, less tasty, or less nutritious for any reason.
4. Medical advice and guardian consent should be obtained before starting weight-loss programs.

Guidelines:
1. Treatment Parents should provide a wide variety of nutritious foods for the foster child, including ethnic preferences.
2. Treatment Parents should avoid imposing personal food preferences on foster children (e.g. vegetarian or sugar-free diets) or fad diets (e.g. eggs and grapefruit for each meal).
3. While some snacks (e.g. sweet snacks) can be sold as a privilege, nutritious snacks such as fruits or vegetables should be made freely available (e.g. apples after school).
4. "Junk food" (chips, Big Macs, etc.) should be available only in moderation. Totally prohibiting "junk food" usually is unreasonable and unenforceable.

Example: Michael returns home late from a visit with his family. Dinner has been over for several hours and the kitchen clean-up is finished. The Treatment Parent tells Michael that because he missed dinner, they will have to fix some something else. The foster father suggests a peanut butter and jelly sandwich and some milk and fruit. Is that okay? Why or why not?

Right to Communicate with Significant Others

Treatment Parents should actively teach foster children how to appropriately communicate with others. Healthy relationships with significant others are desirable for all foster children.

Rules:
1. Foster children have a right to seek help or communicate with significant others such as parents, legal guardians, probation officers, or clergy.
2. Communication with significant others should not be used as a consequence or sold as a privilege (e.g. Because Johnny did not apologize to his Treatment Parents, he cannot call his mother).
3. Treatment Parents should provide methods (e.g. mail or phone) for routine and emergency contact with significant others.
4. Treatment Parents should advocate for each foster child's right to directly present his or her own case in any formal or informal proceeding.

Guidelines:
1. Treatment Parents can exercise reasonable control over the form, frequency (e.g. two long-distance calls per month), and timing of communication (e.g. calling probation officer when child is calm).
2. Control over the form, frequency, and timing of communication should not be unreasonable. For example, even though a foster child is not calm, he or she can call a legal guardian after there has been a reasonable attempt to calm the child.

Example: The foster mother is talking with Sara, who is angry, yelling, and threatening to run away. Sara demands to call her probation officer. The foster mother tries to discourage her from calling while she is so angry. Is that okay? Why or why not?

Right to Respect of Body and Person

Treatment Parents should use interaction styles that are as pleasant as possible and that demonstrate humane, professional, concerned care at all times. Physical contact (e.g. guidance, restraint) is strongly discouraged and should be used only after attempts to verbally calm the foster child have proven ineffective and the foster child is endangering himself or herself or others.

Rules:
1. Corporal (i.e. physical) punishment or threats of corporal punishment should never be used to discipline foster children (e.g. hitting, spanking, or physical exercise).
2. Treatment Parents should use passive restraint only as a last resort, when it is necessary to prevent a foster child from harming himself or herself or others, and only after receiving permission from the Consultant. Mechanical restraints or locking a foster child in or out of a room or house are never used.
3. Any use of passive restraint should be reported to the Consultant as soon as possible.
4. Treatment Parents should avoid sarcasm, labeling, or name-calling; such practices can humiliate a foster child (e.g. discussing John's bed-wetting with members of the family).
5. The use of curse words, threats, or yelling directed toward the foster child is never appropriate.

Guidelines:
1. Passive restraint, if necessary, is most successful when the adult has physical superiority because it prevents injury.
2. The least possible force should be employed when passive restraint is required.

Example: Eleven-year-old José has just been restricted from going to his friend's house because he came in two hours late the night before. He is yelling, cursing, and walking around. José shakes his fist at the Treatment Parent and says, "If you don't let me leave this house, I'll hit you." The foster father then tells José that he is acting like a "baby" and takes the boy by the arm, pushes him into a chair, and holds him there until he calms down. Is that okay? Why or why not?

Right to Have One's Own Possessions

Each foster child has a right to possessions that are in keeping with his or her developmental level and living situation. Treatment Parents should respect a foster child's right to possessions and should create a home atmosphere that encourages the foster child to own personal possessions.

Rules:
1. Treatment Parents should ensure that foster children do not possess dangerous items (e.g. drugs, guns, knives).
2. Treatment Parents should ensure that foster children have the necessary materials for school or a job, and that these are similar to their peers' (e.g. books, clothes, bedding).
3. Treatment Parents should never permanently take away a foster child's possessions (other than dangerous possessions) unless the foster child waives his or her right to the possession or unless the possession is taken away so that it can be turned over to the foster child's legal guardian.

Guidelines:
1. Treatment Parents can exercise reasonable control over the possessions foster children bring into the home (e.g. no illegal or stolen property, no pagers).
2. Treatment Parents can limit the use of personal possessions to reasonable times or places (e.g. no stereo played after bedtime).
3. If a foster child is restricted from appropriate use of his or her personal possessions, he or she should be told how to earn back the use of the possessions.

Example: Thomas has a set of headphones that he likes to wear after dinner. He wears them most of the evening and it is very difficult to talk with him. The Treatment Parents become frustrated and decide to take them when Thomas is at school so that he will stop wearing them so much. They tell their Consultant that they will give the headphones back to Thomas "in the future." Is that okay? Why or why not?

Right to Privacy

Under the right to privacy, Treatment Parents should ensure that each foster child has the rights typically given to people in our society. Each foster child should have adequate personal living space and storage areas. Each foster child's right to physical privacy should be protected.

Rules:
1. Treatment Parents should not open a foster child's mail or listen in on phone conversations without permission from the foster child or a written request to do so from the legal guardian.
2. Treatment Parents should not conduct routine, secret searches of a foster child's room or belongings.
3. Treatment Parents should never search a foster child's body.
4. Treatment Parents can release program records only to a foster child's legal guardian or persons who have written permission from a foster child's legal guardian.

Guidelines:
1. Treatment Parents should assure that privacy is available in the foster child's living space and for his or her belongings (e.g. bed, dresser, clothes).

2. Public searches (which are announced and with the foster child and one other adult present) may take place when there is probable cause to search and with prior permission from the Consultant and Coordinator.
3. While Treatment Parents should not open and read a foster child's mail, a child can be asked to open mail in front of the Treatment Parents when they have probable cause to believe the mail contains dangerous contents (e.g. a foster child receiving drugs from a friend).

Example: Tracy has been caught on several occasions under the influence of drugs. In an effort to curb this drug use, the foster mother and Consultant decide to search Tracy's room after she gets home from school so she can be present. Is that okay? Why or why not?

Right to Freedom of Movement

Each foster child has a right to a wide range of experiences according to his or her age and maturity level. Procedures that physically restrict movement or consequences that don't allow exposure to healthy activities for extended periods of time are generally discouraged.

Rules:
1. Treatment Parents must not use seclusion or isolation as a discipline practice (e.g. child is locked in a room or isolated from the family).
2. A foster child should always be provided with options for earning privileges.

Guidelines:
1. Treatment Parents can limit a foster child's movements to a given area and time (e.g. in school from 8 a.m. to 4:15 p.m., at home from 4:30 p.m. to 6 p.m.).

2. "Time-out" is an acceptable procedure for certain children, provided that it is an approved part of that child's Treatment Plan.

Example: Alex, 10-year-old foster child, disrupts dinner by failing to follow instructions, accept "No," and keep his hands and feet to himself. The foster father finally has had it and sends Alex to his room for the rest of the evening. Is that okay? Why or why not?

Right Not to Be Given Meaningless Work

Treatment Parents should ensure that each foster child lives in an environment where chores, tasks, goals, and privileges are meaningful learning experiences. Ideally, consequences for problem behaviors will have immediate teaching benefits and should not be principally punishing in nature.

Rules:
1. Treatment Parents should never give "make work" tasks (e.g. cleaning a floor with a toothbrush, digging a hole and refilling it, or writing sentences 500 times).
2. Procedures that are designed solely to punish the foster child should not be used (e.g. having the foster child kneel and hold a broom above his or her head, or eat a catsup sandwich as a consequence for squirting catsup on someone).
3. Foster children should be paid according to the prevailing wage and hour laws when performing personal work for Treatment Parents (e.g. doing the Treatment Parents' personal laundry) or doing tasks that benefit the organization (e.g. hanging recruitment posters).

Guidelines:
1. Treatment Parents can assign chores and tasks related to daily living that teach family

or personal values (e.g. making one's bed or doing family dishes).
2. Removal from typical responsibilities (e.g. jobs, athletic teams, clubs, lessons, or church) should not routinely be a consequence for problem behaviors. Note: While a foster child sometimes must be removed from these activities, this should be done only when the behavior is so serious that it negates the benefit of continued participation.

Example: David has been arguing with his foster sister about many things throughout the day. Finally, the foster mother gets fed up with David's arguing and tells him that if he has so much energy for arguing, he needs to go vacuum the van. Is that okay? Why or why not?

Right to See Written Material and to Disagree with Its Contents

Treatment Parents should inform the foster children about what is being written about them in daily paperwork. Written documentation should be consistent with daily treatment strategies and target areas. Good Treatment Parent care means that foster children know their treatment goals and their progress on these goals; when it is appropriate for their age, foster children should be involved in the treatment planning process.

Rules:
1. Treatment Parents should not deny the foster child the right to know what is written in Progress Reports.
2. Treatment Parents should be present whenever a foster child is reviewing file material.
3. Treatment Parents must ensure that all file material is stored in a secure space.

Guidelines:
1. Consultants/program supervisors may routinely have the foster child sign Progress Reports when it is age-appropriate.
2. Sensitive file materials (e.g. psychological evaluations or social histories) should be stored in a central file outside of the foster home. This makes it less likely that the foster child will be exposed to confusing or emotionally laden material.

Example: Christina has read her Progress Report and doesn't think that it was fair. She thinks that her caseworker will get the impression that she isn't trying and will delay her scheduled return home. The Consultant and Treatment Parents encourage Christina to sign the report so that everyone will know that she had a chance to read it. So that the caseworker will understand that Christina doesn't agree with the report, she is encouraged to write her opinion of her progress on the report before it is mailed to her family and caseworker. The Treatment Parents and Consultant then talk with Christina about how the Treatment Plan should be revised to help her meet her goals by the next review period. Is that okay? Why or why not?

Right to Interact with Others

Foster children should be taught skills that enhance their relationships with peers and adults. Foster children should be provided with ample opportunities to interact with peers of the same and opposite sex. Treatment Parents should monitor the foster child's social contacts to ensure that they are appropriate.

Rules:
1. Isolation should not be used as a consequence for problem behaviors (e.g. instructing other children not to talk to a foster child as a consequence for a problem behavior). Time-out may be an appropriate consequence for some foster children; this type of consequence should be an approved part of the Treatment Plan.
2. Treatment Parents must provide the foster child with appropriate opportunities to interact with the opposite sex.

Guidelines:
1. Treatment Parents may limit interactions between foster children and their peers (e.g. foster children with known substance abuse or sexual development problems may be limited or supervised more closely in their interactions with peers until these treatment issues are addressed). Treatment Parents and Consultants will discuss and decide on a case-by-case basis whether teenagers in the program may go on a "date." It is important to remember that the child is in treatment foster care for specific reasons and that he or she should receive close supervision.
2. Treatment Parents may limit when and how the foster child interacts with peers (e.g. no wrestling, no playing in bedrooms with doors closed, etc.).

Example: Mary has an extreme problem with cursing. In order to help her overcome this problem, the Treatment Parents decide on a new rule. It states that whenever Mary curses, no one is to speak to her for an hour. Is that okay? Why or why not?

Right to Basic Clothing Necessities

Foster children should be provided with appropriate dress and leisure clothing in keeping with their age and sex. Treatment Parents should ensure that each foster child's basic clothing needs are met at all times.

Rules:

1. Basic clothing needs should never be restricted as a negative consequence for problem behavior (e.g. foster child doesn't get a replacement coat as a consequence for losing one).
2. Each foster child has a right to the same style, type, and quantity of clothing that is provided for other children in the home.

Guidelines:

1. A foster child's preference in clothing should be strongly considered by Treatment Parents so long as the personal preference is not extremely deviant in regard to style or price (e.g. neither "punk" or gang styles nor designer quality need to be provided).
2. Treatment Parents can limit the style of clothing to be consistent with the treatment goals of an individual foster child (e.g. sexually provocative clothing should not be worn).

Example: David is upset because he received what he thinks is an unfair consequence. He has said that he is going to run away from the program. To keep him from running away, the Treatment Parents take his shoes. Is that okay? Why or why not?

Right to the Natural Elements

Each foster child has a right to natural elements such as fresh air, light, and outdoor exercise. Healthy outdoor activities should be a routine part of every foster child's experience. Treatment Parents should ensure that foster children have the opportunity to experience the natural elements each day.

Rules:

1. Access to the natural elements and indoor light should not be used as a consequence.

Guidelines:

1. Foster children should be provided with the opportunity for outside activities each day (e.g. walking to and from school or playing in the yard).
2. Treatment Parents can regulate the amount of time spent outside and the degree of supervision provided for the foster child.
3. It is acceptable to reduce the amount of play time outside as a consequence. If possible, foster children should be given a chance to earn some of this time back by engaging in appropriate behavior.

Example: For several days, six-year-old Russel has not gotten along with other children while playing in the yard. He appears to become very aggressive with the other children when he thinks they are "not playing fair." The foster mother decides to take away Russel's privilege to play outside for three days as a punishment. Is that okay? Why or why not?

Right to One's Own Bed

Each foster child has a right to a personal bed and a private sleeping area or room shared with another child of the same sex and similar age.

Rules:

1. A foster child's access to a personal bed or bedding should never be restricted during normal sleeping hours.

Guidelines:

1. Treatment Parents may have more than one child share a bedroom provided that ample space (according to state licensing guidelines) and privacy are assured.
2. Treatment Parents may regulate a foster child's access to his or her bedroom during nonsleeping hours or limit privacy of sleeping

arrangements when a foster child is at-risk (especially when a foster child is suicidal).

3. Treatment Parents may use earlier bedtime as a negative consequence or later bedtime as a positive consequence, within reason and in keeping with the foster child's Treatment Plan. As with other consequences, this should be discussed with your Consultant prior to using it with the child.

Example: The foster family is having relatives come visit for the holidays. They don't have enough beds for everyone, so the foster parents decide to have the kids double up in their beds. The 12-year-old foster daughter is asked to sleep with the foster parents' 10-year-old daughter. Is that okay? Why or why not?

Right to Visit Family in the Family Home and to Receive Visits

Rules:
1. Each foster child may visit his or her family and receive visits, unless otherwise stated in his or her Treatment Plan and specified, in writing, by his or her legal guardian.
2. Treatment Parents are expected to help provide or arrange for transportation to and from parental visits if necessary.
3. Foster children do not have to "earn" visits with their families unless the legal guardian agrees in writing that it is in a foster child's best interest to make visits dependent on the child's behavior.
4. The length or setting of the visit can be modified to provide the type and amount of structure necessary to promote a positive visiting environment for the foster child.

Guidelines:
1. Treatment Parents may host the foster child's visits with his or her family in their own (foster parents') home if they volunteer to do so. The foster family is under no obligation to do so or to supervise visits if they occur elsewhere.
2. Treatment Parents should support the foster child in developing the best relationship possible with his or her family and extended family.

Example: Sherri had been living with the Parkers for two weeks when her first home visit was scheduled. The Parkers had read Sherri's social history prior to her placement and they were surprised and saddened that Sherri had gone through so much in her young life. Although the Parkers knew that home visits were a part of Sherri's Treatment Plan, they were convinced that seeing the people who had hurt her would not be in her best interest. The Parkers had met Sherri's parents at the Preplacement Meeting. Sherri was scheduled to have a home visit every other week. When Sherri returned from the home visit, she was argumentative, refused to eat her dinner with the rest of the family, and complained that she was "in prison." The Parkers decided to cancel her next three visits with her family because they felt the visits were too upsetting to her. Is that okay? Why or why not?

Right to Participate in Treatment Planning and to Refuse Any Specific Therapy or Medication Unless Those Rights Have Been Limited by Law or Court Order

Rules:
1. Each foster child is provided care in accordance with his or her reasonable wishes and that of his or her legal guardian.

2. The foster child and his or her guardian are encouraged to participate in the treatment planning process.
3. Should the foster child refuse treatment, he or she will be informed of the consequences, which may include removal from the program. The foster child may be discharged from the program if the staff believe the refusal of treatment or medication jeopardizes the safety of the foster child or the Treatment Family, or is inconsistent with the therapeutic goals of a community-based placement.

Guidelines:
1. Boys Town staff and Treatment Parents are encouraged to make reasonable efforts to resolve the foster child's or guardian's concerns regarding the implementation of treatment.
2. Boys Town staff and Treatment Parents are expected to be sensitive to cultural and racial issues when developing Treatment Plans and selecting professional treatment providers in the community.

Example: Miguel was in a psychiatric hospital for seven weeks before he moved into a treatment foster home. Part of Miguel's Treatment Plan when he was discharged from the hospital included a recommendation that he start individual therapy when he moved to the treatment foster home. Miguel said he would do this if it would help him get out of the hospital. After living in the treatment foster home three weeks, he said he was "tired of being in therapy" and didn't want to "start all over again with a new therapist." Miguel was cooperating with the rest of his Treatment Plan. Should Miguel be forced to begin individual therapy? Why or why not?

The Right to Lodge a Complaint or Appeal
Rules:
1. Each foster child and his or her parent(s) or legal guardian have the right to express a grievance or complaint.
2. Grievances should first be expressed to the foster child's Boys Town Consultant. If the person making the complaint is not satisfied with the response, he or she should next contact the Boys Town Coordinator, then the Site Director, and finally the Regional Director or National Director, to resolve the complaint.

Guidelines:
1. Boys Town staff and Treatment Parents should make every reasonable effort to address and resolve complaints so as to provide the highest level of care possible to the foster child.
2. Reasonable efforts should be made to resolve conflict so that the foster child can experience the least amount of disruptions in his or her placement as possible.

Example: Terrance, who just turned 16, was scheduled to take driver's education at school. He very much wanted to get his driver's license. Terrance talked with his Treatment Parents and Consultant about his desire to drive. They told him that driving a vehicle on his own was against Boys Town policy. Terrance then talked to his parents and they agreed with him. His parents thought Terrance should have the chance to drive like everyone else, and they were willing to buy him a used car if he paid for the insurance and gas.

Terrance and his parents made an appointment and met with the Coordinator of Treatment Foster Family Services. The parents explained their request to the Coordinator, who maintained that it was against the program's policy to allow foster children to drive or own a vehicle. She also explained that treatment foster children are sometimes in our program because of problems with impulsiveness, poor anger control, and/or suicidal thoughts. The Coordinator commented that it was not always easy to know which foster children could safely drive, and which foster child might pose a safety risk. So, Boys Town has a "blanket" policy that foster children cannot drive.

Terrance and his family appealed this decision to the Site Director and finally to the National Director. Boys Town did not change the policy. Terrance and his family were disappointed but decided that it was important for Terrance to remain in treatment foster care and that he would have to wait until he had completed his treatment to own a car and drive. Is that okay? Why or why not?

Additional Standards
Consequences

Treatment Parents should not use or engage in the following:

1. Severe or nonprogram consequences such as having a foster child sit in the car while the rest of the family participates in an outing.

2. Withholding a foster child's personal possessions without contacting the Consultant.

3. Taking away a foster child's allowance or other money as a consequence, unless money is being used as part of the child's Motivation System.

4. Restricting a foster child from talking to his or her parents or other family members as a consequence for misbehavior. If a Treatment Parent believes a foster child cannot have a minimally successful visit with his or her family due to current behavioral problems, the Treatment Parent must contact the Consultant prior to taking any steps to cancel the visit.

Modeling

The following is a list of examples of inappropriate modeling:

1. Inappropriate teasing or humiliation of a foster child (i.e. using racial slurs, put-downs based on religion, background, parents, etc.). This also includes sexual harassment.

2. Indiscreet or excessive use of alcohol; DWI violations.

3. Use of illegal drugs.

4. Swearing at foster children or other family members.

5. Showing movies with sexually provocative or violent scenes to foster children, or allowing them access to such movies (e.g. having X-rated videos in the home).

6. Indiscreet display of sexual behaviors in front of foster children, including pinching, prolonged kissing, and inappropriate dress by parents; extramarital affairs.

7. Verbal aggression toward consumers, including becoming visibly upset in public, yelling or cursing at parents, teachers, or administrators, etc.

Coercion

Examples of coercion or intimidating a foster child to do something include:

1. Coaching a foster child on how to answer the Youth Consumer, which is a part of the Treatment Parents' evaluation process.

2. Offering a foster child bribes of money or other rewards for positive responses on the Youth Consumer.

3. Individually interviewing a foster child about the ratings he or she gave on a Youth Consumer.

4. Telling a foster child what to tell or not tell his or her parents or program staff regarding the foster family.

Neglect

The following are examples of neglect of a foster child's basic care:

1. Neglecting a foster child's medical care.

Examples include failing to give a foster child medication, improperly giving medication, not keeping a medical log, and failing to get the foster child to doctor or dentist appointments.

2. Serving nutritionally inadequate meals. Examples of this include poorly prepared meals, nutritionally poor foods, or lack of variety (all hot dogs, frozen pizza, etc.).

3. Failure to report dangerous behavior of the foster child (including behavior in which the child injures himself or herself), or suicide statements, ideations, or gestures.

4. Failure to adequately monitor the foster child.

Abuse

The following are examples of abuse of a foster child:

1. Using physical restraints (other than safety restraints while driving). (On rare occasions, and with prior approval of and supervision by the Consultant, the Treatment Parent may need to physically assist a foster child who is a danger to himself or herself or others.)

2. Slapping, pushing, shoving, grabbing, punching, hitting, or throwing objects at a foster child with the intent to hurt him or her.

3. Body searches.

Professionalism

The following are examples of lack of professionalism:

1. Failing to report serious incidents regarding the foster child.

2. Refusing to cooperate or being dishonest during a Child Rights Violation Inquiry.

3. Serious or consistent refusal to accept or implement feedback.

4. Mismanaging a foster child's money.

5. Violating confidentiality.

6. Intentionally risky or unsafe driving with a foster child.

7. Openly complaining about the foster care program or other professionals on the foster child's team including the state caseworker, judge, therapist, etc. Concerns of this nature should be addressed with your Consultant. If Treatment Parents have concerns about their Consultant or other staff, these concerns should first be addressed with that staff member and then his or her supervisor if necessary.

Religion

The following are examples of inappropriate behaviors regarding religious activities:

1. Failing to take a foster child to church.

2. Proselytizing; it is inappropriate to make critical statements about a foster child's beliefs or religion.

3. Forcing a foster child to participate in Bible studies or religious discussions.

4. Repeatedly showing religious videos or playing religious music while excluding other forms of entertainment.

5. Overusing God or religion as a rationale.

Sexual Behavior

The following are examples of inappropriate sexual behaviors with or around youth:

1. Indiscreet affection toward a foster child, including dating a current or former foster child, laying on a couch or bed with a foster child, or inappropriate touching of the foster child's genital areas or other parts of his or her body with the intention of becoming sexually stimulated.

2. Talking with the foster child about inappropriate sexual issues, including telling the child about personal sexual experiences or insisting that the foster child talk about his or her past sexual feelings or behaviors. Consultants (or another designated professional) should question a foster child about his or her sexual behaviors if it is necessary to assess risk or other essential treatment issues.

3. Taking a foster child into the Treatment Parents' bedroom is discouraged.

4. Reinforcing adolescent infatuation. This includes giving a child jewelry (necklaces, rings, etc.), attempting to maintain a "special" relationship with a foster child who has left the foster home (a relationship that excludes a spouse), or encouraging a foster child to rely exclusively on the Treatment Parents to the extent that he or she is discouraged from seeking help from others.

Child Rights Violation Inquiries

Any questionable practice reported by a foster child is followed up by a formal inquiry. Inquiries are investigations into suspected inappropriate practices reported by a foster child or a consumer, or observed by program staff or another Treatment Parent. Boys Town Treatment Foster Family Services investigates all reports, regardless of their perceived validity or seriousness. Even relatively minor allegations are investigated to address potential problems early when they can be most easily solved.

All Treatment Parents are responsible for safeguarding the rights of foster children. Any suspected abuse observed by foster children, Treatment Parents, or people outside the program should be reported immediately to a Boys Town staff member and the appropriate program supervisor. When such a report is received, a Child Rights Violation Inquiry is immediately implemented by the program administration. (See Appendix A for more information on this process.) The foster children and the adults allegedly involved are interviewed along with others who may have relevant information. The facts should be established and conclusions reached as quickly as possible. It is our goal to promptly address any danger or discomfort experienced by a foster child and/or any harm to a Treatment Parent's reputation.

It is essential that all Child Rights Violation Inquiries are kept confidential from people who do not have a right to information about the child's care. Total anonymity cannot be maintained because the child's parents or legal guardians have the right to be informed of any allegations regarding their child's care. In cases where serious allegations are made, Child Protective Services agencies also must be notified so they can decide whether or not to conduct their own investigation.

Once the Child Rights Inquiry is completed, there is a debriefing phase. Verbal and/or written reports about outcomes must be provided to protect the interests of the foster child and the reputations of the Treatment Parents. When deciding on a plan of action, every effort is made to be sensitive to the needs of the child and the foster parents while preserving the placement if possible. The program's number one priority is always to provide a safe environment for the child.

Summary

Boys Town is very concerned about protecting and assuring the free exercise of rights of all foster children we serve. The guidelines and processes described in this chapter provide evidence of this concern. Ensuring each foster child's rights comes not only from procedures, but also from the "sense of quality" that is imbedded in each Treatment Parent. Each Treatment Parent's competence in carrying out Treatment Plans and continually monitoring his or her own actions and the actions of others makes the real difference. Rules, guidelines, and procedures are necessary, but it is the commitment to providing the highest quality care possible that guarantees each foster child a safe environment.

CHAPTER 3

The Professional Treatment Parent

Professional: characterized by or conforming to the technical or ethical standards of a profession or an occupation; manifesting fine artistry or workmanship based on sound knowledge and conscientiousness. One who belongs to one of the learned professions or is in an occupation requiring a high level of training and proficiency.

Webster's Third New International Dictionary
Merriam-Webster Inc., 1986

When most people think of "foster parents," they think of a family that provides a home to children who can't live with their own families for awhile. These foster parents are expected to care for the child's basic needs and treat the child kindly. Period. Most foster parents are not asked to participate in meetings where the child's emotional, social, or educational needs are discussed and planned for. As you know by now, Boys Town Treatment Foster Family Services expects Treatment Parents not only to meet the child's basic needs, but also serve as the child's **primary treatment providers**. Treatment Parents are professional members of the child's treatment team.

What does it mean to be called a professional Treatment Parent? How does this change your role, and what responsibilities do you accept?

Professionals are generally viewed as experts who are competent, caring, and cooperative. By engaging in the following professional behaviors, Treatment Parents will earn respect for themselves, their home as an effective treatment environment, and the agency they represent.

Part of becoming a Treatment Parent means that you agree to live by a code of acceptable behaviors and ethics. In the Boys Town program, this code of behavior and ethics includes:

1. Implementing the Treatment Foster Care Technology
2. Appropriate Modeling
3. Respecting Cultural Diversity
4. Positive Consumer Relationships
5. Continued Development of Professional Skills
6. Evaluation of Skills
7. Communication
8. Confidentiality
9. Advocacy

Implementing the Treatment Foster Care Technology

Providing care and treatment to a troubled child in your home can be very stressful and hectic. By thoughtfully implementing the Boys Town program, you can develop a warm, loving relationship with your foster children.

Treatment Parents are strongly encouraged to implement the child's Treatment Plan **every day**. This means focusing on teaching the child the skills identified in his or her plan. Providing treatment also includes using good problem-solving skills, and using logical consequences or a Motivation System for the child that has been agreed on ahead of time. It is essential that you implement the Treatment Plan the way it is written.

Another aspect of being a professional means that you agree to work within the policy and procedures of the organization and not "do your own thing." By using the treatment skills you are taught in Preservice and the follow-up teaching your Consultant will provide, you provide a professional treatment service.

The treatment you provide will be more effective if you carefully schedule your personal and professional time. Treatment Parents need to be sure that daily, weekly, and monthly tasks, meetings, and commitments are routinely and promptly completed or attended. By completing these tasks within specific time lines, you will be more confident that goals that are set for the child and yourself will be met. Good scheduling also means planning time for yourself and your own family. This includes using respite care, where another approved adult cares for the child while you rest and enjoy your family. This allows you to remain rested and keeps you from feeling like you're cheating your own family. As a result of making time or scheduling for your personal needs, you provide a professional level of care to your foster child over a longer period of time.

Appropriate Modeling

As professionals, Treatment Parents are role models for their children and for other Treatment Parents. When you "practice what you preach," you demonstrate your commitment to the child and your confidence in the treatment skills taught by Boys Town. Further, you can show your foster child a variety of skills, including using appropriate humor, expressing anger in a constructive manner, being sensitive to the needs of others, and asking for help when appropriate. These all are skills that will further reinforce the child's and agency's respect for you as a professional.

Appropriate modeling also becomes important when you meet with professionals from other agencies, schools, courts, etc. A very important part of appropriate modeling is showing respect for your foster child by avoiding unfair negative labeling. Examples include calling a child "a brat," "mean," "stupid," or "lazy." You get the picture. Using slang or jargon that negatively labels a child can affect the child's self-concept and other people's view of the child. Instead, it is more professional and helpful for your foster child if you describe the behaviors he or she needs to learn. Although this takes a little longer to say or even to think of, it is more specific, focuses on what the child needs to learn, and describes what you or others can do to help the child.

Exercise 1

What would be another way to describe a child with negative behaviors? For each negative label, describe behaviors the child needs to learn.

Unprofessional	Professional
brat	
mean	
stupid	
lazy	

Other effective professional behaviors include appropriate dress, use of correct grammar, good listening skills, advocacy for the foster child, being on time for meetings, and completing tasks when you say you will. When delays are unavoidable or commitments cannot be kept, Treatment Parents should always let the other person(s) know, request a new time line, and be sure to meet it.

By modeling these skills, you are more likely to receive similar courteous treatment and you are modeling important skills for the children in your care.

Respecting Cultural Diversity

An exciting aspect of being a Treatment Parent is the opportunity to teach children a wide variety of social, academic, and life skills. It is equally important, however, for you to understand and appreciate each child's family, religious, and cultural background. This means valuing differences, becoming educated about them, and presenting them to your own family as a positive learning experience. By respecting and nurturing the child's ties to his or her family and community, you can help promote the child's sense of identity and feelings of self-worth. In addition, your modeling of the child's special history or culture as an asset or strength brings a richness to your life as well as to the child's.

Positive Consumer Relationships

In Boys Town Treatment Foster Family Services, we use the term "consumer" for any group or person who has a relationship with a child in Boys Town's care. In general, these consumers include people who have referred the child to the program, court systems, schools, employers of the child, the child's parents, therapists, and especially the child in care.

In order for any child's treatment program to be effective, these people must work together. One part of the Treatment Parents' role is to develop cooperative relationships with consumers by using the professional behaviors we present in this chapter.

There are a number of general guidelines that can help Treatment Parents begin and maintain relationships with any consumer. These guidelines, along with the importance of informal and formal feedback systems, are reviewed in this section.

Beginning Relationships

- Help others understand your role by describing your organization's program to people who may be unfamiliar with it. This includes the agency's treatment approach to foster care.
- Express concern for the child and appreciation for the person's involvement.
- Emphasize how much you value and need feedback, positive and corrective, to help the child get the best treatment available.
- Encourage communication by phone and letters, and through visits.

Maintaining Relationships

- Talk regularly, share good news, and ask for the person's opinion about how he or she thinks the child is doing.
- When you are given feedback, thank the consumer for his or her concern and opinion. A pleasant, professional response helps ensure that the person will continue to communicate with you.
- Show courtesy for others by calling ahead for appointments, being on time, and dressing appropriately.
- Present your information clearly, getting to the point promptly.
- Ask for information in a nonthreatening manner, listen without interrupting the speaker, and ask for suggestions.

This general style of interaction conveys respect and allows the person or team to focus on the issues.

Continued Development of Professional Skills

Training

As society changes, the needs of children change. Treatment foster family care has come to represent an extremely broad array of services because treatment needs of children vary widely. In order to meet this increasing challenge, all Boys Town Treatment Parents complete Preservice Training, attend ongoing training, and receive in-home training and regular support services. Most other treatment foster care programs also have policies and procedures that outline the agency's expectations for training.

Feedback

For professional growth to occur, Treatment Parents must **value**, **request**, and **respond** to feedback from others. Giving and receiving feedback appropriately is essential to professional growth and success of Treatment Parents.

We define feedback as information about the effects of one's behavior on other people and on the environment. Feedback can be given to tell you what you are doing well or given to correct a problem. For example, moving a switch turns on a light that helps you see in a dark room. A friend may say, "Thanks for turning on the light!" That is a form of positive feedback. Someone else saying "Oh, that's too bright; turn it off!" is corrective feedback. That person is giving you information to change or correct something.

Feedback is essential on a day-to-day basis for everyone in Treatment Foster Family Services. It is a must for learning. Feedback provides information about behavior that is appropriate or needs to be corrected.

Naturally, most people would prefer to give and receive positive feedback. A lot of what people notice about each other may involve personal behaviors, and if some of them are negative, we feel uncomfortable talking about them. Also, many people are not used to receiving corrective feedback from others. When they do, they may feel offended or insulted because they feel they are being criticized personally.

Corrective feedback in this program is given in the spirit of trying to help people improve their skills so they are more effective professionally. You were selected to be a Treatment Parent because you have solid judgment and a commitment to children. No matter how good we are at helping children, no one is expected to be perfect. In providing a professional treatment service, we **must** be willing to accept corrective feedback so we can change and, as a result, help the child get better. This means appropriately giving and receiving feedback; the skills involved must become second-nature to every Treatment Parent.

Giving Feedback

Giving feedback is very important for building relationships, sharing information, and solving problems. Good relationships depend upon open communication and the mutual respect that grows out of caring enough to share sensitive information. Also, just ignoring most problems won't make them go away. Usually, feedback must be given to help find solutions to problems. Given the importance of feedback and how often it is used by Treatment Parents, it is important to learn how to give feedback in a sensitive and constructive manner. Using this process will ensure that information is presented in a tactful, pleasant, and concerned manner, and will encourage the person's understanding and acceptance of the information.

Receiving Feedback

Receiving feedback also requires a special set of skills. Given the importance of feedback and the difficulties many people have in giving feedback, it is important for Treatment Parents to model these skills and to encourage and request feedback. Treatment Parents come to realize that the only feedback that really hurts them is the feedback *they do not receive.*

Most people think they accept feedback well, but they do not realize that arguing or defending themselves or offering long explanations actually *punishes* people for giving them feedback. If Treatment Parents are not regularly receiving feedback from a variety of people, they need to check if they are somehow punishing people for sharing such information. This can be done by asking for input (e.g. "Is there anything else I could be doing?" or "Could I have handled that situation differently?"). Also, when others care enough to give positive or corrective feedback, they need to be sincerely thanked for taking the time to express themselves. A professional is careful not to do anything to discourage the flow of information.

Accepting feedback gracefully, in a professional, nonpersonal manner, is not always easy. Yet it is crucial to your growth as a Treatment Parent and to the success of the overall program. Corrective feedback helps Treatment Parents solve problems and continue to develop more sophisticated skills. Both forms of feedback must be encouraged, reinforced, and responded to appropriately if a program is to succeed with each child in its care.

Here are the steps for giving feedback and receiving feedback:

Giving and Receiving Feedback

1. Give your full attention
- Make eye contact
- Look interested and open (e.g. smile, don't cross your arms)

2. Describe or listen to the situation
- Be specific when describing a concern
- Give reasons for your concern
- When being given corrective feedback, avoid giving excuses
- Ask questions to clarify the information
- Thank the person for listening or giving you the information

3. Discuss solutions
- Ask for possible solutions to the problem
- Decide on a practical solution or decide to make a decision at a later time

4. Follow up to see if the solution works
(optional)
- Set up a time to review whether the solution is working
- Thank the person for working with you to find a solution

Requesting Feedback

Requesting feedback on a routine basis means that lines of communication will be open if and when problem situations arise. Also, by routinely requesting feedback, you are more likely to find out what it is that consumers appreciate.

The following examples illustrate ways to request feedback:

"Are you comfortable with our meeting?"
"Are we communicating enough?"
"Were you comfortable with this discussion?"

The more informed Treatment Parents become, the better services they can provide. In spite of problems that may develop, the child's treatment goals can be achieved when Treatment Parents and other team members can give and receive feedback in a professional, nondefensive manner. The following examples show how problems can be resolved using feedback skills. In each example, the situation is described and followed by behaviors for giving and receiving feedback. The corresponding step in the process precedes each behavior.

Example 1

A foster mother is concerned because the foster child's stepfather has been late picking up the child for several visits. The foster mother decides to talk with him about it when he brings the girl back from a visit.

Step: Give your full attention
Behavior: The foster mother smiles and makes eye contact with the stepfather.

Step: Describe the situation
Behavior: "It's nice to see you Wayne. I hope you had a nice visit. When you came to get Neosha today, you were a half hour late. You might not realize it, but when you are late, Neosha starts to worry that you won't come, and she is very upset by the end of the half hour."

Step: Discuss solutions
Behavior: "How about if you call me from a pay phone next time you are going to be late to let me know? I know this would help Neosha not worry and she probably would be happier during your visit. Do you think this would work or do you have another idea?"

Giving feedback this way gives the stepfather an opportunity to focus on a solution instead of just feeling like he's being criticized. By using a pleasant voice, smiling, and making eye contact, the foster mother is clearly communicating that she wants to help the stepfather, not just point out his mistakes.

Example 2

A foster father received a note from school saying that his foster son, Paul, had missed math all week. The foster father calls the school to discuss the problem. He is frustrated that he just learned that Paul has skipped the class so many times. He takes a couple of deep breaths to relax and calls the guidance counselor.

Step: Give your full attention
Behavior: "Hi, Mrs. Arroyo. I appreciate you taking my call because I know you are very busy."

Step: Describe the situation
Behavior: "I didn't know that Paul had skipped his math class all week until I got the note from his teacher today. I'm concerned that I didn't find this out sooner. I'm worried about what Paul was doing during that time and that he will be so far behind in his assignments."

Step: Discuss solutions
Behavior: "Would it help if I gave Paul a school note? He would need to have his teachers sign the card each day to show he went to all his classes. This wouldn't involve too much time for the teachers, and I could follow up at home more quickly. Do you think this would work, or do you have a different suggestion?"

The foster father is pleasant and understanding, yet gets to the point quickly, explains his concern, and suggests a solution. He also asks if the counselor has another suggestion that will help the child. This is a positive way of asking someone to work with you to help the child.

Example 3

Most children feel their visits with their families are extremely important. It is very difficult for most children when these visits are canceled with little or no notice. In this case, Linda, the child's mother, called the foster mother a day after she did not come to get her daughter for a visit. The foster mother feels rather angry at the mother for not calling sooner and not coming to the visit. The foster child, Carol, was very upset for several hours when she realized her mother was not coming. Not only is the foster mother feeling a little worn out from teaching to all of Carol's behaviors, but she also feels bad for Carol. But the foster mother reminds herself that nagging at the mom will not make things any better. She tries to keep her voice pleasant and focuses on how to help.

Step: Give your full attention
Behavior:
Foster mother: "I'm glad you called, Linda. How are you doing?"

Linda: "I'm okay. I just realized that yesterday was my visit with Carol and I was scheduled to work. I wanted to call and see about setting up another visit."

Step: Describe the situation
Behavior:
Foster mother: "I appreciate you calling to let us know what happened. I know that Carol really looks forward to her visits with you. When you don't show up for the visit, Carol thinks you don't care about her. I know neither of us wants her to think that."

Step: Discuss solutions
Behavior:
Foster Mother: "So Carol doesn't feel so disappointed in the future, what do you think would help you know ahead of time whether or not you can come for a visit?"

The two women work out a plan for scheduling visits around the mother's new work schedule.

The foster mother then has Carol come to the phone so she can talk to her mother for a few minutes. The foster mother tries hard to keep a pleasant voice tone on the phone so Carol's mother will feel free to call if problems develop again. At the same time, she was honest with the mother about how the "no show" affects Carol. When the foster mother is sure Carol can't overhear her, she calls her Consultant and reports the phone call from the mother. The foster mother expresses her frustration that Carol's mother isn't more responsible. Later that evening, the foster mother talked to Carol about how her mother felt bad that she had missed the visit.

These are all examples of working out problems professionally. In each situation, the Treatment Parent could have ranted and raved about how the other person was irresponsible and had created problems for the Treatment Parent. While that might have felt good at the moment, it wouldn't have helped the child at all. Controlling your emotions, developing a solution, and expressing your frustrations to your Consultant or spouse all are ways of helping the child and not getting sidetracked.

The following is an example of how a Treatment Parent can accept corrective feedback in a professional manner.

Example 4

The foster mother, Michelle, receives a phone call from the principal at her foster son's school. Michelle is trying to get dinner on the table so the family can leave for a church program. The principal tells Michelle that the foster son, Nathan, has lost the right to ride the bus to school. He tells Michelle that he is quite disappointed with Nathan because today while riding the bus, Nathan swore at other children and made sexual comments to several girls. Nathan had not told Michelle about this when he came home, so this was the first she learned of the problem. Immediately, Michelle begins thinking of the arrangements she would have to make to take Nathan to school every day and how much more difficult it would make her morning routine. She has suspected that the school principal wasn't happy about enrolling Nathan at the school and wonders if he is being unfair to Nathan by kicking him off the bus so fast. At the same time, she knows it won't

help the situation to argue with the principal. This is how Michelle responds:

Step: Give your full attention
Behavior: Michelle takes a deep breath and thanks the principal for calling. She asks if he can hold for a minute while she turns the stove down.

Step: Listen to the situation
Behavior: When she comes back, she keeps her voice pleasant and asks him to describe exactly what Nathan said on the bus. She tells the principal that she certainly understands why this is not acceptable and that other children should not be bullied on the bus. Michelle does not make any excuses for Nathan. She tells the principal that she appreciates him calling to let her know about the problem the same day it occurred.

Step: Discuss solutions
Behavior: When Michelle has gotten all the information about what happened, she asks the principal if Nathan could earn his way back on the bus. The principal responds that he would have to think about it. Michelle suggests that Nathan could apologize to the students whose feelings he hurt and possibly do some volunteer work at the school. The principal said he thinks that could be arranged. They agree to meet the next day with Nathan to draw up a contract about what he needs to do to earn his way back onto the bus.

Step: Follow up to see if the solution works
Behavior: Michelle then arranges to make a follow-up call to the principal the following week to make sure Nathan has fulfilled the contract.

So while this was a very stressful phone call for Michelle, she remained pleasant with the principal and tried to focus on a solution that would help Nathan take responsibility for his behavior and learn from this problem.

Evaluation of Skills

One very important component of a treatment foster care program is evaluation. A description of the Boys Town Treatment Foster Family Services evaluation and certification process is included in Appendix B. If you work with a program that is not affiliated with Boys Town, it would be important for you to discuss its evaluation process while you are in Preservice Training.

Communication

Clear, frequent, and pleasant communication is a hallmark of professionalism. With it, work can be completed smoothly. Without it, confusion and misunderstandings develop and result in unpleasant and unproductive working relationships. One communication skill that is bound to help you have a good working relationship with anyone is "being positive." A positive, "can do" attitude is respected and appreciated. Someone who cheerfully tackles new tasks, avoids complaining excessively, and easily and sincerely recognizes the work and achievements of others is a valued member of any professional group.

As Treatment Parents, you need to have a close working relationship with your Consultant and the Treatment Foster Family Services program. This means that you must feel comfortable communicating frequently with your Consultant, especially early in a child's placement. Communication of this kind includes face-to-face meetings with staff and phone calls about the child's behaviors and needs. It also includes reporting the child's behaviors every day using the Parent Daily Report (adapted from Chamberlain & Reed, 1987) and/or other methods that help determine whether a child is getting better. Appendix C explains in more detail the type of documentation that Treatment Parents must complete. This written communication to Boys Town administrators is extremely important and is a professional expectation that goes along with your role as a treatment provider.

We also encourage Treatment Parents to honestly communicate with their Consultant about personal or professional issues that may affect their ability to provide treatment to their foster child. Consultants and other Boys Town staff understand that foster parents are real people, and real people have problems and frustrations from time to time. The staff can help you more effectively if you trust them with your frustrations or concerns. Arranging respite, adjusting Treatment Plans, or doing other problem-solving together are part of the services Consultants are ready to provide.

Finally, Consultants are trained to use the feedback steps when working with Treatment Parents, and we encourage you to use them with Boys Town staff. It is our experience that when people use these steps to work out problems or express positive feedback, relationships remain respectful and ultimately the children in care get the treatment they deserve.

Confidentiality

We would like to add a few more words about professional communication. Treatment Parents have access to a great deal of information about each child and his or her family, background, etc. Confidentiality is extremely important in maintaining professional relationships with everyone on the team. As a Treatment Parent, you must be sure that confidential information is shared only with persons who have a legitimate need for it and a right to it. Maintaining confidentiality preserves your integrity and develops a sense of trust with the agency as well as with outside organizations. As a rule, the positive accomplishments of a child may be shared with others, but individual child problems should be discussed only with the appropriate individuals. Your Consultant will work with you to decide what information about your foster child can be shared with others (i.e. school, therapist, other Treatment Parents).

In Exercises 2 and 3, we'll take a look at the right way and the wrong way to respond to someone's questions about confidential information.

Exercise 2

The first situation is an example; fill in the responses to the situations that follow.

Your brother-in-law asks you, "Why do you think Michael's parents put him in the hospital? I heard he tried to hurt himself...."

Unprofessional response: "Yeah, Michael has had a lot of trouble. He has tried to kill himself twice, both times with pills. His psychiatrist said he was getting better."

Professional response: "I appreciate your interest in Michael, but the reasons he is in our home are private. Would you mind if Michael practiced his basketball shots on your hoop until we get one up this weekend?"

The school nurse says, "I hear Sara was at the police station about some sexual problems in the family. What did they tell you about this?"

Unprofessional response: "They told me that her dad had sex with her for years. They even think her older sister was sexually abused by him, too. The sister had a baby a few years ago, but I think she gave it to another family to raise. I think the whole family has trouble."

Professional response:

Your neighbor says, "I really am amazed that you would be willing to let that boy (your foster son) in your home. I've heard that he has been causing trouble for years. I heard that he was yelling at some teachers at the school last week. Is that true?"

Unprofessional response: "Michael thought the teacher was 'on him' too much. He can really get mad sometimes. I think his dad used to yell a lot and that is where Michael learned it. His dad has a pretty bad drinking problem from what I understand."

Professional response:

Your best friend says "I really admire your willingness to be a Treatment Parent." She watched your kids for you while you went through the Preservice Training. When your new foster child moves in, she asks, "Has he been involved in gangs? He sure has a lot of tattoos. Don't you worry that he'll be a bad influence on your own kids?"

Unprofessional response: "Yeah, he's been in a gang for about a year now. I think we got him just when he was going to be initiated. He wanted to get out but he didn't know how. His aunt helped raise him. She works at the City Hall."

Professional response:

Exercise 3

Treatment Parents also should protect the confidentiality and dignity of their fellow Treatment Parents by responding professionally to rumors or gossip. A Treatment Parent who hears someone discussing personal information about others should respond professionally by not probing for details and not sharing the information. A professional response also might involve having that person speak directly to whoever is the subjects of the rumor, expressing discomfort about the rumor, or trying to drop or change the subject. Professional responses to gossip and rumors can help limit this kind of behavior.

As in Exercise 2, think about some of the professional and unprofessional ways Treatment Parents can respond to rumors and gossip.

Another Treatment Parent mentions this to you after an inservice training class: "I heard that Karen and Paul Murphy are having marital problems. They didn't seem to be talking to each other much tonight. I'm just sure that Samuel is at the heart of it. I told her she shouldn't take that boy – he's been a troublemaker from the start!"

Unprofessional response: "I think you're right. Karen seems to spend a lot of time with Samuel and Paul is the jealous type. I think they looked pretty stressed tonight. I wonder if their Consultant knows how bad their marriage is?"

Professional response:

Two Treatment Parents are talking on the phone. One says, "I heard the Mitchells may not pass certification. I think some of the people they work with at the school and Juanita's parents have been upset with them. I'm not sure they are cut out for the program."

Unprofessional response: "I had no idea that they were having so many problems. Juanita seems like such a sweet girl. I can't image what they have done to make her so unhappy in their home. You might be right about them not cutting it in the program."

Professional response:

Two Treatment Parents run into each other at a school program. One says to the other, "I just saw the Lees yesterday at a football game. Have you ever met their own daughter, Michelle? You remember them; they were in our Preservice Training. I think that girl has some problems. They held her back a year in school and now I think they take her to counseling. If they are having trouble with her, I wonder how they got to be Treatment Parents?"

Unprofessional response: "Really? I didn't know she had so many problems. They sure do keep it a secret. I sure wouldn't apply to be a Treatment Parent if I had so many problems with my own kids."

Professional response:

Advocacy

Advocacy: the action of advocating, pleading for, or supporting.

Webster's Third New International Dictionary
Merriam-Webster Inc., 1986

To "get along" with people, Treatment Parents do not merely "go along" with what other people want. Treatment Parents must be willing to advocate for the best interests of the foster child in their care. The concept of "assertive advocacy" should guide all your activities when you interact with teachers, agency personnel, police, and others who share responsibility for the child. You must advocate for a foster child in ways that do not alienate people or close off channels of communication. That is what professionalism is all about. **Advocacy** defines the content or subject of the communication with others. **Professionalism** defines the process or style of the communication. That is why the manner in which Treatment Parents give and accept feedback is critical to maintaining communication channels and, ultimately, to the treatment of each child.

Court Contacts

Many children who enter a treatment foster care program do so through the court system. Some may become involved with the juvenile court system while in the program. This means that the agency and the Treatment Parents will need to work cooperatively with the courts, while advocating for the child's best interests. Treatment Parents and their foster child should be prepared for any court appearance. Preparing a child for a court appearance involves careful teaching with the child ahead of time. The child needs to know how to dress, how to respectfully answer questions, and how to make a positive statement on his or her own behalf. Most importantly, the child needs to clearly understand that his or her behavior greatly influences the judge's decisions.

Treatment Parents also need to be well-prepared for any court appearance. They need to model appropriate dress and behavior. In particular, they need to be prepared to make a positive statement about the foster child, including describing the

child's progress and accomplishments. The basic principle is always the same: Act in a way that truly promotes the child's best interests. Sometimes a child's actions or requests do not reflect what is in his or her best interest. The child's best interests should always prevail.

School Contacts

Treatment Parents need to be very involved in each child's school program. Frequent contacts with teachers through phone calls, meetings, school notes, and/or classroom observations help Treatment Parents understand a child's educational needs. Regular communication also helps them determine how well skills that are being taught in the home are being used by the child in school. Treatment Parents also must stay informed about the child's progress in school to help develop and review the child's specific education plan. Using the professional skills described earlier will help Treatment Parents develop and maintain cooperative relationships with the child's educators.

Mental Health Providers

Many of the children who are in treatment foster care receive the services of mental health providers at some time during their placement. Mental health providers who Treatment Parents work with include psychiatrists, psychologists, and social workers.

A *psychiatrist* is a physician who is trained in a medical school and a hospital. A psychiatrist has completed a four-year undergraduate degree program, usually in biology and chemistry. This training is followed by several years of medical school training, one year of internship, and three years of residency in psychiatry. A psychiatrist holds an M.D. (Medical Doctor) degree. Psychiatrists and psychologists have many similar responsibilities, but a psychiatrist is more likely to be involved with treating hospitalized patients. As a physician, a psychiatrist can prescribe medication.

A *clinical psychologist* is trained in a university or professional school. Training includes completion of a four-year undergraduate degree program (usually in psychology), plus four to five years of graduate training in clinical psychology and one year of internship. Most clinical psychologists have a Ph.D. (Doctor of Philosophy) degree. A clinical psychologist may work in a variety of settings – private practice, a mental health clinic, or a hospital. Psychologists perform a variety of activities, including psychotherapy, psychological assessment, and teaching. A clinical psychologist cannot prescribe medication.

Social workers usually are trained in a university-based school of social work. Training includes completing a four-year undergraduate degree program in the social sciences, plus one to two years of graduate training in social work. Social workers usually have an M.S.W. (Master of Social Work) degree. A social worker may conduct psychotherapy, and/or work with individuals who need help getting services. For instance, a social worker may help find placements for retarded or handicapped people, refer people to psychiatrists or psychologists for psychotherapy or assessment, or help people find financial assistance (Saccuzzo & Kaplan, 1984).

When working with mental health providers, it is important to respect the therapist's skills, training, and ability to provide special therapeutic assistance to the foster child. Therapists can help children resolve issues of loss, trauma, depression, etc. This can help the child heal more rapidly and best take advantage of the relationship and teaching you can provide. When a foster child is receiving services from a mental health provider, it is important for the rest of the team, including the Treatment Parents, to understand the type of treatment the child is receiving. Treatment Parents should not be afraid to ask the mental health provider questions about treatment the child is receiving and how it can be coordinated with the treatment they are providing in the home. Treatment Parents should talk with their Consultant if they feel that the mental health provider is not able to satisfactorily answer their questions or is unwilling to listen to their information or input. Differences should be resolved with the goal of providing coordinated services that ultimately benefit the child.

Summary

Treatment Parents have an extremely important role in helping children heal so that they can go on to enjoy happy and satisfying lives. This chapter has presented some essential skills that will help ensure that the child in your home will have a positive, successful experience. Implementing the program in your home, modeling positive and professional behavior, communicating effectively by both giving and receiving feedback, maintaining confidentiality, and advocating for your foster child are key elements in providing effective care and treatment. Using these professional skills and embracing the values explained in this chapter will help both you and your foster child reach your goals.

CHAPTER 4

Religion in Family Life

"Unless the Lord builds the house, in vain do they labor who builds it."

Psalm 127, Verse 1

This chapter is a brief introduction to the central place that religion plays in family life in Boys Town's programs. We hope you will be inspired and encouraged by the goals that are explained here.

When children come to us, they are suffering from abandonment, neglect, physical abuse, psychological abuse, sexual abuse, and many other problems. All the helping techniques that are described in the following chapters, important as they are, will only help you make changes in the exterior behavior of boys and girls. Though a child may appear to have made a good deal of progress during the first few months in a Treatment Foster Family Home, our work is not done. When a child experiences the miracle of healing in the heart, only then can the beauty, goodness, faith, hope, and love that are God's gracious gifts be released. And it is only then that we are able to complete the process of making the child whole again.

Father Flanagan said: "Every boy must learn to pray. How he prays is up to him." By prayer, Father Flanagan meant raising our minds and hearts to God. He believed, as we do, that the success of Boys Town's programs will not be complete without this. Thus, religion has a definite priority in our program of care for boys and girls who come to live with us in Treatment Foster Family Homes. We respect the religious traditions of children who come to us and strive to enhance them, but we do not proselytize or try to convert them to our own church or faith.

Treatment Parents bear the responsibility of teaching sound religious practices while at the same time exercising care not to engage in conversion tactics. Treatment Parents need to encourage a child to worship God in such a manner that the child's family religious traditions are honored and enhanced. To assist Treatment Parents, Boys Town has established eight specific goals for the religious development of children.

Goal 1: Each child should learn to appreciate and cherish a fundamental relationship with the God who loves and understands him or her. Treatment Parents are "images" of God for the children who live in their homes. Their primary obligation is to help the children realize that God loves and understands them. So often in their lives, their experience of religion has been negative or nonexistent. The difficulties that have plagued their homes — alcoholism, stressful divorce, domestic violence, physical or sexual assault — all have made God seem far away and indifferent to them. They need to see positive, warm images of God, and their Treatment Parents are there to provide those images.

Goal 2: Treatment Parents should be role models of faith for foster children. Treatment Parents have to lead the way by being religious role models for their children. Role models are respected, admired people who make a life of faith attractive by encouraging others in gentle and joyful ways to witness to their faith. As role models, it is important for

Treatment Parents to encourage religious life in the home by attitude, word, and deed.

Goal 3: Each child should attend religious services. To be good role models, Treatment Parents are strongly encouraged to attend religious services with their foster child. If a child is placed in a home that practices a faith that is different from his or her faith, Treatment Parents are encouraged to attend services with that child in his or her church. Or, the Treatment Parents can arrange for a neighbor, friend, or the child's parents to attend that church with the child. By their attitude toward religion and their attendance and behavior at church, Treatment Parents can enhance the worship experience for their children and help them view it as a very important, vital family activity.

Goal 4: Each child should learn about religious faith and practice. Religion is just as important to a child's spiritual development as food and drink are to a person's physical development. Children need to receive religious instruction in the church they regularly attend – CCD for Catholics and Sunday School for Protestants. As good role models, Treatment Parents need to become involved with the religious instruction in church and continue that instruction in their homes. All Boys Town staff should take the special responsibility of helping children grow in their faith without trying to influence the children to accept the Treatment Parents' personal denominational preference.

Goal 5: Each child should pray regularly and appreciate the religious significance of special events. Children should be taught the fundamentals of prayer and its practice so that prayer becomes a part of their home life. Treatment Parents should teach prayer by example, by direct instruction, and by praise and appreciation. For example, there should be prayers at mealtime as well as morning and evening prayers.

Goal 6: Each child should develop sound religious habits for home. Religious habits help create an atmosphere of warmth, the kind of atmos-

phere that we would like to pervade our homes. These habits include times for reflection, for private prayer, and for reading the Holy Scriptures and other devotional books. They also include Christian service projects that are sponsored by the church the family attends.

Goal 7: Each child should have the opportunity to develop a positive relationship with a priest, minister, rabbi, or other clergy. We encourage children to develop warm relationships with clergy and to discuss their concerns with pastors as an integral part of religion in family life. They may request the opportunity to speak with a priest or minister at any time and the request is to be honored. Obviously, these matters must be handled with the utmost confidentiality; the content of disclosures may not be revealed to anyone, including the Treatment Parents, without the child's permission.

Goal 8: Each child should be encouraged to live a spiritually balanced life, without overexaggeration or underexaggeration. It should be clear by what you have read so far that Treatment Parents are asked to be true religious leaders in their homes. They are encouraged to draw out and use what the child has learned in religious instruction and put it into practice at home. They should practice good, sound religious principles and project warm images of God and His relationship with each one of us. In this way, Treatment Parents clearly function as key people for the religious development of children committed to their care.

The religious development of each child should be balanced, meaning without overemphasis or underemphasis.

Examples of **overemphasis** would be:

- excessive use of religious terms in every conversation with the child.
- using God as the exclusive reason for all behaviors.
- allowing only religious music in the home.
- allowing only religious books in the home.
- misuse of prayer (e.g. as a consequence).
- sermonizing instead of discussing.

Examples of **underemphasis** are:

- discouraging the use of religious talk or conversation.
- avoiding the use of God as a reason for any behavior.
- not allowing or encouraging religious music in the home.
- not praying before meals.
- not taking an active part in religious projects.
- not helping with religion class homework in a positive, approving fashion.
- being negative or unenthusiastic about Sunday services.

Treatment Parents teach their children how to worship appropriately and how to behave properly in church. We ask this of all Boys Town parents for the following reasons:

- Boys Town is convinced that helping children grow spiritually is essential to their lives and well-being. Learning how to worship is a big step in that direction.

- Children who are taught how to worship appropriately will be more likely to actively participate in religious services because they will enjoy it and not be so self-conscious or awkward.

- Participating in religious services gives children opportunities to praise God by using the skills they are developing (e.g. reading, speaking, and singing).

- Teaching children to worship appropriately will give them a way to show respect for the House of God.

- Children who listen and participate will derive more meaning from the service.

- The service will be more enjoyable and meaningful to the Treatment Parents if they can concentrate more on the message and less on their child's behavior.

Boys Town's attitude toward the role of religion in children's lives is perhaps best summarized in our creed.

Boys Town Creed

Boys Town was founded on the conviction that the hope of the future lies in the wholesome development of the young men and women of today. Boys Town is dedicated to helping all young men and women realize their full potential for God, self, and society.

WE BELIEVE in God, our Creator and loving Father.

WE BELIEVE in the sanctity of human life from its conception to its entrance into eternal life.

WE BELIEVE that every young man and woman should pray; how he or she prays is a matter of personal concern.

WE BELIEVE in helping young men and women of any creed and ethnic background and in developing the total person: the physical, mental, social, and spiritual.

WE BELIEVE in helping physically handicapped as well as socially deprived young men and women and in respecting the human rights of each individual.

WE BELIEVE in the pursuit of truth within a framework of religious principles.

WE BELIEVE that our Boys Town motto, "He ain't heavy, Father... he's m' brother," characterizes our concern for every young man and woman, whatever his or her burden.

Punishment vs. Teaching

Foster children who come to your Treatment Foster Family Home have much to learn and unlearn in a relatively short time. They may have problems controlling their anger or not doing what you or other adults ask them to do. They may have tried to hurt themselves, failed in school, or used alcohol, drugs, or sex to forget their problems. How can Treatment Parents make a difference in such a troubled child's life? **Frequent, direct, and skillful teaching is the key to success.** The model you will use to help young people is based on Boys Town's many years of experience of helping troubled foster children. We have learned that teaching **skills** is the critical difference between real treatment and just providing physical care.

By focusing on teaching social skills, Treatment Parents help foster children learn new ways of behaving that are alternatives to past problem behaviors. Because foster children in a Treatment Foster Family Home are directly taught new ways of behaving, they can more successfully and comfortably adapt to society's expectations and can get their needs met in socially acceptable ways.

Direct, frequent, and concerned teaching also helps Treatment Parents. This teaching approach provides a specific, effective, and positive way to deal with problem behaviors. Because teaching is a positive approach that works well and is liked by foster children, Treatment Parents can avoid punishing approaches that could damage relationships.

In fact, research has shown that the more teaching staff does in group homes, the more the children like the program and the less involved they are in delinquent activities (Bedlington, 1983). This also is true for foster care. We at Boys Town have shown through evaluation research that our therapeutic foster care program produces positive changes in a variety of areas (Mott, Authier, Shannon, Arneil, & Daly, 1995).

With that in mind, this chapter will focus on different forms of discipline and how teaching allows Treatment Parents to correct the children in their care without resorting to methods that can harm children and relationships in the home.

Discipline

Discipline is commonly misunderstood. To parents, it may mean a number of different things — punishment, correction, and/or guidance. Before we discuss Boys Town's approach to discipline, please take a moment to answer the following questions about the way you deal with your children or foster children and their problems. Indicate your answers with a check mark.

Exercise 1

	YES	NO
1. Do you find yourself arguing with your children or foster children?	—	—
2. Do you feel like you're always correcting your children or foster children?	—	—
3. Do you often get your child or foster child to promise that he or she won't do something again?	—	—
4. Do you sometimes respond with a big punishment for a relatively minor misbehavior?	—	—
5. Do you sometimes threaten action that you know you won't carry out?	—	—
6. Do you find yourself saying things to your child or foster child that you later regret saying?	—	—
7. Do you repeat instructions time and time again?	—	—
8. Do you often give in to your child's or foster child's demands?	—	—
9. Do you find that the more you punish, the more your child or foster child misbehaves?	—	—

If you answered "Yes" to most of these questions, you're definitely using punishment with children in your care. If you answered "Yes" to two or more of these questions, you're using some methods of punishment. You're not alone. As a recent survey on parenting indicated, most parents use punitive or unpleasant responses when their own children misbehave. This means they yell, scold, call their children names, or use physical punishment. The use of punishment is commonplace. And, we won't try to convince you that punishment doesn't work. It does in the short run. In the long run, however, a child can actually develop more behavior problems as a result of being punished. Punishment is not the best way to discipline children or foster children.

We understand that there are certain situations where some parents feel that punishment can be effective and useful, if for no other reason than they feel that something has to be done immediately. For example, when your three-year-old runs into the street, grabbing him quickly out of the street and giving him a swift swat on the bottom can show him how dangerous that situation is. If a swat was used for each misbehavior, however, it would lose its effectiveness. Also, as children get older, punishment becomes less effective. Swatting a 16-year-old usually results in some type of retaliation and long-term problems for both the parent and the child.

Inappropriate Punishment

For our purposes, we define inappropriate punishment as something that is harsh and unreasonable, violent, or harmful. Corporal punishment such as hitting, slapping, or punching hurts children, emotionally as well as physically. In most states, Treatment Parents are not allowed to use physical punishment with foster children. In our program, physical punishment is NEVER allowed. But there are other **inappropriate** punishments – yelling, belittling, ridiculing, or isolating the foster child – that parents may resort to when they become frustrated or angry. Any form of inappropriate punishment is harmful to a child's development. And the parents feel bad for losing their cool.

So why do parents use inappropriate punishment so often? There are several reasons. The first is because it seems to bring about an immediate change in behavior. Sometimes, it results in short-term changes that seem effective. The first few times a parent yells at a child, the child gets quiet. Yelling has to work, right? Wrong. In the short run, inappropriate punishments can accomplish what the parent wants, but over time, they cause all sorts of problems for parents and children. For example, once a child gets "used" to being yelled at, she will stop responding, which will make the parent yell even more.

A second reason parents use inappropriate punishment is that they are not sure what else to do in those situations. They are angry and frustrated and react to what the child said or did, almost like it was automatic. Hitting, yelling, and spanking are common punishments parents use when they react without thinking.

The third reason involves a feeling all parents have had – fear of losing their authority. Parents are afraid that if they aren't tough enough, their children will run roughshod over them, and the children will be in control instead of the parents. As parents feel the need to become tougher, to let the children really know "they mean business," it leads them to use inappropriate punishment.

The last reason parents use inappropriate punishment is because no one taught them any other way. They learned how to discipline from their models – their own parents. There's nothing wrong with this; we all learned from our parents. But if a person's parents used inappropriate punishment, it is likely that that person will use the same punishment (or do just the opposite and be overly permissive).

Here are some other negative side effects of inappropriate punishment:

- It hurts children's self-esteem; children don't feel good about themselves after being hit, yelled at, or verbally put down. This is especially true for foster children who already have experienced abuse. In most cases, they already think they are pretty bad children and more inappropriate punishment makes them feel that way again.

- Punishment damages relationships between Treatment Parents and their foster children. After awhile, foster children may want to avoid their Treatment Parents altogether. When this happens, children miss opportunities to learn social skills, values, and problem-solving skills. This is an essential part of being in a therapeutic home.

- Punishment often results in revenge. Children want to get back at the person who punished them. Many foster children resent being taken out of their homes and they miss their own parents. When they feel unfairly punished in a foster home, they are less likely to want to stay there. They may not care a whole lot if their efforts to "get revenge" result in them being removed from the home.

- Punishment can have a snowball effect. If one punishment doesn't work, parents often try a harsher one; a parent's response can escalate from requests to commands, to yelling, and even hitting. This type of parenting is not consistent with the goals of treatment foster care and is destructive to a Treatment Parent-foster child relationship.

Exercise 2

Take a few minutes and jot down some of the times you remember misbehaving as a child and how your parents responded to you.

Misbehavior

1.

2.

3.

Parents' Response

1.

2.

3.

Now write down some of the things your own children or foster children do that you dislike, and how you respond to their misbehavior.

Misbehavior

1.

2.

3.

Parents' Response

1.

2.

3.

Appropriate Teaching

The focus of this entire book is on showing you how to teach your children and foster children in a better way, without having to resort to the use of punishment. In the Boys Town Family Home Model, we use what we call **appropriate teaching**. All of the skills outlined in this book provide the foundation for appropriate teaching to take place.

Appropriate teaching provides a positive and effective approach to problem behavior. It is:

- **Specific** – you let your foster children know exactly what they did wrong.

- **Consistent** – you help your foster children understand the relationship between what they did and the result of their actions.

- **Concrete** – you give your foster children clear examples of how to improve in the future.

- **Positive** – you help your foster children learn self-discipline (to be in control of their actions and expressions of emotion).

- **Interactive** – you give your foster children a chance to show what they have learned. You are an active part of the learning process. You and your foster children work together toward a common goal.

- **Informative** – you become the teacher and the coach as you give information that helps your foster children learn to solve problems.

In other words, appropriate teaching helps build self-esteem, teaches foster children to get along well with others, and gives them the skills to make their own decisions.

Appropriate teaching uses guidance rather than control. Foster children are much more likely to learn when they are treated with affection and pleasantness than when they are treated with anger and physical punishment. Appropriate teaching provides a positive framework for necessary learning.

Appropriate teaching also tells foster children what they did wrong and how to correct it. If you are pleasant, firm, consistent, and able to give clear messages, you will be teaching effectively.

Exercise 3

Indicate whether the parent used appropriate teaching or inappropriate punishment.

1. Mike is playing the TV video game. Johnny doesn't want to wait his turn, so he unplugs the game. Mike hits him with a Ping-Pong paddle. The foster mother hears what's going on, comes in, lifts Mike up, shakes him, and says, "Don't hit your foster brother!"

____ Appropriate Teaching
____ Inappropriate Punishment

2. Sally and her friend walk into the living room. They are talking about the new girl in school. Sally's foster mom overhears Sally tell her friend that they shouldn't play with the new girl any more because she doesn't wear neat clothes. The foster mother asks the girls to sit down, and they talk about how clothes shouldn't determine how someone feels about another person. The foster mother says it is what's inside a person that is important, not what's on the outside.

____ Appropriate Teaching
____ Inappropriate Punishment

3. Dad tells Ty that he can't go outside to shoot baskets because Ty has homework to finish. Ty gets angry, stomps his feet, and complains how unfair his foster father is. The father tells Ty that they need to talk about Ty's behavior. First, he tells Ty that he needs to calm down and stop yelling. Moments later, after Ty has settled down, the father explains why Ty needs to learn how to accept "No" for an answer.

____ Appropriate Teaching
____ Inappropriate Punishment

4. Felicia draws a picture on the living room wall with a red crayon. She finds her foster mother, shows her the picture, and asks her if she likes it. The foster mother tells Felicia that she is "a very bad girl" and sends her to her room. She also tells Felicia that she doesn't draw very well.

____ Appropriate Teaching
____ Inappropriate Punishment

In Exercise 3, appropriate teaching was used in examples 2 and 3. Was it easy to recognize the difference between appropriate teaching and inappropriate punishment?

Now complete Exercise 4. As we explain more about appropriate teaching, it might be interesting to come back and read the answers you gave here.

Exercise 4

Describe what you would do if your foster child behaved like the children in the following examples.

1. Mike, your 15-year-old foster child, is 30 minutes late coming home from his friend's house. When you tell him you were worried and that you feel it's important for him to be home on time, he yells, "I'll stay out as long as I damn well please!" and stomps down the hall to his room.

What would you do?

3. Pat is an active six-year-old boy who frequently climbs on furniture, despite being told not to. You're on the phone when you hear him jumping from the coffee table onto the couch. Suddenly, you hear a crash in the living room.

What would you do?

2. Bridget, your 11-year-old foster child, received a detention in school for throwing a pencil at a fellow student and arguing with her teacher.

What would you do?

4. Bobbie, age four, knows how to get her way, especially at dinner. She throws her food and screams whenever anyone tries to talk to someone other than her. She just threw her mashed potatoes into the middle of the table, spilling some of the drinks.

What would you do?

Summary

The key to becoming an effective Treatment Parent is teaching your foster child new ways of behaving and interacting with others. While punishment may seem to be a useful teaching tool initially, in the long run it usually doesn't work. In the next chapters, we'll look at tried and true ways to effectively change behavior by:

- Being clear and specific when teaching.
- Understanding how to change behavior by using consequences.
- Using strategies that help the child succeed, including "catching 'em being good."

CHAPTER 6

Clear Messages

"You've got a lousy attitude!"
"Shape up, Judy. Stop being so naughty."
"You were a good boy at the store."

These are common statements made by parents and Treatment Parents. But do children really understand what they mean? We must remember that children are concrete thinkers; they don't grasp the full meaning of words that are abstract or vague. Telling a child he has "a lousy attitude" does not give him enough information to know what needs to be changed. A clearer message to the same child might be, "You walked away from me when I asked you to do something, and mumbled 'Get off my back.'" This gives the child specific information. One of your goals as a Treatment Parent is to give your foster children messages they understand.

Giving clear messages is one key to appropriate teaching. Treatment Parents need to specifically tell their foster children what needs to be done and how to do it. They need to tell their foster children when they've done something well. They also need to correct their foster children when they mess up and help them learn from their mistakes. Finally, Treatment Parents need to teach their foster children how to think for themselves and solve problems.

But before this can happen, Treatment Parents must know how to communicate clearly with their foster children. They must be specific, focus on what their foster children are doing or saying, and describe the foster children's behaviors.

Everyone has a general idea of what behaviors are. But to make sure we're on the same wave-

length, let's take a look at a definition that can help Treatment Parents give clear messages.

Describing Behaviors

Behavior is what people do or say – it is an action that can be seen, heard, or measured.

Here's a descriptive list of behaviors:
1. My foster child talks on the phone for one hour at a time.
2. When I ask my foster son to do something, he rolls his eyes and walks away.
3. When my foster children come home from school, they put their books away and ask if there's anything that needs to be done around the house.
4. When I tell my foster daughter her jeans are too tight, she whines and screams, "Why are you such a bitch?"
5. My foster son helped me put away the dishes. Then he swept the kitchen floor.

It is easy to understand what we mean by actions that can be seen or heard. You **see** your foster child slap his brother. You **hear** your foster child singing to her baby sister. But what do we mean by **measuring** a behavior? Think of it this way: You can measure how long a person lays on a couch by the length of time that passes. Laying on the couch is a behavior; it's something a person does. But you can't measure how long a person has been "lazy." Laziness is a perception; it is an interpretation, and is not behaviorally specific.

Exercise 1

List four behaviors you might expect your child or foster child to demonstrate. Remember to focus on what is said and done.

1.

2.

3.

4.

Terms like "hyperactive," "naughty," or "irresponsible" are far from clear, concrete descriptions. These words describe perceptions; people see or hear something and form mental impressions of another person. As that person's behaviors are observed, perceptions are formed. The problem is that when these perceptions are conveyed to others, they can easily be misunderstood and can mean different things to different people. This can be confusing to foster children, and may result in arguments. To one Treatment Parent, "irresponsible" may mean not coming home on time or leaving the kitchen a mess. To another Treatment Parent, "irresponsible" may mean not helping around the house or not putting the lawn mower away. When Treatment Parents teach their foster children, they need to describe **behaviors**, not perceptions, in order to give clear messages.

To give clear messages, you must first watch what a child does or says. Then, clearly and specifically tell the child what he or she did or did not do. Use words that you know the child will understand. For younger children, use short sentences and easily understood words. As they get older, adjust your language to fit their age and level of comprehension.

Have you ever listened to a sporting event on the radio? If you have, you know that a good sports announcer enables you to visualize what is happening through his descriptions. You can see every play in your mind. He is giving a verbal replay of the action taking place. As a Treatment Parent, you must be just as clear with foster children.

In order to give clear messages, it will help to describe the following:

Who – Who is involved, who is being praised, whose behavior is being corrected.

What – What just happened, what was done well, what needs to be improved or changed.

When – When the behavior happened, when you want something.

Where – Where the behavior occurred.

How you give messages also is very important. Here are several points that will help you convey clear messages to your foster children:

1. Have your foster child look at you. It's more likely that he or she will hear what you say and follow through on any requests. Our experience has taught us that eye contact is a key to giving and receiving clear messages.

2. Look at your foster child. This shows that you are paying attention and allows you to see his or her reaction to what you say. Give your foster child your full attention.

3. Use a voice tone that fits the situation. Your voice should be firm when giving correction, friendly when giving compliments, etc.

4. Be aware of your facial expressions and body language. For example, you might smile when you are happy about something your foster child has done, or frown when you are displeased.

5. Eliminate as many distractions as possible. Try to find a quiet area where you can talk to your foster child.

6. Try to position yourself so that you are at eye level with your foster child. Avoid intimidating your foster child by standing over him or her.

One final thought about clear messages: The most important part of being specific when describing your foster children's misbehavior is that they understand that you dislike their **behavior, not them,** and that you are upset and displeased with the way they are acting. You must convey that you still care for them; that's why you are taking the time to teach another way to behave.

Exercise 2

Circle the statements that give clear messages.

1. "Billy, why can't you act your age when company comes?"

2. "When we get to the store, please be a nice girl."

3. "Jim, would you please rake the backyard, put the leaves in a big plastic bag, and put the bag on the front curb?"

4. "That was a nice story you wrote for English class, Sam."

5. "Sally, you need to stop talking right now."

6. "Reggie, don't eat like a pig."

7. "Veronica, when you chew your food, you should keep your mouth closed."

8. "Chuck, after school you are to come right home. Don't stop to play."

9. "Billy, thank you for sitting still and not talking in church."

Statements 3, 5, 7, 8, and 9 are examples of clear messages. The other statements are not clear. They didn't describe specific behaviors.

Now let's change the vague statements so that they give the child a clear message:

1. "Billy, you're whining about your sister taking your toy. I'd like you to go in the family room and pleasantly ask her to give it back."

2. "When we get to the store, remember that we aren't buying any candy. Okay? I'd like you to help me pick out the things on our list and put them in the cart. You can also push the shopping cart. Okay?"

4. "Sam, you did a nice job on that story for English class. You used complete sentences and all of the grammar was correct. The topic of prejudice was excellent! It was really interesting."

6. "Reggie, you're eating with your fingers and making grunting noises while you eat. I'd like you to eat with a fork, take small bites, and not make any noises."

These statements include descriptions of what each foster child said or did. When a child's behaviors are described this way, the child is more likely to understand what needs to be changed.

Framework for Giving Clear Messages

If you noticed, most of the statements in Exercise 2 followed a general pattern. There's a reason for that. We've found that giving Treatment Parents a framework really helps them give clear messages. There is a two-part framework for both correcting a behavior and praising a behavior.

When correcting behavior:

Describe what happened. Tell your foster child what needs to be changed or stopped. Say something like, "What you're doing now is...," or "You did...," or "You said...."

Describe what you want done. Your foster child needs to know what you expect of him or her. Say something like, "What I'd like you to do is..." or "Please go and ...."

Examples

Describe what happened – "Johnny, you left the milk out on the counter, and there are potato chip crumbs on the floor."

Describe what you want done – "Please go out to the kitchen and put the milk in the refrigerator. Then sweep the floor and throw the crumbs in the trash."

Describe what happened – "Mrs. Johnson called and said that on your way home, you rode your bike through her flowers."

Describe what you want done – "We are going to go back over to her house and you need to tell her you are sorry. Then ask her if you can do anything to make up for going through her flowers."

Describe what happened – "Sandy, your music is too loud."

Describe what you want done – "Please turn it down and shut your door."

Describe what happened – "Right now you are arguing with me."

Describe what you want done – "I'd appreciate it if you would be quiet and let me finish talking. Then you can have your turn to speak. Okay?"

When praising a child's behavior:

Show your approval. Say something like, "You really did a nice job with...," or "Thanks for..." or "That's fantastic! You...."

Describe what was done well. "...sweeping and mopping the floor," or "...playing quietly with your sister," or "...studied hard all week and got a 'B' on your test."

This can be done in one sentence. For example, "Thanks for taking the shovel back to Mr. Jones." This may sound very basic, but it is extremely important that your foster child hears your approval and knows exactly what was done right. Remember to give clear, positive messages!

Examples

Show your approval – "You really did a great job!"

Describe what was done well – "It took a lot of time and effort to study for your math test."

Show your approval – "Thanks for helping out."

Describe what was done well — "You took the time to help me make a grocery list and cut out the coupons. I really appreciate it."

Show your approval – "Awesome catch!"

Describe what was done well – "You stayed right in front of the ball and kept your eye on it. It was really hit hard!"

Show your approval – "Wow! You're downstairs already!"

Describe what was done well – "You set the alarm clock last night and got up on your own. That's three days in a row!"

Show your approval – "You did a fantastic job on this English paper."

Describe what was done well – "You wrote the paper neatly, you used proper grammar, and you expressed your ideas clearly."

Exercise 3

Read these situations. In place of the vague comments, write specific comments that give clear messages. The first two are done for you.

1. Situation: Your two foster children are arguing about who had a toy first.
Vague: "Cut that out!"
Specific: "You two are arguing with me about who had the toy first. What I'd like you to do is give me the toy and sit quietly."

2. Situation: Your three-year-old foster child is using his spoon to eat his food.
Vague: "You're being such a good boy."
Specific: "All right! I'm so happy. You're using your spoon to eat! You're keeping all of the food on the spoon. Good job!"

3. Situation: Your teenage foster daughter throws her books on the kitchen table.
Vague: "What do you think you're doing?"
Specific: (Describe what happened.) (Describe what you want done.)

4. Situation: Your 17-year-old foster son spends 45 minutes on his homework instead of talking on the phone.
Vague: "Gee, what got into you?"
Specific: (Show your approval.) (Describe what was done well.)

5. Situation: Your 13-year-old foster daughter argues about taking out the trash.
Vague: "Don't you talk to me that way!"
Specific: (Describe what happened.) (Describe what you want done.)

6. Situation: Your nine-year-old foster son put his toys away. He also picked up his clothes and put them in the laundry basket. Now he wants to go play.
Vague: "Thanks for being so neat. Sure, you can go out and play."
Specific: (Show your approval.) (Describe what was done well.)

7. Situation: Your 15-year-old foster son comes home one hour late.
Vague: "Can't you tell time? You'll never go out again!"
Specific: (Describe what happened.) (Describe what you want done.)

8. Situation: Your 14-year-old foster daughter comes home with the highest grade she's ever received on a math test.
Vague: "Oh, that's nice."
Specific: (Show your approval.) (Describe what was done well.)

9. Situation: Your seven-year-old foster son leaves his bike in the driveway.
Vague: "You're so irresponsible with your things."
Specific: (Describe what happened.) (Describe what you want done.)

Now, try this at home with your children or foster children. Watch what they do and say for the next day or two. When you correct or compliment them, use the framework you just practiced. If you describe what your child or foster child does or says, you'll give clearer messages. Congratulations. Giving clear messages is the first step toward effective treatment parenting.

In the next several chapters, you'll learn another valuable technique – giving consequences. We'll also show you how to teach your foster child specific social skills such as "Following Instructions," "Accepting 'No' Answers," and "Accepting Criticism." You will find that as we move through the book, these techniques are used in many different situations. They give Treatment Parents a practical way to help their foster children. By learning thcsc and other skills, your foster child will be able to make a more successful adjustment to your home and achieve his or her treatment goals.

Welcome to treatment parenting.

CHAPTER 7

The ABC's of Behavior

When we think of changing a foster child's behavior, we usually think of what we can do in **response** to his or her behavior. Many times, this is effective. But you actually have **two** opportunities to change a foster child's behavior. Sometimes we can change what is happening just **before** the behavior occurs. We call these the **antecedents** – the events or conditions you observe before a behavior. You also can look at and change what happens **after** a behavior occurs. This is called the **consequence**.

So in looking for opportunities to change a foster child's behavior, you actually should look at all three parts – the ABC's – of the child's behavior:

A = Antecedents: what comes before the behavior

B = Behavior: what you can see, hear, or measure

C = Consequences: the actions or results of the behavior

Antecedents

In this chapter, we'll discuss antecedents and their role in changing a child's behavior. The following chapters will look more closely at consequences, both positive and negative.

Here are some examples of antecedents and how they can be changed:

- If you give a foster child a sweet snack at 4:30 p.m., she probably won't eat much dinner. You would be changing the antecedent if you give her a smaller nutritional snack earlier in the afternoon. Then the behavior of eating dinner would probably improve.

- When it is time for your foster child to go to bed, she may argue or complain, especially if she is doing something fun. You may begin nagging her to get her to stop the activity and get ready for bed. But you could change the antecedent if you told her to finish what she was doing by saying, "Ten more minutes, then it will be time to go to bed; if you get to bed late tonight, you'll have to go to bed earlier tomorrow." The arguing and complaining would probably decrease.

If you are considering changing the situation **before** a problem behavior can occur, here are some questions you can ask yourself:

Who is present when the behaviors occur?

When does the behavior occur?

Where does the behavior occur?

What activity is the foster child engaged in when the behavior occurs?

What may have been said, and how it was said, to the foster child?

Exercise 1

List three problem behaviors that your children or foster children have that can be changed by altering the antecedent (what comes before it).

1.

2.

3.

Here is a frustrating situation many Treatment Parents can relate to. After describing the situation, we'll discuss the ABC's of the child's behavior and options available for changing it.

The foster mother, Karen, and her eight-year-old foster daughter, Sally, are at the grocery store. After 30 minutes of shopping, they head down the candy aisle and Sally asks for a candy bar. Karen says "No." Sally begins to argue and insists that she "always gets" a candy bar. As Karen continues to tell Sally "No," Sally's behavior goes from arguing to demanding and crying. Sally says that her "real mom" bought her candy whenever she wanted, and if Karen loved her, she would too. Karen becomes frustrated and wants to tell Sally that if she were her "real mom," she would be tempted to spank her when they left the store. Instead, Karen threatens to take Sally's privileges away for the rest of the day.

When Karen and Sally finally reach the check-out, both are clearly very frustrated. Sally grabs a candy bar from the shelf and demands that Karen buy it for her. Karen gives several more warnings and tells Sally to put the candy back. Sally refuses. Karen then takes the candy bar away. Sally drops to the floor and screams. Karen has never had one of her own kids throw such a tantrum in public and she is very embarrassed and frustrated. Finally, Karen decides this must end, no matter what it takes, so she hands

Sally the candy bar. Karen says, "Here, now you'd better stop crying." Sally takes the candy bar and stops crying.

What are the antecedents?
Who is present? Karen, Sally, and people in the store.
Where are they? In the grocery store.
When? This starts on the way down the candy aisle and peaks at the check-out stand.
What is the activity? Karen and Sally are shopping.

What are the behaviors?
Continual asking, crying, demanding, takes candy off the shelf, refuses to return the candy, drops to the floor and screams.

What are the consequences?
Sally does not get the candy during shopping but she does get Karen's attention, and probably that of others in the store.
Sally gets attention from everyone in the check-out lane and then gets the candy.

What could Karen have done to change the antecedents so that Sally was less likely to have a tantrum in the store? She could do some or all of the following:

1. If Karen was willing to buy Sally a snack, she could tell Sally **exactly** what she must do to earn the snack. For instance, she could tell Sally to wait until they got to the check-out lane before she asks for candy, or to politely ask for some candy, without whining.

   If Karen does not want Sally to have candy, she could let her earn something else by displaying positive behaviors while shopping. These rewards might be playing dolls together later in the day, going to the park for 15 minutes on the way home from the store, etc.

2. Let Sally pick out a nutritional treat before they get to the candy aisle.

3. Avoid the check-out lane where candy is displayed.

4. Give Sally lots and lots or praise for good behavior (not whining, not complaining, standing quietly in the check-out line, etc.)

Summary

One key to being an effective Treatment Parent is the ability to observe the antecedents, behavior, and consequences of a child's actions and change what happens before or after the behavior. Many times, it is most effective to change the antecedents in order to either increase or decrease a child's specific behavior. Clearly identifying antecedents and learning how they relate to a child's behavior is a major factor in providing effective treatment.

CHAPTER 8

Teaching Social Skills

You have just learned how to give clear messages to children and how to identify the elements of behavior, which are some of the basic building blocks to teaching children new behaviors. This chapter will explain how to use what you've learned in order to teach children what you want them to do differently in the future.

What Are Social Skills?

First, let's review what we mean when we talk about social skills. Social Skills can be defined as **"the ability to interact with others in specific ways that are socially acceptable and, at the same time, personally or mutually beneficial"** (adapted from Combs & Slaby, 1977). This means that social skills help us all function within the rules of our community and society. Our parents taught us social skills when they talked to us about how to be a student, a friend, or an employee. We learned what we needed to do to get along with others in our family or community.

While the basic elements of a social skill usually remain constant, how a skill is used may vary from situation to situation. For instance, you would not greet the mayor of your community in the same way you would greet an old friend. With the mayor, you would show more formal respect. If you greeted your friend that way, he or she probably would think you were joking around. This is an example of how we adjust our social behaviors or skills to match the situation we are in.

Why Emphasize Social Skill Teaching?

Many of the children we help have not had the benefit of the informal social skills training that we received from our parents and teachers. For example, a foster child may appear very uncomfortable and awkward when meeting new people. Or, if you give a new foster child a compliment, he may look away and mumble something like, "Oh, yeah, I guess it's okay." Even more troubling is the fact that foster children frequently have difficulty using essential social skills such as "following instructions." When told to do something by an adult – a teacher, parent, or a police officer – these children may argue, complain, or simply refuse to comply.

In fact, the link between poor social skills and other problems is clear. Children with social skill deficits experience a variety of problems, including aggressive and antisocial behavior, juvenile delinquency, learning problems and school failure, mental health disorders, and loneliness and despondency (Gresham, 1981). Research evidence also indicates that if social and behavioral deficits are not corrected in childhood, they frequently carry over into adulthood (Steinberg & Knitzer, 1992). Without appropriate opportunities to learn better social skills, children fail to correct the deficits on their own (Stephens, 1978). It is easy to see why teaching social skills is very valuable to any child.

Our job is to directly and clearly teach foster children how to use appropriate social skills. This goal must be reached in a short time. While our own parents had many years to teach us the "people skills" we needed to be successful when we left home, the children you will work with may be in your home only a few months or more before they return to their family or are placed in a more permanent home. By teaching social skills in a planned, clear way, you can help a child learn many social skills in a short period of time.

Treatment Parents can make this learning process easier for children if they adjust their techniques, vocabulary, and behaviors to mesh with the learning style of the child in their home. **We cannot overemphasize the need for social skills instruction to give children meaningful alternatives to their behaviors.** When we ask you teach a child new social skills, we are asking you to teach a new set of behaviors.

Social Skill Components

We defined social skills as "the ability to interact with others in specific ways that are socially acceptable...." This means being able to perform a series of behaviors, not just one. When you are teaching social skills, you will be describing several behaviors or components that make up each skill. There are four steps to this process (adapted from Cartledge & Milburn, 1980):

1. Describe the skill by identifying the desired outcome or goal. For example, **"Telling the truth."**

2. Identify the essential component behaviors of the goal or skill.

3. State the skill's elements in observable terms.

4. Put the component behaviors in an order of performance. For example, to tell the truth, you should:

   • **Look at the person you are talking to.**
   • **Tell the person exactly what happened if he or she asks for information.**
   • **Answer any other questions. This can include what you did or did not do, or what someone else did or did not do.**
   • **Don't leave out important facts.**
   • **Admit to mistakes or errors if you made them.**

Appendix D, "Skills for Children and Teens" lists many of the basic skills that you will teach a child in your home. Teaching these skills will give children a positive way to get their needs met and to correct inappropriate behavior. Your Consultant will give you specific suggestions about which skills you should focus your teaching on. These skills, which are described in the child's Treatment Plan, will be chosen in order to help you get as many inappropriate behaviors as possible under control quickly. For instance, skills that can be generalized to many different situations will be taught first. "Following Instructions" and "Staying Calm" are just two of these skills that are frequently part of a new foster child's Treatment Plan. You will be the child's primary teacher for these alternative or positive skills.

Let's look at an example of which skills can be taught in response to a child's inappropriate behaviors.

Example 1
Inappropriate behavior

1. The foster child argues, "I didn't do it; you didn't see me," when you describe his inappropriate behavior.

   Skill: Accepting Criticism
   Disagreeing Appropriately

2. The foster child flops down in a chair and pouts after you tell her she can't stay up late.

   Skill: Accepting "No" Answers

3. The child walks into the kitchen and says, "Gimme some lunch money, I'm late for school."

   Skill: Asking for Help

4. The foster child kicks another child for barging in front of him to get into the van.

   Skill: Staying Calm
   Getting Along with Others
   Disagreeing with Others

5. The foster parent remarks that she likes the child's new haircut and he mumbles, "Yeah? Well I hate it!"

   Skill: Accepting a Compliment

6. The child stays seated when the Treatment Parent brings a visitor over to meet him.

   Skill: Greeting Others

Exercise 1

This exercise will help you practice how to choose the skills you want to teach. Match the skill or skills with the situation that follows.

Staying Calm
Following Instructions
Apologizing
Accepting a Consequence
Telling the Truth

Child refuses to put his coat and shoes on when it is time for school
Skill:

Child argues when you tell her she lost some TV time for not doing her chore
Skill:

Child does not apologize for breaking another child's toys
Skill:

The child screams and slams doors when he is angry
Skill:

The child makes up a story to explain why she was late getting home from school
Skill:

Exercise 2

List some inappropriate behaviors that you have seen your own children or other people's children engage in. Then list some skills that you would want the child to use instead of the inappropriate behaviors. (If you are unsure of the skill components, refer to Appendix D.)

1. Description of behavior and circumstances:

Skill:
Skill Components:

2. Description of behavior and circumstances:

Skill:
Skill Components:

3. Description of behavior and circumstances:

Skill:
Skill Components:

4. Description of behavior and circumstances:

Skill:
Skill Components:

5. Description of behavior and circumstances:

Skill:
Skill Components:

Now it is your turn to practice describing a child's behavior and thinking of the skill you would teach so that the child could behave appropriately in the future.

Summary

In this chapter, we've discussed how and why you should teach children social skills. By describing the specific components of a skill, the child will learn to recognize when, where, how, and with whom to use these new behaviors. The child also will learn that using these new skills will help him or her get needs met appropriately. As the child practices and uses these new skills, he or she will be more successful in your home, in school, and eventually in his or her own family. Ultimately, this will give the child a better chance of successfully returning home or moving on to another living situation.

CHAPTER 9

Consequences

Consequences are at work all the time. We run into them every day – at work, at home, with friends, and so on. If we compliment a friend, he returns the pleasantry. If we don't get our work done, the boss criticizes us. If we don't remember to take the dog outside, he leaves a calling card on the carpet. Consequences affect all of us, positively and negatively.

As Treatment Parents, it helps to understand why giving consequences to our foster children is so essential. Consequences teach foster children to think. Consequences help foster children learn that their actions lead to results, both positive and negative. They learn that life is full of choices and the choices they make greatly influence what happens to them. Foster children whose Treatment Parents give appropriate consequences learn successful ways to behave.

Consequences Change Behavior

As a Treatment Parent, you must know how to use consequences to teach foster children. If consequences have the power to change behavior, it makes sense that they should be used to help our foster children. You've probably used consequences frequently. "Grounding" your child or foster child, letting your teen go out on a weekend night because she finished her homework early, using time-out, and offering dessert only after a child finishes his vegetables all are examples of consequences.

Simply giving a consequence doesn't mean you are automatically going to change a foster child's behavior. Throughout this book, we emphasize the importance of learning to use a combination of clear messages and consequences when teaching your children and foster children. They need to understand the relationship between their behavior and consequences in order for them to change behavior. This combination, coupled with your love and affection, leads to effective treatment parenting.

Effective Consequences

Let's look at some of the basic elements of effective consequences. There are two basic kinds of consequences – positive and negative.

Positive consequences are things people like and are willing to work to get. Behavior that is followed by a positive consequence is more likely to occur again (or will occur more frequently). Rewards are a form of positive consequences.

Negative consequences are things people don't like and want to avoid. Basically, negative consequences encourage people to change their actions so that they won't receive more negative consequences. Behavior that is followed by a negative consequence is less likely to occur again (or will not occur as frequently). Removing a privilege is a negative consequence.

Let's look at qualities to consider when choosing an effective consequence:

Importance. The consequence has to mean something to your foster child. One way to find out what is important to your foster children is to watch what they do when they have free time. For example, if a child likes to watch TV, invite friends over to your house, and ride his bicycle, then these activities are important to your foster child. These everyday and special activities can be used as consequences. Taking away or giving something the child isn't interested in will probably have little effect on the behavior.

Immediacy. This means giving a consequence right after a behavior occurs. If you can't give the consequence right away, give it as soon as possible. Delaying a consequence reduces its impact and weakens the connection between the behavior and the consequence. If you took play time away from your five-year-old for something she did last week, she would be confused and think that you were tremendously unfair. You may decide to take away something that will happen in the future, like a trip to the park scheduled for the weekend. In this case, your child or foster child should be told of the consequence right after the behavior occurs.

Frequency. This refers to the number of times a consequence is given. If you give the same consequence too often or give it inconsistently, it loses its effectiveness. Changes in the foster child's behavior will help you determine whether you are using a consequence too often or inconsistently. For example, if you were to give your foster child a fruitcake (assuming he loved fruitcake) each time he helped around the house, he soon would get tired of fruitcake and have less interest in helping.

It is helpful to know that when you are teaching a new behavior, you should give a positive consequence for the positive behavior **each** and **every time** it occurs, **immediately** after it occurs. Once the foster child has learned the new skill and can use it without being reminded, you can begin to give the positive consequence **intermittently** (ever other time or occasionally). This will help ensure that the behavior continues to happen and will allow you to move your attention to teaching new skills.

Degree. Degree refers to the severity or size of the consequence. Typically, Treatment Parents should try to give the smallest consequence they think will be effective. This works for both positive and negative consequences. If you think that allowing your foster child to have a friend stay over Saturday night will be incentive enough for her to keep her room clean during the week, use that as the positive consequence. On the other hand, grounding a foster child for a month for not cleaning her room would be too big a negative consequence. A less severe consequence (not allowing her to have her friend stay over) would probably get the job done. Giving too much of a positive consequence may result in a "spoiled" foster child, one who gets too much for doing too little. On the other hand, giving too much of a negative consequence may result in a foster child who always feels punished or who "gives up" trying to change because the consequences are too great if she makes a mistake.

Contingency. This is commonly called "Grandma's rule" because grandmothers used this long before it ever showed up in a book. Basically, it means that one activity (a privilege your foster child likes) is available after your foster child finishes an activity that you want done. For example:

"You can watch TV after you have finished your homework."

"You can go outside after you make your bed and put your dirty clothes in the laundry basket."

"When you're finished with the dishes, you can call your friend."

These are all examples of "Grandma's rule" – giving a privilege after, not before, a specified task is completed. This contingency rule can be used with foster children of all ages. As a quick practice, fill in the following blanks to complete statements you could make to your foster child that uses the rule.

"You can _____ after
                    (something your foster child likes)

you _____
          (something you want your foster child to do)."

"When you're finished with _____,

you can _____."

58

Exercise 1

Think of the positive and negative consequences you now use with your child or foster child and list three of each below.

Negative consequences:

1.

2.

3.

Positive consequences:

1.

2.

3.

When Consequences Don't Work

Occasionally, Treatment Parents tell us that no matter what they try, consequences won't work with their foster child. There could be several reasons for this. We'll touch on a couple here.

Treatment Parents sometimes give many negative consequences, but neglect to give enough positive consequences. As a result, the negative consequences lose their effectiveness because there isn't a balance between positive and negative consequences. The foster children, logically, go elsewhere to get positive consequences. It's just too darned unpleasant being around their Treatment Parents.

The second reason is that Treatment Parents don't always give consequences enough time to work. They often expect a consequence to change a behavior the first time it is used. This isn't the case. Change takes time. Foster children didn't learn to

behave the way they do, good or bad, overnight. Therefore, Treatment Parents need to be patient, look for small improvements, and give the consequences time to work.

A third reason is that Treatment Parents may not make clear the connection between a child's behavior and its consequence. The child or foster child does not change his behavior because he doesn't understand that a certain behavior results in a consequence each and every time (consistently and immediately).

A final reason is that some Treatment Parents mistake privileges for rights. Of course, most foster children will try to convince their Treatment Parents that everything is a right. But if Treatment Parents treat privileges as rights, they limit what they can use for consequences. The rights of foster children include the right to nourishment, communication with others, clothing, and so on. (See Chapter 2.) Watching TV, going out with friends, and using family possessions all are privileges that can and should be monitored by the Treatment Parents and used by the foster child with their approval.

Thinking Ahead

It's wise to set up both positive and negative consequences in advance. For example, when your foster child does not do her chores, know what negative consequences you plan to use and tell her what those consequences will be. If your foster child does what is expected, know what positive consequences you will use and tell her what they are. Your Consultant will talk with you before the foster child comes to live with you about suggestions for positive and negative consequences that may be appropriate for that specific foster child. As you get to know your foster child better, you will learn which positive and negative consequences are most effective. Just like with your own children, this list changes over time as your foster child changes and grows.

Your foster children should be aware of planned consequences. Don't hesitate to post established consequences, both positive and negative, on your refrigerator door or in your foster children's rooms. Consequences shouldn't be surprises. In fairness to your foster children, they should be aware of what they will get for behaving well and what they will lose for misbehavior. In the chapter on Motivation Systems, we talk about helping your foster child set and reach reasonable goals. Treatment Parents tell us that this also is a good way to spell out positive and negative consequences for a foster child. Again, your Consultant will help you establish these rules and expectations for your foster child.

Giving Consequences

Later chapters will outline steps for effectively giving consequences to your foster child. Until you finish those chapters, these few basic components will help you become aware of how to deliver consequences that will affect a child's behavior.

When delivering a consequence, remember to:

Be clear. Make sure your foster child knows what the consequence is and what he or she did to earn or lose it.

Be consistent. Don't give a big consequence for a behavior one time and then ignore the same behavior the next time.

Another part of being consistent is deciding when a behavior is inappropriate enough to merit a consequence. There is a fine line for most of us between what is accepted and what is NOT accepted as appropriate behavior. We refer to this line as the **tolerance level**. A Treatment Parent with a low tolerance level gives consequences as soon as the misbehavior begins and before it becomes severe. A Treatment Parent with a high tolerance level waits until after a behavior occurs repeatedly or is severe before giving a consequence.

Each Treatment Parent makes decisions about when "enough is enough." Spouses may generally agree on where to draw the line with foster children's misbehavior, yet it is impossible to always agree about everything. The important thing is to talk with your spouse about when to start giving consequences for misbehavior, and then **consistently follow through**. The foster children will be less confused, they will view you as being fairer, and

in the long run, it is less likely that one Treatment Parent will be viewed as the "good guy" and the other as the "bad guy."

Occasionally, Consultants will suggest that Treatment Parents make adjustments in their tolerance levels so that teaching occurs sooner or is more consistent. The goal here is to help the Treatment Parents experience success sooner in changing certain types of behavior or avoiding situations in which one is seen as "nice" and the other as "mean."

Be brief. This is especially true with younger foster children. Clear messages usually get lost when you lecture.

Follow through. If you set up an arrangement for your foster child to earn a positive consequence, be sure he gets the reward after he's completed his task. Likewise, if you give a negative consequence, don't let your foster child talk you out of it (unless you decide that the consequence you gave was totally unreasonable or given out of anger).

Be as pleasant as possible. This is generally easier when you give positive consequences, but keep it in mind when you give negative consequences as well. Yelling and screaming are not effective. Foster children can't hear your words, they can only hear your anger. Our research tells us that foster children are more likely to respond positively and learn more from adults who are calm and reasonable, even when the adults are giving negative consequences.

Warnings

One last pointer about consequences. Many Treatment Parents have fallen prey to giving too many warnings – "For the third time, I'll take your game away if you don't stop that." While a single warning may be effective, repeated warnings that are not followed by consequences usually do not work and become a source of frustration for the Treatment Parents. If you have to come back time after time and deal with the same behavior, you may be talking too much and not giving enough consequences. If you told your foster child that you would take the game away for a certain misbehavior, and the misbehavior occurs, then take the game away. This helps the child understand what rules are in effect in your family. Otherwise, rules become confusing and turn obedience into a guessing game for your child – "Can I get away with it this time? Mom warned me three times and nothing's happened yet."

Summary

It always amazes us how creative and effective Treatment Parents can be once they learn how to give consequences. All they need is a little push in the right direction and a little confidence that what they are doing will work. In the next two chapters, we will talk about the different types of positive and negative consequences you can use.

CHAPTER 10

Positive Consequences

Positive consequences can be a Treatment Parent's best friend because they are used to increase positive behavior. Positive consequences also can be referred to as **rewards** (or reinforcers). Generally, rewards are things that people like or enjoy and will work to earn. Therefore, when we use the term "reward," we mean any type of consequence that makes behavior occur again (or occur more often).

In the last chapter, the two basic principles you learned were:

- **Positive consequences are used to increase desirable behavior.**

- **Negative consequences are used to decrease and stop problem behavior.**

It's human nature to focus on the negative; just read today's newspaper or watch the evening news. Most stories report negative events. As Treatment Parents, we sometimes fall into the same trap when it comes to our foster children; we focus on their negative behaviors. Foster children make mistakes and they don't do everything we'd like them to do. But, they also do many good things. Everyone benefits when Treatment Parents focus on what their foster children do well.

Using positive consequences is one way to focus on what foster children do well, and to increase the amount of time that they spend doing positive things. If Treatment Parents give only negative consequences, they run the risk of becoming a negative consequence themselves. In such situations, foster children may want to avoid their Treatment Parents. The alternative is also true. When you give positive consequences, your foster children find that spending time with you is more enjoyable. This gives you even more opportunities to use praise and positive consequences.

Treatment Parents who balance negative and positive consequences are viewed as more fair and reasonable by their foster children. (Plus, it's a heck of a lot more fun and rewarding for Treatment Parents when they give positive consequences.) Treatment Parents who consistently use positive consequences are more pleasant and effective and foster children are more likely to listen to them.

Positive Consequences That Work

Something that is a reward for one person may not be a reward for someone else. It's sort of like the old saying, "Different strokes for different folks." Exercise 1 should help you find positive consequences that will work with your foster child. Using the examples as a guide, identify what your foster children like to do and write those preferences in the blanks provided.

(All Treatment Parents enjoy consequences that don't cost money. We know you can't run out and buy something every time your foster child behaves well. Even if you could, it isn't healthy for your foster child. In Appendix E, we've included a list of items that are "freebies." Some of these may help you complete the following exercise.)

Exercise 1

Take a few minutes to think about what positive consequences you could use with a child:

Activities – What everyday activities does your child or foster child like (e.g. Nintendo®, baseball, watching sitcoms, baking cookies, reading)?

First child

Second child

Possessions – What material articles does your child or foster child like (e.g. sweatshirts, baseball cards, money, dolls, music cassettes)?

First child

Second child

Special activities – What special activities does your child or foster child like (e.g. going to a ball game, visiting a zoo, going to a movie, having a friend stay overnight)?

First child

Second child

Food – What are your child's or foster child's favorite foods and beverages (e.g. popcorn, Popsicles, pizza, cola, candy, fruit juice)?

First child

Second child

(Note: Do NOT use meals as a negative consequence. As stated in Chapter 2, foster children have the right to proper nutrition. "Food" consequences refer to special snacks or "extras."

People – Who does your child or foster child like to spend time with?

First child

Second child

(Note: A foster child's opportunity to visit with his or her family is not a reward; it is a right unless the court or the foster child's caseworker has determined that seeing the family would be harmful to the child. This is especially true if the family visits are court-ordered. So, foster children should not earn or lose visits based on their behavior, except under certain circumstances.)

Attention – What specific kinds of verbal and physical attention from you and others does your child or foster child like (e.g. hugs, smiles, compliments, high five's, thumbs up, praise)?

First child

Second child

Other rewards – Is there anything else that your child or foster child likes, is interested in, or would like to spend time doing? Is there a favorite chore, or something that he or she has wanted to do but hasn't yet done?

First child

Second child

Exercise 1 gave you a list of consequences that can be used to encourage your foster child's positive behavior. Now, let's look at how to use them.

Exercise 2

In this exercise, list four behaviors you want your child or foster child to use more often or more consistently. Then assign a positive consequence or reward you identified earlier to each behavior, and how much of the reward you are going to give.

1. Behavior:

    Consequence:

    Amount:

2. Behavior:

    Consequence:

    Amount:

3. Behavior:

    Consequence:

    Amount:

4. Behavior:

    Consequence:

    Amount:

Shaping

Sometimes, using positive consequences may not be enough to get a foster child to change his or her behavior right away. This is particularly true if you are trying to teach a new set of behaviors that a foster child is having difficulty learning. In these situations, **shaping** is a procedure that can be used to effectively teach and reinforce new behavior. Basically, shaping means that you praise or reinforce the foster child's **attempts** to use the new skill you are teaching. For example, if your foster child is not used to making his bed and cleaning his room, you would enthusiastically praise and reward him for pulling the covers up on the bed, and putting his toys in the corner of the room. This may be less than you ultimately want, but the foster child is making an effort to clean his room. Next time, you may ask the foster child to put his dirty clothes in the hamper in addition to making the bed and cleaning the floor. Eventually, the foster child will be able to clean his room on his own; you will have shaped this skill through specifically teaching, praising, and rewarding the child's attempts. This helps the foster child feel that he can accomplish what is expected of him. So many foster children with low self-esteem give up before they really try. Shaping helps the foster child "bite off a little at a time" until his or her confidence has improved.

Bribes

The idea of using positive consequences (rewards) to change behaviors is viewed with skepticism by some foster parents. To them, it seems that foster children are being bribed or paid off for doing what they're expected to do. However, rewards are a natural part of daily life. They can include anything from the obvious, like merit raises at work, to subtle things, like a smile or a wink. These are given for acceptable behavior, behavior that is expected to be repeated.

Bribery occurs when rewards are given for **inappropriate** behavior. Giving a child a candy bar to make him stop crying in the grocery store check-out lane is a bribe. (It may seem necessary for your sanity, but it's still a good example of a bribe.) The parent feels forced to do anything to stop the foster child's negative behavior – "Okay, you can have the candy. Just stop crying!" The child is rewarded for being "a brat." If this scenario occurs frequently enough, the result is a foster child who always wants a reward before she'll behave as the parent wants. The reward worked in quieting the foster child, but guess what happens the next time the parent is in the checkout lane? Right – the child cries and demands a candy bar. The child has learned that inappropriate behavior will earn a candy bar; she has been bribed and wants another bribe before acting appropriately. Therefore, don't give rewards for inappropriate behaviors – those are bribes. **Give rewards for positive behaviors.**

Using the same example, here's how the candy bar could be a reward. You may tell your child or foster child that if she stays next to the cart, does not touch things on the shelf, and does not complain while shopping, she can have a candy bar when you're finished. This way, you are rewarding or reinforcing positive behavior, not bribing.

Summary

The more you use positive consequences, the more likely you are to see positive behavior. Please remember that the most powerful rewards for foster children can be praise and positive attention from their Treatment Parents. Continue to focus on the positive things your foster children do – positive consequences work!

CHAPTER 11

Negative Consequences

"I hate you."
"I don't have to do anything I don't want to!"
"I was only an hour late. What's the big deal?"
"Why do I have to clean my room? I just cleaned it last week."

Okay, so you won't give positive consequences for all behaviors. Children are going to say and do things we don't like. We all realize children are going to misbehave. When they do, they should receive negative consequences. If the consequences are given in a firm, fair, and consistent manner, they will be effective (and so will you).

As a Treatment Parent, one of your first goals should be to find out what negative consequences work with your foster child. Just as with positive consequences, different negative consequences are effective with some foster children and not with others. One key to look for when determining the effectiveness of a consequence is the result: Did the negative behavior stop or occur less often?

We will concentrate on using two forms of negative consequences – taking away a privilege, and adding work related to the misbehavior (for example, vacuuming the carpet after tracking dirt in).

Removing Positive Consequences

When a problem behavior occurs, one type of negative consequence is the removal of a privilege. Some situations are tailor-made for this. For example, if your foster daughter comes home an hour late, you may remove part of the privilege (coming home an hour earlier next time she goes out). If this

is a frequent problem, she may lose the entire privilege of going out for a period of time. Similarly, if two children are arguing about which TV show to watch, you can shut off the TV until they settle their differences, or they can lose TV privileges for the evening.

Using the method that we presented in Chapter 6 ("Clear Messages"), you can combine clear messages with negative consequences. You could say to your foster daughter, "Sarah, you're one hour late. As a result, you can't go out tomorrow night." To the two children arguing over the TV, you could say, "Bob and Ray, you're arguing about which show to watch. Please shut the TV off until you can calmly come to me with a solution."

Always keep in mind the qualities that make consequences effective. During the first few weeks that your foster child is living with you, you may not be real sure what negative consequences will be effective. By talking with the foster child about his or her interests and talking with people who have cared for the child before, you will probably get some good ideas. As you get to know your foster child better and work with your Consultant, you will probably improve your list.

In deciding what consequence to use, you should ask these questions. (We'll use the situation with Sarah coming home late as an example.)

Was the consequence:

Important? – Does Sarah really like to go out?
Immediate? – Did you give the consequence right away?

Frequent? – Has she lost the privilege of going out so often that she doesn't really care anymore?

The right amount? – Was losing one night out with her friends enough (or too much) of a consequence?

Contingent? – Did you use Grandma's Rule? "If you come home from school on time for two days in a row, you can earn the privilege of going out on Friday night."

Exercise 1

Now, identify some of your child's or foster child's problem behaviors. Then list the negative consequences (removal of privileges) you would use in each situation. The first one is done for you.

1. Behavior: Didn't do homework

   Consequence: No TV

   Amount: Rest of night

2. Behavior:

   Consequence:

   Amount:

3. Behavior:

   Consequence:

   Amount:

4. Behavior:

   Consequence:

   Amount:

Adding Work

This is an effective method for teaching responsibility. It takes time and effort for foster children to correct problems, and if added work cuts into their play time or takes away time for doing something fun, the children will try to avoid that consequence by changing their behavior. Many times, the consequence relates directly to the problem; in fact, the consequence actually is designed to "make up" for the misbehavior. Other times, you can provide a negative consequence simply by adding a chore. So, instead of removing a privilege, you're having your foster child do something constructive in order to get your message across.

The process of adding work is simple. For example, if your foster son constantly leaves his clothes laying on the floor, he must pick them up before he gets to do what he wants to do (Grandma's Rule). Or he must gather the dirty clothes from every family member and put them in the hamper. Adding work is another way of teaching responsibility.

Here are some other examples of how to add work as a consequence.

- Your foster son throws his clean clothes in a wadded-up ball in the corner of his closet. He must fold those clothes as well as help you fold the next load of laundry.
- Your foster daughter doesn't take her lunch bag to school, so you have to take it to her. The next day, you get her up 15 minutes earlier to make sure she has enough time to make her lunch and put it in the bag.
- Your son and foster child are fighting about who last put away the clean dishes. To help them learn how to get along, you have them wash the dishes together the next two nights.

It is important to keep your Consultant informed about what "work" consequences you are using with the foster child. **While most of these chores are corrective and very acceptable, it is possible to overdo it. Telling your Consultant what work consequences you are using helps avoid concerns about a child rights violation.**

Exercise 2

In the following situations, decide how you would correct your foster child by adding work:

1. Your foster child left a mess on the dining room table.

2. Your foster son jumped on a chair. The chair fell over and broke a lamp.

3. Your foster child left a pan of soup on the stove and it boiled over, making a mess on the stove.

4. Your foster son tells you he left his books at school so he can't do his homework.

5. Your foster child and son argue over who has to set the table.

Giving Negative Consequences

The effectiveness of your consequences depends, in part, on how you give them. An angry response is not going to work; it may even result in more problems. Our experience tells us that children respond better and learn more from adults who are pleasant and positive, even when they are giving negative consequences.

With that in mind, we use a process called Corrective Teaching®. Corrective Teaching combines clear messages with consequences and practice to help Treatment Parents respond to problem behavior. Treatment Parents have found that Corrective Teaching gives them a formula for using consequences to deal with routine negative behavior.

For now, it's enough to only mention Corrective Teaching, which is described in detail in Chapter 15. But we do want you to know that negative consequences are given as part of this focused, organized teaching process.

Is the Consequence Truly Negative?

Sometimes, Treatment Parents make the mistake of assuming that a consequence is negative. We encourage them to look at the effects of the consequence on the behavior they want to change. If the behavior **stops or decreases in frequency**, you've given a **negative consequence**. If the behavior **continues or occurs more often**, you've given a **positive consequence**. For example, one mother told us that her six-year-old continually fidgeted and talked in church. She told him that he couldn't come with her next time if he continued causing problems in church. Sure enough, that kid fidgeted like crazy and talked more than ever. He didn't want to be in church to begin with! His mother's "negative consequence" actually encouraged more problem behaviors. The behavior she wanted to stop actually increased. She had given him a positive consequence.

In this situation, the mother could use one of the following:

- **Remove a privilege** – The boy can't play with his friend after church if he fidgets during the service.
- **Use Grandma's Rule** – If the boy sits quietly, the family can stop for ice cream on the way home from church.

Actually, the mother used both methods, and they worked. The young boy learned to sit quietly in church.

Pay close attention to the effect a negative consequence has on the behavior you want to change. If the problem behavior has decreased or ended altogether, you gave an effective consequence.

The Snowball Effect

One problem with negative consequences is that Treatment Parents can lose sight of when to stop. If one consequence doesn't work, they often try another that is harsher. This can create an upward spiral where the Treatment Parent ends up grounding the foster child for the next five years, or something totally unreasonable like that. Usually, this happens when Treatment Parents are frustrated and upset. Foster children know which buttons to push, and Treatment Parents can sometimes quickly lose their patience. That's when the "snowball effect" usually takes place.

Consider this situation: Amy didn't clean her room so her foster dad took away her telephone privileges for a weekend. Her room was messy the next day. For this, she lost a week of TV privileges. The room didn't get any cleaner, so her dad added another month without phone privileges, another week without TV, and told her that she couldn't come out of her room until it was spotless.

Whew! This wasn't just the snowball effect; it was an avalanche! In three days, this girl lost just about all communication with the outside world! This is a good example of how Treatment Parents can get carried away with ineffective negative consequences, and risk violating the foster child's rights in the process. So instead of repeating negative consequences in rapid-fire succession, step back and look at the effects of the consequence on the behavior. Change the consequence if necessary, but don't continue to pile consequence upon consequence. More is not necessarily better. We strongly encourage you to call your Consultant if you are feeling this frustrated. Since the consequences given by this foster father were unreasonable, we suggested that he go back, talk to Amy, and set up the following plan:

1. He helps Amy clean her room.
2. In return, Amy helps him clean the garage.

If these two parts of the plan were completed, Amy could have her privileges back. To help Amy keep the room clean consistently, the foster father found a way to use Grandma's Rule: Each day that Amy cleans her room, she gets to use the phone and watch her favorite TV show. This practical solution worked. Amy's room was not spotless, but it was clean much more often than it was dirty. And the foster father knew exactly what consequence he could use depending on whether the room was clean or dirty. He learned how to avoid the snowball effect and still give a negative consequence that worked.

It helps when Treatment Parents are willing to look at their own behavior when they are giving negative consequences. They need to determine if they are giving too many negative consequences or if the consequences are too extreme. Again, Consultants can be very helpful in figuring out negative consequences that will help change the behavior and keep the foster child motivated to work on his or her behavior. If you find that you are going overboard when giving negative consequences, alter them. Remember, the consequence needs to fit the behavior. One consequence that works well with younger foster children is "time-out." For a description of how to use it, see Appendix F at the end of the book.

Summary

Finding effective negative consequences is a challenge for Treatment Parents, but it is not impossible. If your foster children misbehave, do one of the following – remove all or part of a privilege, or add work. Be logical, fair, and consistent, and you'll be on the road to using effective consequences.

CHAPTER 12

Effective Praise

When foster children come to your home, do they feel good about themselves? Can they identify their talents and strengths? Do they think they are good learners? Are they calm and self-confident? We've found that this rarely is the case. Most children coming into a new foster home feel adrift and alone. They usually feel responsible for the break-up of their family and overwhelmed by the task of trying to make it better. They frequently think they are "bad kids," deserving whatever bad treatment they get. They think they are stupid and unlovable. Remember that emotional abuse is one of the most damaging types of abuse. The legacy of being emotionally abused is that you believe you are not worthy of being cared for or loved. How can Treatment Parents begin to fill in this foster child's self-image with something positive and meaningful? **Effective Praise** is a very powerful tool in helping foster children develop or restore a positive view of themselves. Praise is nourishment for the foster child's mind and self-esteem.

Focus on the Positive

Praise is not a new concept; we're all familiar with it. But many of us don't use it as often as we should. Why? One of the reasons is that we have been trained to see negatives. It is easy to see what people do wrong. Unfortunately, some untrained foster parents often focus on the negative. It's easy for them to see the mistakes and shortcomings of their foster children. And so many of the children who come into foster care are so unfamiliar with praise, that when they do hear it from Treatment Parents, they don't believe the compliments at first. They may reply, "Oh yeah, sure" or "You are just saying that to be nice or because you have to."

At Boys Town, we have found one thing to be true time and time again – **praise works wonders.** When Treatment Parents use praise consistently, foster children change dramatically. When Treatment Parents "zero in" on as many positive things as they can, foster children begin to feel better about themselves.

Some Treatment Parents tell us that they praise their foster children, but it just doesn't seem to work. Usually, we find that these Treatment Parents praise only outstanding achievements or momentous occasions. We tell them to look for little things to praise, too. After they begin praising small improvements, they notice many positive changes in their foster children's behavior. This is not a coincidence. Praise works.

Other Treatment Parents ask, "Why should I praise my foster children for something that they're supposed to do?" Good question. We answer them with these questions: "Do you like being recognized for the things you do well, regardless of whether you're supposed to do them? Do you like to hear your boss tell you what a good job you're doing?" Most Treatment Parents say, "Of course." And then add, "And, I wouldn't mind hearing it a little more often." Enough said. We **all** like to hear about things we do well.

When praising your foster children, it helps to look closely at three areas:

1. **Things your foster children already do well** (and maybe you take for granted).
2. **Improvements**, even small improvements, in problem areas.
3. **Positive attempts at new skills**.

For example, praise your foster child for coming home from school on time, or cleaning her room, or turning off the lights, if you haven't mentioned your appreciation for a long time. Most likely, he or she will continue to do these things since you took the time to notice.

If your foster child tries hard to learn something new, praise the effort. Praise any step in the right direction. Learning a skill requires learning small parts of it, then putting all of the steps together. When your own child was learning to walk, you probably praised each and every improvement – from first standing alone, to taking that first awkward step, to finally putting a series of steps together. When foster children first come to your home, there is so much for them to learn. You may have so many new expectations for them that you tend to take for granted – eating at the table as a family, getting up for school on time, or sleeping in pajamas. If you praise positive attempts to learn or try a new skill and other improvements, the same level of enthusiasm and the same attention to trying can carry over to many areas of your foster children's lives. Seize every opportunity to recognize positive attempts to learn.

Steps to Effective Praise

The easiest way to praise someone is to say things like, "Fantastic!", "Great!", or "Keep up the good work!" This is a good start, but we suggest you take it a little further to make sure your foster child receives a clear message. That's why we make a distinction between praise in general, and what we call Effective Praise.

Effective Praise allows you to:

- **Recognize your foster children** sincerely and enthusiastically for the progress they are making.

- **Specifically describe** what you like.

- **Give a reason** why you like it.

In the chapter on clear messages, we talked about a framework to use when teaching your foster children. This is the basis for Effective Praise. Here are the steps:

1. **Show your approval.** Smiling and a pat on the back are enthusiastic ways to show approval. A brief praise statement such as "Great job" also is effective.

2. **Describe the positive.** Give clear, specific descriptions of what your foster child did well.

3. **Give a reason.** Tell how that behavior helps your foster child, or why that behavior is appreciated by others.

4. **Optional reward.** A reward can be given, depending on the situation and the behavior or skill the child used.

Consistently using Effective Praise will result in more positive behaviors from your foster children. Consistently "catching 'em being good" results in foster children who like themselves and grow in self-confidence.

Let's look at an example of Effective Praise. Your teenage foster son just called to tell you where he is.

Show your approval – "Thanks for calling me, Tom."

Describe the positive – "I'm really glad that you let me know where you were and why you'll be a little late."

Give a reason – "Calling me shows responsibility and shows that I can trust you."

Optional reward – "For checking in, you can stay out an extra 15 minutes the next time you go out."

In this brief scenario, your foster child learned specifically what he did right and why it was so important. You increased the likelihood that he will call the next time he's out.

Let's look more closely at these relatively easy steps and see why they are important.

Show Your Approval

Foster children are like the rest of us. They not only like to hear nice things said about them, but they'll also work harder to get more praise in the future. As we mentioned earlier, many foster children have been emotionally neglected or abused. They are really starved for someone to notice them and their abilities. When you combine a sign of your approval with specific praise, the praise is that much more meaningful.

There are numerous words that show your approval and, for goodness sakes, show a little excitement! Awesome! Terrific! Wow! You're right on target! I'm impressed! Super! Amazing! That's great! Wonderful! Magnificent! Excellent! (Doesn't it make you feel better just saying these words?)

There also are numerous actions that convey your approval to children: Hugging them. Winking or smiling at them. Giving them a "thumbs up" or an "A-Okay" sign. Ruffling their hair. Giving them "five." Nodding your head. Clapping for them.

Showing your approval lets foster children know that you're excited about what they're doing. Every foster child gives us something to be happy about. Every foster child does something that deserves praise. Let's make sure we recognize it, and most of all, let's tell them.

Describe the Positive

After you have given a praise statement, describe the specific behaviors you liked. Make sure your foster children understand what they did so that they can repeat the behavior in the future. Give them clear messages. Praise what you just saw or heard your foster child do well. For example, "Sue, thanks for washing the dishes and helping me put the leftovers away," or "Eddie, I'm glad you washed your hands after you went to the bathroom."

Along with specifically describing the behavior, you also will want to identify the skill. For example, "Sue, thanks for cleaning the dishes and helping me put the leftovers away. You did a nice job of following instructions."

Remember to use words your foster children understand. Make the statements brief and to the point. Just let your foster child know what was done well.

Give a Reason

Foster children benefit from knowing why a behavior is helpful to them or others. It helps them understand the relationship between their behavior and what happens to them. When foster children first come into placement, it is more effective to use explanations that deal with short-term effects. For instance, "It's important to share your toys so other children will want to share with you." As foster children develop and begin to internalize the gains they have made, you can use reasons that point out long-term effects or begin using reasons that include concern for others. An example is, "It's important to share your toys so the other children will feel welcome and want to come back to see you again." This helps foster children learn empathy for other people and understand how their actions affect others.

Here is another example of how to give a reason: Your teenager volunteers to clean up the family room before guests come over and completes the job. In order to explain why that behavior is helpful, you could use one of the following reasons:

"Cleaning the family room really saved us a lot of time. We have time to get everything finished before guests come over."

"Helping others is a real plus. If you do that on the job, your boss is more likely to give you a raise."

"Since you helped out, I'll have time to take you over to your friend's house when you want to go. I don't know if I would have had time if you hadn't helped."

Giving your foster child a reason for using a certain behavior shows the relationship between the behavior and the consequences or outcomes. Unfortunately, most foster children have not been taught this relationship. A child may say that his teacher gave him poor grades "because she didn't like me," rather than because he was frequently absent or didn't turn in their homework. Reasons are particularly meaningful when they can demonstrate the benefits your foster child may receive, either immediately or in the future. The reasons should be brief, believable, and age-appropriate. Giving a reason such as, "Because I said so," is not helpful to children because it does not help them see how they can benefit from the behavior.

Optional Reward

Occasionally, you may want to add a fourth step – a reward – when you give Effective Praise. When you are especially pleased with a certain behavior, or when your foster child has made a big improvement in a certain area, you can reward him or her with a special privilege. (Refer to the list you made in Chapter 10, "Positive Consequences," for privileges or activities you can use.)

Rewards can be big or small; that's up to you. If possible, give rewards that are related to the type of behavior you want to encourage. Rewards also will help make your praise more reinforcing over time.

Many children coming into foster care feel lonesome and homesick at times. They also have missed out on spending time with adults who put the child's needs first. So, spending extra time together doing simple activities is one of the biggest rewards you can give, and also is important for that child's treatment.

Here are some examples of how the statements can be completed:

1. It's important to answer the phone politely because it may be your mother or caseworker.
2. It's important not to make excuses to your teacher because it looks like you're not willing to take responsibility for your homework.
3. It's important to be on time to see the caseworker because she has set aside time for you and we want her to know we appreciate it.
4. Picking up your things is important because if you do, people won't step on them.
5. Sharing your toys with others is helpful because then they will want to share their toys with you.

Let's take a look at some examples of how Effective Praise can be used:

1. **Show Approval** – "Michael, that's great!"
   Describe Positive – "You tied your tennis shoes all by yourself!"
   Give Reason – "Now, you won't have to wait for me to do it for you."

2. **Show Approval** – "I'm so proud of you!"
   Describe Positive – "You did your homework before watching TV."
   Give Reason – "Now, you won't have to do it late at night."
   Optional Reward – "You're sure welcome to some popcorn while you watch the movie."

3. **Show Approval** – "Kathy, what a nice job!"
   Describe Positive – "You told me you and Susan were having trouble sharing your toys. You told me before any hitting started."
   Give Reason – "When you come to me for help right away, neither of you have to go to time-out."

Exercise 2

In the spaces below, write down something your child or foster child did recently that deserved praise. Then complete the Effective Praise steps for each behavior.

1. Behavior –

   Show Approval –

   Describe Positive –

   Give Reason –

2. Behavior –

   Show Approval –

   Describe Positive –

   Give Reason –

3. Behavior –

   Show Approval –

   Describe Positive –

   Give Reason –

4. Behavior –

   Show Approval –

   Describe Positive –

   Give Reason –

Summary

Parents who have used Boys Town's Model with children in group homes, with their own children, or with foster children have consistently told us that Effective Praise has had a lasting impact on their families. Treatment Parents find themselves being more positive about their foster children. Foster children, in turn, are more positive about their Treatment Parents. With Effective Praise, everyone wins.

CHAPTER 13

Preventive Teaching

Ben Franklin once said, "An ounce of prevention is worth a pound of cure." Old Ben was right; society's reliance on preventive measures is proof of that. We have fire drills; we have our cars tuned up; we go to the doctor for a physical exam. We do all of these precautionary things to prevent problems. While practicing a fire drill may not keep a fire from starting, it could prevent a catastrophe such as the loss of life in a fire. Prevention is both necessary and important.

An Ounce of Prevention

We've taken Ben's wisdom and applied it to treatment parenting. We call our method **Preventive Teaching®**. Preventive Teaching is our "ounce of prevention." It means that Treatment Parents can spend time teaching skills **before** their foster children need to use them, and can help foster children prevent problems from occurring. When foster children know what is expected of them, and have the opportunity to prepare, they will be more successful.

You've probably used Preventive Teaching many times before – teaching your own child how to safely cross the street, what number to dial in case of emergency, what clothes to wear when it's cold, and so on. Preventive Teaching helps you anticipate and prevent problems while setting up your foster child for success. Preventive Teaching means teaching your foster child what he or she needs to know for a future situation and practicing it in advance.

There are two specific times when you can use Preventive Teaching:

- **When your foster child is learning something new.**
- **When your foster child has had difficulty in a past situation.**

Of course, the Preventive Teaching areas you focus on will vary with each foster child. But all foster children can learn something new or improve behaviors that have caused problems in the past. You may want your young foster child to learn how to use better table manners or how to answer the phone. You may want him to improve in areas where he has had difficulties before, like playing nicely with others or getting to bed on time. For a young teen, you may want to teach her how to improve her school grades or how to apply for a job. You may want her to improve in situations where she loses her temper or doesn't know how to respond to a teacher who is offering criticism.

Many of the children who are placed in foster care have experienced too much criticism and too little success. They also have a lot of new rules and expectations to adjust to when they move to a new home. Preventive Teaching provides an excellent opportunity to set up foster children for success in a new home. It helps them learn what the expectations are before they goof up or get a negative consequence simply because they didn't know what was expected of them.

Preventive Teaching occurs during the **absence of problem behaviors**, when anxiety levels and emotions are under control. The learning process is helped by a comfortable, supportive, and relaxed environment. In effect, the foster child has an opportunity to experience success without ever having to experience failure!

Exercise 1

Think of areas in which your child or foster child needs to learn something new. List these in the following spaces:

1.

2.

3.

Think of areas in which your child or foster child might have difficulties and would need to improve. List these in the following spaces:

1.

2.

3.

Preventive Teaching helps you take care of these situations and increases the likelihood that your foster child will do well. It's a simple concept, but untrained foster parents usually don't use it as often or in as many situations as they could. Many of the children in foster care have not had adults teach them the social skills they will need to be successful within their family, at school, or other social settings. So you should not assume that children who come to your home know exactly what you expect. This is why teaching specific skills is so important. When you take the time to teach children skills, such as

"Following Instructions" or "Accepting 'No' Answers," they will know what you expect, and in turn, will be better able to meet those expectations.

As we discussed in Chapter 8, in order to help children learn these skills as quickly as possible, it is essential that you explain to them the specific steps to these different skills. For example, a common skill that most children need to learn when they come into the program is "Following Instructions." While it may seem like common sense to you, many children do not know what you expect when you ask them to pick up their books from the floor. A child may assume he can do it tomorrow or can throw the books on the kitchen table. Describing the steps to the skill helps the child know what is expected. For instance, when you teach a child to follow instructions, you could say:

"When I tell you to do something, I want you to look at me, show me you understand by nodding or saying 'Okay,' do what I ask, then check back with me. That way I know it is done and then you can go out to play with your friends."

Your Consultant will help you continue to identify the skills that your child needs to learn. Each child's Treatment Plan will focus on two to three skills that are especially important for the child to practice and use.

Steps to Preventive Teaching

The steps to Preventive Teaching are:

1. Describe the skill or behavior you want
2. Give a reason
3. Role-play (practice)

Describe the Skill or Behavior You Want

Before your foster child can do what you want, he or she must first know what it is you expect. Break the skill down into specific steps. Make sure the child understands. For example, if your foster daughter argues with her teachers and gets sent to detention, you would teach her how to appropriately respond to the teachers before she goes back to school. You might say, "Sharon, tomorrow at school when the teacher asks you to do something and you want to argue with her, you need to remain calm. Try keeping your mouth closed, take a deep breath, and don't argue with her."

Give a Reason

Foster children, like adults, benefit from knowing why they should act a certain way. Reasons help a foster child understand why new skills and appropriate behaviors are useful and important. They also teach how inappropriate behaviors are harmful. The best reasons, of course, are those that relate directly to the person's life. Simply saying to your foster children, "Do it because I said so," is a command, not a reason. Foster children are more likely to use the skill long after they leave your home if they understand why and **how it will help them accomplish what is important to them,** rather than because they did something simply because the Treatment Parents said so.

Sometimes it is difficult to come up with reasons that mean a lot to foster children at that time. Even if they don't immediately agree with what you are saying, at least they will know why you think it is important. That means a great deal since reasons are indications of fairness and logic. Foster children are much more likely to comply with what you say when you give reasons. If reasons are personal to the child, they are more likely to accept what you are teaching. In the earlier example with Sharon, a reason for her to not argue with teachers could be: "When you yell or get upset with the teacher, you have to go to detention and you can't spend time with your friends after school."

Role-Play (practice)

Knowing what to do and knowing how to do it are two different things. Any new skill needs to be practiced. You can tell your foster child how to ride a bicycle, but that hardly will ensure that she could hop right on and take off. It takes practice to become good at almost anything. We call practicing a new skill "role-playing."

Foster children occasionally are reluctant to practice, especially when being taught a new skill. They may feel embarrassed, or lack self-confidence, or think that practicing is a waste of time. The fact of the matter is that practice actually eases embarrassment and raises the child's confidence in his or her abilities. If you are enthusiastic about practicing, your foster children will be more willing to practice. Encourage them as they practice and use a lot of praise for trying. Most practices should be fun, yet realistic. This isn't the time to be super-serious; otherwise, the practice will become drudgery for you and your foster child.

In the earlier example with Sharon, you might have her practice staying calm when a teacher corrects her by saying: "Okay, Sharon, let's practice staying calm. Pretend I'm the teacher and I just asked you to stop talking in class. Show me what you'll do to stay calm. Okay?"

Practice can be an enjoyable time with your foster children, especially when they understand that you are practicing because you care about them. Praise areas that your foster child did well in and encourage him or her to improve in areas that need improvement. Don't expect perfection the first time you practice. Remember the idea of shaping? Maybe when you begin role-playing with Sharon, she takes a big breath to start calming down, but continues to argue under her breath. By having her practice how to take a big breath and remain silent, she eventually will stop mumbling to herself and simply do what the teacher asks. If you make the practice fun and perhaps provide a reward for a good effort, Sharon will be willing to role-play several times before she goes back to school. The more you practice on a new skill, the more likely Sharon will be to use it at school the next day.

If you are practicing a complex skill or a difficult situation, such as how to say "No" to peer pressure and using drugs, never promise that the real situation will work out perfectly. Explain to your foster child that you are practicing possible ways to handle a situation and the outcome won't always be the same. This is no different from what we go through in our daily lives. We know that a certain way of dealing with one person won't work with another person. As a Treatment Parent, remember that you cannot ensure your foster child's success in every situation; you can only improve the odds. Your foster children will learn that every situation is different, but they won't be defenseless. You will help them learn more and more ways to solve problems, until they have several solutions to choose from.

After finishing any teaching situation, it is wise to encourage the child to use the skill in the future. A few words of encouragement can motivate your foster child to use what he or she has learned in real situations. As the child learns the skill, it will not be necessary to go through each step of Preventive Teaching.

Opportunities for Preventive Teaching

As we mentioned earlier, Preventive Teaching can be very helpful when you are trying to help a foster child become adjusted to a new home, school, and neighborhood. Some other opportunities to use Preventive Teaching are:

- **When teaching skills** you and the Consultant identify as part of the foster child's Treatment Plan.
- **When teaching or discussing house rules**. This is a critical part of every foster child's introduction to a new home. (House rules are covered in more detail in Chapter 24, "Caring for the Sexually Abused Child.")
- **When teaching basic safety**. The foster child may not be familiar with certain potential hazards in your neighborhood, such as traffic, lakes, or farm animals. They also may be unfamiliar with appliances or special recreational equipment.
- **When discussing or planning home visits**. Preventive Teaching can be used before a foster child goes on a home visit or to visit other relatives. Let's imagine that the foster child's referral behaviors included "difficulty asking permission" and "accepting 'No' for an answer." The Treatment Parents could do some extra practices on those skills with the foster child before the visit. This will help the foster child focus on those skills and prepare for a more successful visit.

Let's look at some examples of Preventive Teaching:

Situation: Robbie, your foster son, is about to go outside to play; he's had difficulty coming in when he's called.

Describe the skill or behavior you want

Treatment Parent: "Robbie, let's talk about following instructions. When I call you to come in for dinner, please let me know that you heard me and pick up your toys right away before coming in."

Give a reason

Treatment Parent: "If you come in right away, I'll be more likely to give you permission to play after dinner."

Practice

Treatment Parent: "Let's pretend I've just called you in. What are you going to say and do?"

Robbie: "I'm going to put my toys away and come in the kitchen."

Treatment Parent: "Great! Now run and have fun. Remember to come in right away when I call."

Situation: Your teenage foster daughter, Michelle, wants to spend an overnight visit with her family, but her caseworker has not approved the visit. Michelle wants to call the caseworker to explain her request and ask her to change her mind.

Describe the skill or behavior you want

Treatment Parent: "I know you really want your caseworker to change her mind, but she may not. Let's talk about how you should accept a 'No' answer in case that happens. If she says 'No,' you need to say 'Okay' and calmly ask for a reason if you don't understand. If you disagree, you can bring it up with her next week when she comes for a visit."

Give a reason

Treatment Parent: "If you show her that you are learning to disagree appropriately, she may be more willing to let you spend more time with your family in the future because she will be more confident that the visits with your folks will go better."

Practice

Treatment Parent: "Let's pretend that you just asked to go on the overnight visit and your caseworker said 'No.' What are you going to say?"

80

Michelle: "I'm going to say 'Okay' and ask her why she said 'No.' I can talk with her more about it next week when she comes to see me."

Treatment Parent: "Very good. I think she will be very impressed that you can disagree with her in such a mature manner."

Now complete Exercise 2 in the other column.

Preventive Prompts

Experience adds skills. Eventually, when your foster child is faced with situations in which the same skill can be used, you may just have to provide a reminder – a preventive prompt. For example, let's say that you have practiced these steps with your foster daughter on how to stay calm when she gets upset with her friends: "Remember, Sharon, stay calm just like we practiced for school. Don't say anything and take a few deep breaths. Then walk away from them if you have to." Then just before your foster daughter goes out to play with her friends, you could give a preventive prompt: "Remember what we practiced, Sharon. You'll do just fine."

The purpose of a preventive prompt is to get your foster child focused on what you have practiced. Your praise and encouragement during the whole Preventive Teaching sequence will help your foster child remember important skills to use.

Summary

Preventive Teaching is a valuable tool for both Treatment Parents and foster children. By using it with your foster children, you can help them prepare for unfamiliar situations and promote gradual behavior changes in areas where they may be having problems. Preventive Teaching can increase your foster children's self-esteem by showing them that they can learn how to change their behaviors and avoid problems. And perhaps most importantly, Preventive Teaching allows you and your foster child to work toward goals together. Taking the time to be with your foster children and showing them that you care helps improve relationships, and that benefits the whole family.

Exercise 2

Think of three situations in which you can use Preventive Teaching. In the spaces below, use the steps of Preventive Teaching to write what you would say to your foster child.

1. Situation –

   Describe the skill or behavior you want –

   Give a reason –

   Practice –

2. Situation –

   Describe the skill or behavior you want –

   Give a reason –

   Practice –

3. Situation –

   Describe the skill or behavior you want –

   Give a reason –

   Practice –

CHAPTER 14

Staying Calm

Many Treatment Parents tell us that the biggest challenge they face in dealing with their foster children's problem behaviors is staying calm. We all know there are times when our foster children are going to make us upset and angry. They can be sarcastic, defiant, rebellious, and possibly violent. Treatment Parents have to prepare themselves for times like these and learn to keep their cool.

This doesn't mean you won't get angry. That's impossible, maybe even unhealthy, since anger is a basic human emotion. We are simply saying that blowing your top over your foster child's behavior can make situations worse. Adults who have many confrontations with their foster children frequently reinforce inappropriate responses or cause confrontations to occur. Research has shown that three-fourths of the time, aggressive behaviors of children have been modeled by the parents and others in the child's environment (Patterson, 1976). The way we look at it, anger is only one letter away from "danger." Our experience tells us that staying calm and controlling angry responses is much more effective in teaching foster children how to behave.

The First Step

Knowing what makes us angry is the first step in being able to respond calmly to our foster children's problem behaviors. What you do when talking to a foster child who is upset can influence how the child acts. Do you remember reading about antecedents earlier in the book? By being aware of

your own actions, you can avoid behaviors that can trigger a negative response by your foster child and thus decrease the chances of having confrontations with the child.

Parents may do many things when they are angry. They may yell or cuss at their children, or they may hit something, or throw or kick things. Some parents even hit their child in anger. As you learned in Chapter 2, "Creating a Safe Environment," **Boys Town policy prohibits physical discipline of foster children.** But many untrained foster parents are totally convinced that these angry responses work with their children or other foster children. And they are right. Such responses do temporarily stop the problem behavior. But what did their foster children learn? To yell or hit, or to throw or kick things when they are upset. All children are significantly affected by role models. You can help reverse your foster child's inappropriate expressions of anger and frustration by modeling and teaching healthier ways to deal with his strong emotions.

The Boys Town Family Home Model teaches Treatment Parents to stay calm in tense situations. When they stay calm, Treatment Parents report that:

- The temper tantrum or problem behavior **stops sooner**.

- The **behavior does not last as long** and is **less severe**.

- The **Treatment Parent feels better** about the way he or she handled the situation.

In one particular case, a Treatment Parent told us, "You know, that 'calm' thing really works. My foster son used to run away frequently, and I didn't handle the situation too well. I came close to losing my temper each time. After I learned how to stay calm and not get so frustrated, we both stayed more calm and were able to work things out without him running away."

Of course, staying calm was just one of the effective changes this man made in his parenting style. But staying calm was the first step. He learned that his anger got in the way of what he wanted to teach his foster son. As he learned to remain calm, he was able to put his other parenting skills to work. This led to a dramatic, positive change in the relationship between this man and his foster son.

Exercise 1

What does your child or foster child do that makes you downright angry? List three of these behaviors below.

1.

2.

3.

How do you respond to these behaviors? List your answers.

1.

2.

3.

Calming Down

Staying calm isn't always easy at first for some parents. They have to work at it. Here's how some of them say they calm down in tense situations.

- "I count to 10 – very slowly. I concentrate on doing that regardless of what my foster son is yelling."

- "I put my hands in my pockets. I tend to be really demonstrative with my hands, especially when I'm angry. Before I learned to do this, I think my foster daughter thought I was going to hit her. I wasn't, but she viewed my behavior as a threat."

- "I sit down. If I'm standing, I begin to tremble. Sitting calms me for some reason. I can still tell my foster child what he's doing wrong, but I say it a lot more calmly."

- "I take a deep breath and let it out slowly. This kind of serves as a safety valve for me. It's like I'm letting steam out of my body."

- "I just leave the situation for awhile. I go in another room until I can handle myself. I figure if my kid's that mad, taking a little time to regain my control won't hurt anything. I can deal with it a lot better that way. Sometimes, he even calms down by the time I get back."

- "I call someone like my wife or Consultant. By talking about the situation, I can go back in and deal with it more calmly."

So far, we've talked about ways to calm down when you're already angry. An even better suggestion is to calm down as soon as you recognize you're getting angry.

Exercise 2

What do you do when trying to stay calm? Do you have any methods of anger control that work for you? If you do, please list them below.

1.

2.

3.

We all have little signals that warn us that we're getting angry. Recognizing these signals allows us to think before we act. It's much easier to find a solution to a problem when you're calm. Listed below are some ways people react or feel when they start to get angry.

Tensing muscles
Sweating
Speaking faster and/or louder
Feeling flushed
Grinding or clenching teeth
Pounding heart
Quivering lips when you speak
Ringing in your ears
Trembling or shaking
Clenching fists

Exercise 3

Please take a few minutes and think about the little signals that your body gives off to tell you you're getting angry. List them below.

1.

2.

3.

Now, let's take a look at how you can use these signals to help you stay calm in tense situations with your foster child. In the next exercise, we're going to combine:

1. Your foster child's problem behaviors.

2. Your early warning signals.

3. A way of staying calm that works for you.

Use this information to prepare yourself for the next time you are upset with your foster child's behavior.

Exercise 4

Following the example below, complete the sentence using the three elements we just discussed. We have found that when Treatment Parents think about a plan and write it out, they are more likely to remember and use it during a real situation.

Example: The next time Johnny **talks back to me and refuses to go to bed** (child's problem behaviors), and I start **feeling my heart pound** (my warning signals), **I will take a deep breath and let it out slowly before I correct him** (what I will do to stay calm).

The next time my foster child _____
(problem behaviors)

_____

_____

and I start _____
(my warning signals)

_____

_____

I will_____
(what I will do to stay calm)

_____

_____.

More Tips on Staying Calm

Learning to control your negative reactions will take some time and practice. Here are some tips that have helped other Treatment Parents:

- **Don't take what your foster child says personally**. This may be very difficult when your foster child is calling you every name in the book. But remember that this child hasn't yet acquired the skills necessary to deal with anger or frustration. Don't react when a child calls you a name, accuses you of being a rotten parent, or negatively compares you to other caretakers with whom the child has lived. Learn how to let negative, angry comments bounce off you, and your teaching will become more effective.

- **Use the "take five" rule**. Instead of saying something out of anger or frustration, tell yourself to take five minutes to think about what is happening. It is remarkable how that "cooling off" period can help a person regain self-control and put things in perspective. Also, if a consequence is warranted, it is more likely that you will choose one that is fair if you are calm. Simply leaving the scene can help to defuse a volatile situation. You may want to call your spouse or Consultant. If you cannot leave the situation, monitor your own actions. It is helpful to use a calm voice, use appropriate language, and stand an arm's length away from the foster child. Match the foster child's general posture (i.e. standing or sitting), and maintain a nonconfrontational appearance (don't point fingers, clench your fists, or put your hands on your hips).

- **Focus on the child's behavior instead of why you think the child is misbehaving**. Don't look for motives; instead, deal with the way your foster child is acting. You can drive yourself batty trying to figure out reasons for a child's negative behavior. Also, it is important for the child to realize you are frustrated only with the behavior, and that you don't think that he or she is a bad person. After the problem is solved, take time to talk to your foster child about what happened and why.

- **If you get angry and say or do something you regret, go back and say that you're sorry**. This teaches your foster children how to behave when they make a mistake. Apologize, say what you did wrong, and tell the child what you're going to do differently next time. Some untrained foster parents worry about apologizing because they think they lose some of their parental control. We've found that apologizing helps foster children realize that everyone, young and old alike, makes mistakes. The best thing is to admit your mistake and do your best not to let it happen again. If you think your behavior was inappropriate or may have violated the Child Rights policy, call your Consultant to discuss your concerns.

- **Staying calm does not mean you are totally passive**. There are times when you will raise your voice – but you can use a firm, no-nonsense voice tone. And what you say involves specific descriptions, not judgments or feelings. Staying calm means you don't react to misbehavior in an angry, aggressive manner. Yelling in anger at a foster child is not appropriate.

Summary

1. Stay calm.
2. Look at your own behavior.
3. Identify what makes you angry.
4. Know what you are going to say and do.
5. Control negative responses and deal with them quickly.
6. Remember that your self-control is a key to effective teaching.

CHAPTER 15

Corrective Teaching

Foster children are constantly testing limits. In many respects, this is healthy. Testing limits is one way they learn and grow and find out about the world around them. Foster children test limits so they can find out how their new family functions. Testing limits helps them learn about the boundaries between grown-ups and children. They also learn how fast those boundaries are set, who sets them, and the type of consequences that are used. And as you know, actions speak louder than words. However, when foster children continually test the limits set by Treatment Parents, it can cause problems for the whole family.

The problem behaviors of foster children vary from one child to the next. For each of your children or foster children, what behaviors aggravate you the most? When do these behaviors take place? Where do these behaviors take place? How often do they take place? **The more clearly you specify the problem behaviors, the more likely you are to find a solution to them.**

Corrective Teaching is the method we use to deal with many of the problems Treatment Parents face. It is a proven, effective process for helping children change their inappropriate behaviors. It works so well, in fact, that many Treatment Parents can't wait for us to present this section in training.

The need for such a method stems mainly from the frustration untrained foster parents feel when working with the children in their care. Here's just a sample of some of the frustrations those foster parents have shared with us:

- "I always have to ask two or three times whenever I want my foster child to do something."

- "It seems like my foster children argue all the time. And about the dumbest things. They just pick, pick, pick at one another until one of them gets mad."

- "She gets so angry sometimes. She threatens to run away and she screams at me when I confront her about her lying. I worry that I'm not up to the job of being a Treatment Parent."

- "I can't get them to help with the dishes unless I threaten to take away a privilege."

- "When I ask my foster son about his homework, he says it's done or he left it at school. Sooner or later, he gets a down slip from school."

- "He argues with me about everything. I can't remember when I asked him to do something and he actually just went and did it."

- "She likes to shock me by talking about sexual things she knows about. Unfortunately, the other children are usually around, too. I never feel like I handle it very well and she continues to do it."

Well, you get the picture. One foster parent summed up the frustration many foster parents feel when she said, "What can I do? I've had it! I feel like all I do is yell or punish him all day. He thinks I'm an ogre but I can't get him to do a thing!"

Like most concerned foster parents, this woman was looking for a constructive, effective way to respond to her foster child's constant misbehavior.

We taught her Corrective Teaching.

What Is Corrective Teaching?

Corrective Teaching is a five-step process that combines clear messages with consequences and practice to help Treatment Parents respond to problem behaviors by teaching children new skills. It is very similar to what you have practiced in the previous chapters – just a little more detailed.

Basically, you use Corrective Teaching any time your foster children are not following instructions or are displaying inappropriate behavior. Simply, when they are:

- doing something you've asked them not to do.

- not doing something you've asked them to do.

- doing something that could result in harm to the foster child or to other people.

This includes things that are morally or legally wrong, or that are dangerous.

Here are the steps for Corrective Teaching. You have already learned steps 3, 4, and 5 in Effective Praise and Preventive Teaching. Corrective Teaching has two additional steps. An explanation of each one and how it works in Corrective Teaching follows.

1. **Stop the problem behavior**
2. **Give a consequence**
3. **Describe what you want/label the skill**
4. **Give a reason**
5. **Practice what you want**

Stop the Problem Behavior

Most parents find it most effective to get a child's attention by using a calm voice tone and an empathy statement. The child is more likely to listen and want to hear what you have to say if you speak in a pleasant voice tone and express sincere concern. It is helpful to try to have the child look at you, but you can continue the teaching process even if the child doesn't comply. As mentioned earlier, you must be aware of your physical behaviors – pointing your finger, putting your hands on your hips, and other similar actions may be perceived by the child as aggressive behaviors.

A calm, reassuring approach should always be used when you begin teaching; otherwise, the child may come to view you as a person who is unpleasant to be around, quick to criticize, and slow to appreciate or understand a child's frustrations. A calm, caring approach will help you build a relationship with the child, even when he or she is having difficulties.

Once you have the child's attention, you can then give clear instructions about how you want the child to stop the problem behavior. This may be something as simple as an instruction like, "Please sit down" or "Please lower your voice."

It also is very helpful to briefly describe the child's behaviors before you continue the teaching process. This lets the child know exactly what behavior you are addressing with your teaching.

If the foster child refuses to follow your instructions or begins to act out more, you will use the steps described in the next chapter, "Teaching Self-Control." Corrective Teaching is used to help children correct behaviors when they respond fairly quickly to your instructions and teaching.

Give a Consequence

You will have discussed options for consequences with your Consultant and the child as part of creating the Treatment Plan. The important thing to remember is to give a consequence that is closely related to the behavior that is being addressed. That way, the child knows that the consequence is a direct result of his or her inappropriate behavior.

Describe What You Want/Label the Skill

Labeling the skill you want the child to use the next time a similar problem arises helps you teach effectively. It reinforces the consistency of your teaching by describing a skill that has already been introduced to the child during treatment planning and Preventive Teaching. Describing the skill's steps and reinforcing their correct use will help get the child to use it more frequently and with greater consistency. You also can help the child understand how those specific steps can be applied to the situation at hand. For example, teaching the child the specific steps of how to get along with others makes it more likely that he or she will use that skill in a similar situation in the future.

Give a Reason

It is important to help the child understand how inappropriate behaviors can cause problems and how changing the behaviors can help him or her. For example, you might tell a child who takes toys away from others that other children will not want to play with him because of that behavior; you might add that the child will have more friends if he shares toys while playing. Remember that using reasons that a child can easily understand will help motivate him or her to learn new, appropriate behaviors to replace problem behaviors.

Practice What You Want

Treatment Parents have told us that children are more likely to begin using a skill if they practice the skill at the end of Corrective Teaching. Practice is most effective when it's brief and pleasant for the child; using praise and humor helps accomplish this.

Practice also helps you determine how effectively you are teaching. By watching a child practice, you can determine whether or not he or she is learning the skill you are teaching.

How to Choose a Consequence

Oftentimes, it's hard to remain objective when deciding on a negative consequence for a foster child's inappropriate behavior. This is especially true if the behavior is aggressive, repetitive, or harmful to others. Consider the following factors in order to arrive at a fair consequence:

1. **Frequency of the problem behavior**
   (How often does it occur?)
2. **Duration of the problem behavior**
   (How long does it last?)
3. **Intensity of the problem behavior**
   (How disruptive is the behavior?)

4. **Severity of the problem behavior**
   (How dangerous is the behavior?)
5. **Location and time of the problem behavior**

If you believe the situation is complicated and you are confused about what type or size of consequence is appropriate, you should call your Consultant for advice.

Here is a reminder of consequences that are **prohibited** in Boys Town Treatment Foster Family Services:

- Corporal punishment. This means no hitting, spanking, pushing, or threatening any of these punishments.
- Overcorrection, such as cleaning the floor with a toothbrush.
- Violating a foster child's right to nourishment, communication, and respect of body and self.

Using Corrective Teaching

Now let's look at two examples of how the five steps of Corrective Teaching can be used to correct problem behaviors.

Example 1

In this example, a Treatment Parent observes his foster son breaking another foster child's toy after he overhears them arguing about who could play with the toy.

1. **Stop the problem behavior**
   - Calmly get his attention
   - Give a clear instruction
   - Describe what happened or is happening
   - Use empathy to let the foster child know you understand what he or she is feeling

"Michael, please come sit down. I know you are very upset right now. I just saw you break the ship Tony made from blocks."

2. **Give a consequence**
   - Relate it to the problem behavior

"For breaking Tony's ship, you will not be able to play with the blocks the rest of the day."

3. Describe what you want/label the skill

- Be specific
- Describe the skill you want the child to practice (i.e. Following Instructions, Accepting "No" Answers, etc.).

"The next time you think somebody has taken some of your blocks, you need to **ask for help.** You do this by coming to get me. I can help you solve this problem so you won't end up losing the blocks for the day."

4. Give a reason

- Relate it to the foster child

"It's important to take care of other kids' toys, so they'll take care of yours."

5. Practice what you want

- Keep it brief
- Praise during practice

"Now here's a chance for you to show me you can do what we've talked about. You've done a good job listening so far. Okay, pretend you think Tony has taken your blocks. What would you do?"

Example 2

In this example, the foster daughter walks up to strangers in the grocery store and asks if she can go home with them.

1. Stop the problem behavior

- Calmly get her attention
- Give a clear instruction
- Describe what happened or is happening
- Use empathy

"Sara, you need to come here. I know you're just being friendly, but you just walked over to that lady and asked her if you could go home with her."

2. Give a consequence

- Relate it to problem behavior

"You will have to ride in the cart now instead of walking around."

(With young foster children, Treatment Parents report that they find it helpful to have the foster child sit on a chair or in this case, the grocery cart, first. After the foster child sits for the required time, then they tell the foster child what to do in future situations. For a detailed description of time-out, see Appendix F.)

3. Describe what you want/label the skill
- Be specific
- Describe the skill you want the child to practice

"I want you to **follow instructions** when I ask you to stay with me. You can say 'Hello' to another person and then walk back to me."

4. Give a reason
- Relate it to the foster child

"I want you to be safe, so you need to stay with me."

5. Practice what you want
- Keep it brief
- Praise during practice

Foster father: "Let's pretend that we're at the store and you walk next to somebody. What is it okay for you to say?"

Sara: "Hi!"

Foster father: "Very good! Now what are you going to do?"

Sara: I'm going to come over to you."

Foster father: "Very good, Sara. I'm very proud of you!"

Exercise 1

Write down a situation involving one of your child's or foster child's problem behaviors and how you would respond with each of the Corrective Teaching steps.

Situation:

1. Stop the problem behavior

2. Give a consequence

3. Describe what you want/label the skill

4. Give a reason

5. Practice what you want

Now that you have given Corrective Teaching a try in writing, practice it with your spouse or another adult until you feel confident in your ability to do the steps. Practice leads to confidence and confidence leads to success.

Tips for Using Corrective Teaching

Here are some important things to keep in mind when using Corrective Teaching:

Remain calm. This is easy to say, but not always easy to do. Treatment Parents consistently tell us this is one of the most important pieces of the puzzle. Sometimes, foster children misbehave so often that Treatment Parents respond angrily. Or the behavior itself is so annoying that Treatment Parents react abruptly or negatively. Please remember – stop and think about what you need to do. Use a matter-of-fact voice tone, one that's not harsh or accusing. Be careful of your posture and gestures. You are much more likely to effectively change your foster child's behavior when you remain calm.

Respect the foster child's privacy. All of us probably can remember being disciplined in front of our brothers or sisters, or even worse, in front of our friends. The embarrassment made it pretty hard to concentrate on why we were being corrected. The same is true for foster children who already feel that they are different from other children. Once you have stopped the misbehavior, do Corrective Teaching where there won't be an audience. You are much more likely to have the foster child's undivided attention and preserve your relationship.

Stick to one issue. We don't know about your foster children, but most children are masters at getting adults sidetracked. Some foster children can get Treatment Parents so far off the topic that they forget what the topic is. Familiar lines like these are particularly effective:

"I hate you!"

"My parents didn't make me do that. They're nice."

"I don't want to talk about that, and you can't make me!"

"You can take away anything you want. I just don't care!"

"I can't wait until I'm out of a Boys Town foster home. I thought you were supposed to help me!"

Certainly, these types of comments could go straight to your heart. We've all wanted to tell our children or foster children all the nice things we do for them, or to prove what good parents we are. Don't try to justify your existence. Stick with what you want to teach. When foster children bring up other issues as they are being corrected, they are usually trying to avoid the consequences of their own behavior. It is your job not to get sidetracked by getting into the "content" of other issues the foster child would rather focus on. **This is very important.** Let your foster children know that if they really want to talk about other topics, they can bring them up after the main issue is resolved and they have accepted their consequences.

Give them a chance to earn something back. If your foster child is attentive and works to make up for the misbehavior, and you are pleased with the attempt, don't hesitate to give some part of the consequence back; this is called **positive correction.** Many foster children can easily give up on trying to correct their behavior. They may even feel like they can't do anything right. When foster children have an opportunity to earn back some of the consequence, they are less likely to give up. An added bonus is that it strengthens your relationship, because the foster child sees you as fair. For example, during Corrective Teaching, you take away one hour of TV time because your foster son and foster daughter were arguing. After you finish teaching, both of the foster children apologize and say they will work together to wash the dishes. If they cooperate, you could give back 15 or 20 minutes of the TV time you took away. Doing this allows you to give them a positive consequence for working on the problem. This is an effective way to teach foster children to make up for mistakes or misbehaviors.

Treatment Parents are encouraged to let foster children earn **up to half** of the consequence back. By earning up to half of the consequence back, the foster child remains motivated to work on correcting the behavior, but still has to accept and experience the negative consequence.

Some foster parents may be uncomfortable with the idea of letting children earn back some of their lost privileges. They are concerned that the child will view them as being "weak" or "easy." In reality, a child frequently views the foster parent as "fair" and "willing to help with problems" when given a chance to earn back some of what was lost. It is important to remember that children who have experienced severe or unreasonable punishments in the past may easily give up because they feel powerless. Giving children an opportunity to earn back privileges helps motivate them not to give up and as a result, helps them accomplish their treatment goals sooner.

Be consistent. For foster children who come from chaotic homes, the benefit of living with Treatment Parents who can provide consistency is enormous. After the "honeymoon" is over, many foster children find it difficult to adjust to consistency. You are strongly encouraged to stay with it; the foster child eventually will begin to test the limits less and less. One of the most therapeutic benefits of treatment foster care is consistently applying house rules and consequences (both positive and negative) every day. When foster children do cooperate with you, use Effective Praise and some creative rewards. The more consistent you are, the more consistent your foster children will be. You need to provide stability in your foster children's often hectic lives.

Be flexible. Just when we said to be consistent, we throw you a curve and talk about flexibility. What we mean is that you should consistently use Corrective Teaching, but vary the way you use it. As you get to know the foster child better, you will learn what rewards and negative consequences work the best. If you think the child will learn more if you put the consequence at the end, then give it a try. We encourage you to discuss your observations with your Consultant before you make these changes.

A few points are important with this approach. Learn and use the steps the way they're presented, then adapt them. They are presented this way for a reason; it works for most Treatment Parents this way. Plus, it's easier to adapt something after you know what you're adapting.

Keep track of behavior. To determine if your teaching is working, your Consultant will help you develop a tracking system. Keeping careful records helps us document the implementation of the foster child's Treatment Plan and progress. Also, some foster children's progress can be slow, so record-keeping is a way to see change over longer periods of time.

Summary

Treatment Parents who take the time to use each of the steps of Corrective Teaching are amazed at how easy it is and how it helps to change problem behaviors. Their attitude about parenting takes an about-face. They don't hesitate to correct their foster child's misbehavior and teach a better way to behave. Treatment parenting certainly is no less of a challenge, but now they're able to see constructive results. They take the opportunity to teach whenever possible, and they use Corrective Teaching comfortably and confidently. Corrective Teaching will work for you, too.

CHAPTER 16

Teaching Self-Control

"You're a complete idiot. I can't stand you!"
"Get outta my face, you asshole!"
"No way! I ain't gonna do it, and you can't make me!"

One of the more frustrating aspects of being a Treatment Parent is dealing with an angry, defiant foster child who simply refuses to do what you ask. The child may be yelling, hitting, arguing, throwing objects, or threatening you. This type of behavior can make you feel powerless, emotionally drained, or just plain furious.

If you have ever felt like this, you're not alone. Many Treatment Parents face these situations frequently. One thing is certain, however: Foster children must learn that negative, aggressive behavior is not acceptable. And, it can be harmful to them and others. The sooner foster children learn to control their actions, the more they will benefit. When children do not respond to Corrective Teaching and continue to misbehave or refuse to cooperate, it's time to use a process called Teaching Self-Control.

Like most Treatment Parents, you will want to manage most problems that come up with your foster child without consulting someone else first. However, it is important that you and your Consultant decide under which circumstances you will be expected to call the Consultant to report that the foster child is not following your instructions and that you are beginning to use Teaching Self-Control. Also, the Consultant will let you know ahead of time when it is appropriate for him or her to come out and help you, and will explain his or

her role in supporting **you** as the primary adult the child must obey. Since Teaching Self-Control is part of the foster child's treatment, it will be specifically laid out in the child's Treatment Plan. The Consultant will review this plan with you and the child, and also will discuss when an Incident Report or Morning Event Report should be completed.

What Is Teaching Self-Control?

There are two key parts to Teaching Self-Control: **1) helping your foster child calm down,** and **2) follow-up teaching**. We'll explain each part in detail, but let's first take a brief look at what often happens when a foster child yells at a Treatment Parent or refuses to do what is asked.

In these situations, a foster child is certainly not interested in, and in some cases not capable of, discussing the situation rationally. Generally, a great deal of talking by the Treatment Parent does little to improve the situation. Often, the more the Treatment Parent talks, the louder the child yells. The more the foster child yells, the louder the Treatment Parent talks, and eventually, the Treatment Parent is yelling, too. This continues until one of the two decides that the argument is too painful and drops out. It can be the Treatment Parent, who walks out of the room in disgust and anger, or it can be the foster child, who stomps off to the bedroom and slams the door shut. In either case, the problem has gotten worse, not better.

If you've had to deal with a situation like this with a child, you know how helpless you can feel. Teaching Self-Control gives Treatment Parents a way to respond that can help resolve these situations in an orderly manner.

Exercise 1

Describe what happened the last time your child or foster child lost self-control, and what you did.

We all get angry at times. But when anger is vented through aggressive behavior, it becomes harmful to everyone involved. We want to teach our foster children self-control so they can identify how they're feeling and learn how to deal with these emotions in ways that won't lead to aggressive or harmful behavior.

The goal of Teaching Self-Control is to teach your foster children how to control their behavior when they get upset.

The first part of this teaching method is geared toward helping the Treatment Parent and the foster child become calm. This way, both can work to resolve the disagreement rationally, without yelling and shouting. Very little can be accomplished if anger takes the place of logic.

The second part of Teaching Self-Control gives the Treatment Parent an opportunity to teach the foster child some acceptable ways of behaving – some options – when he or she is upset. Like the other skills you have learned, Teaching Self-Control emphasizes giving clear, specific descriptions of the child's behaviors, using consequences, and teaching the desired behavior.

How to Teach Self-Control

Each part of Teaching Self-Control is made up of smaller steps that are designed to calm the child and get him or her to respond to the Treatment Parent's teaching. You will recognize many of these steps from other types of teaching you have already learned. Let's look at the steps first; an explanation of each one follows.

Part 1: Calming Down

1. **Describe the problem behavior**
2. **Give clear instructions**
3. **Allow time to calm down**

Part 2: Follow-Up Teaching

4. **Describe what your foster child could do differently next time**
5. **Give a reason**
6. **Practice what your foster child can do next time**
7. **Give a consequence**

Calming Down

1. Describe the problem behavior

Briefly tell your foster child exactly what he or she is doing wrong. We emphasize "briefly" here. Your foster child may not be interested in listening to what you have to say at this time, so saying a lot won't help. You will have time to describe the problem in detail once your foster child settles down. Remember to be clear and specific with what you do say. You should talk in a calm, level voice tone. Don't speak rapidly or try to say too much. For example, saying, "Marcus, you're yelling at me and pacing around the room," gives the foster child a clear message about what he is doing.

At times, untrained foster parents say judgmental things when they dislike their foster child's behavior. "Quit acting like a baby" and "You have a lousy attitude" are just two examples. Remember that these are perceptions, and do not describe specific behaviors. We suggest that you simply and quickly describe what your foster child is doing wrong without becoming angry or accusatory. Say as little as possible while still getting your point across. A good rule of thumb is to describe the behavior in 10 words in 10 seconds or less.

It also is helpful to use empathy. As we said earlier, empathy means showing that you understand the other person's feelings. For instance, you might tell a child, "I know you are upset right now. And, I know what happened made you unhappy." This starts the teaching sequence positively and shows your foster child that you care. Plus, it often helps you focus on your foster child's behavior rather than your own emotions.

Exercise 2

For the situation you described in Exercise 1, write down the specific behaviors you could have described to your child or foster child.

Are you satisfied that your descriptions are clear and specific? Are they brief? Could you have used an empathy statement? Did you use words that the child could easily understand?

---

2. Give clear instructions

Your purpose here is to help your foster child regain self-control. So tell the child exactly what you want him or her to do. Simple instructions like, "Please come over here and sit down," or "Please stop yelling at me," clearly state what your foster child needs to do. Don't give too many instructions or repeat them constantly, or you will appear to be lecturing or badgering the child. Simple, clear, calm instructions keep the focus on having your foster child regain self-control.

You also can continue to give instructions like, "Take a few deep breaths and try to settle down," or "I'd like you to go to your room until you feel you can talk more calmly about your feelings." Again, be brief and remember to stay calm. By doing so, you will be setting a good example for your child. Showing you are calm and in control is likely to help him or her calm down, too.

Exercise 3

Using the behaviors you described in the first part of Exercise 2, write down instructions you could have given your child or foster child.

It is very important that Treatment Parents practice these first two steps (describing the problem behavior and giving clear instructions). The emphasis is on using clear messages to help calm your foster child. Practicing this skill is time well spent. Besides giving your foster child important information about his or her behavior, clear messages help keep you on track.

We have one more suggestion for helping to get certain situations under control. It's called the **"five-second rule."** This rule means that other children must leave the area within five seconds. When the foster child is so upset that he or she may pose a threat to himself or herself or others, or is likely to "blow up" quickly, we suggest that you tell any other children who are around that the five-second rule is in effect. This ensures that no other children will get hurt and that you can give the foster child your complete attention. It also helps the child calm down because he or she doesn't have an "audience," and doesn't feel like he or she will lose face by backing down in front of the other children.

Be sure to discuss the foster child's uncooperative behaviors with your Consultant. The Consultant can assist you if necessary, and will discuss whether an Incident Report or Morning Event Report needs to be completed.

3. Allow time to calm down

Treatment Parents tell us that this is the most important step in the whole process. If they remain calm, it's more likely that their foster child will calm down faster. Treatment Parents also tell us that remembering this step has helped them focus on their foster child's behavior. Simply saying, "We both need a little time to calm down. I'll be back in a few minutes," can be very effective. Remember, sometimes giving your foster child a little "space" helps him or her "save face."

As you take time to calm down, think of what skill you are going to teach next. This also allows the foster child to make a decision – to continue misbehaving or to calm down.

Come back to the child as often as necessary. Ask questions like, "Are you ready to start following instructions?" or "Are you calmed down enough to talk to me?"

Move to the second part of Teaching Self-Control when the child is able to answer you in a reasonably calm voice and pay attention to what you say. You're not going to have the happiest foster child at this point, but it's important that he or she can talk without losing self-control again.

Take your time. Give descriptions and instruc-

tions as needed. Most of all, be calm and in control of your emotions.

Follow-Up Teaching

4. Describe what your foster child could do differently next time

Give your foster child another way to express frustration or anger. Foster children have to learn that when they "blow up" every time something doesn't go their way, it leads to more negative consequences. We teach many of our Treatment Parents to rely on the "Instead of..." phrase. It goes like this: "Instead of yelling and running out the door, just look at me and say 'Okay.'"; "Instead of cussing, try taking a deep breath and think of how to answer me"; "Instead of pacing the floor, why don't you sit on the couch?"

The purpose of this phrase is to get foster children to think. The next time they're in a negative situation, if they just think about what happened, possibly something will click, and they will remember not to make the situation worse.

Exercise 4

Using the situation in Exercise 1, write down what you could tell your child or foster child to do differently next time.

---

5. Give a reason

Give your foster child a reason why it's important for him or her to act differently the next time. For example, you could say, "If you just look at me and say 'Okay,' I'll be more likely to listen and let you go the next time you ask."

The purpose of giving foster children a reason is to help them begin to see how changing their behavior can benefit them. Giving a reason every time increases the chances that they will behave appropriately in the future. This not only benefits them, but also makes your job as a Treatment Parent easier.

Exercise 5

Using the situation in Exercise 1, write down what reason you would give your child or foster child for using this new skill.

---

6. Practice what your foster child can do next time

Now that your foster child knows what to do, it's important that he or she knows how to do it. By practicing, you are more likely to see the behavior you want the next time your foster child starts to get upset.

After the practice is over, let your foster child know what was done correctly and what needs improvement. **Be as positive as you can be**, especially if your foster child is making a real effort to do what you ask.

Exercise 6

Using the situation in Exercise 1, write down how you would have the child practice the new skill.

---

7. Give a consequence

This is a crucial part of Teaching Self-Control. If there is a common mistake made by the Treatment Parents we work with, it is that they forget to give a consequence. They get so wrapped up in stopping their foster child's negative behavior, or they are so pleased once all the yelling stops that giving a consequence doesn't cross their minds. Others tell us that they just didn't have the heart to give a consequence because they didn't want to upset the child any more than he or she already was. These Treatment Parents don't realize that not providing a consequence for misbehavior means that the misbehavior is very likely to occur again. Consequences help change behavior – use them!

There are several good reasons for waiting until the end of the teaching to give the child a consequence. The child is calmer and more likely to accept the consequence. The Treatment Parent also is calmer and more likely to give a **fair** consequence. It is very human to let our emotions of anger or frustration influence our decisions about consequences. It easy to overreact and give too severe a punishment. When you are both calm, giving a consequence is much more likely to have the desired result – changing negative behavior.

When a foster child is placed with you, you help the Consultant gather information about the foster child's behavior. Within a few weeks, the Consultant will write a Treatment Plan that will clearly state when and what consequences should be given for certain misbehaviors. It is extremely important that the Treatment Plan – including consequences – be implemented as written.

Exercise 7

Using the situation in the earlier exercises, write down a consequence you would give.

Example 1

Let's take a look at an example of using Teaching Self-Control. Here's the situation: A foster mom has just told her 10-year-old foster son, Shawn, that he can't go over to his friend's house because he hasn't finished cleaning his room. He yells, "You idiot! I hate you! You never let me do anything!" Then he runs to his room screaming and cussing.

Part l: Calming Down

1. Describe the problem behavior

- Describe what happened or is happening
- Clearly tell the foster child what he is doing wrong
- Use empathy statements

"I know you wanted to go to your friend's house, but you are yelling and swearing."

2. Give clear instructions

- Describe what the child should do
- Give options for calming down
- Focus on praising the child for approximations and for following instructions

"I want you to stop yelling and sit in your room and calm down. Thank you for going to your room like I asked."

3. Allow time to calm down

- Give everyone a chance to calm themselves
- Decide what to teach next (Leave the area for a few minutes. Come back and ask if the child if he is willing to talk.)
- Check for cooperative behavior

"Are you ready to talk about this calmly?" or "I can see that you're still upset. I'll be back in a few minutes."

When your foster child is following instructions and is willing to talk with you about the problem, you move from the calming-down phase to follow-up teaching.

Part 2: Follow-Up Teaching

4. Describe what your foster child could do differently next time

- Think of a better way your foster child can react when he gets upset

"Shawn, let's look at what you can do the next time you get upset. What I'd like you to do next time you think you will start yelling and swearing is to ask me if you can go to your room and calm down."

5. Give a reason

- Relate it to the foster child

"If you learn to calm yourself down without

yelling and cursing, we can get the problem solved faster and you won't lose any of your privileges."

6. Practice what your foster child can do next time

- Practicing will make it more likely that your foster child will do what is expected

Foster mom: "Why don't you give that a try? I'm going to tell you 'No' when you ask me if you can go out and play, and you start to get really angry. What should you do?"

Shawn: "Ask if I can go to my room to chill for awhile."

Foster mom: "Great! Okay. Let's try it."

- Let him know how he practiced

"Okay. Good. You asked me if you could go to your room. And, you asked me in a nice voice tone. Thanks a lot."

7. Give a consequence

- This will help prevent the problem from occurring again

"As you know, we have a consequence for yelling and swearing and not accepting 'No.' You will not be able to go to your friend's house for two days. Please go wash your hands for dinner. If you want to earn back some of the time at your friend's house that I've just taken away, we could do some more role-playing after the dishes are done."

Remember, this is an example. In real-life situations, your foster child probably won't cooperate this quickly. He or she may go from being uncooperative, to being calm, and then to suddenly being uncooperative again. Some foster children have a lot of stamina when they're upset. You also may have to deal with other distractions in these situations; for example, your other children need something, the phone rings, the soup is boiling over on the stove, and so on. Interactions with your foster child do not occur in a vacuum. Continue teaching. In these instances, use the skills you learned in Chapter 14, "Staying Calm," and adapt the teaching steps and your teach-

ing style to the situation. Stick to simple descriptions and instructions, continue to use empathy, and stay calm. And remember that you are a member of a TEAM. If you need some help, call your Consultant.

Why Teach Self-Control?

Let's think about this for a minute. If your four-year-old throws himself on the floor and kicks and screams to get his way every time he gets frustrated or upset with someone or something, how do you think he will try to get what he wants next time? Right. He will throw a tantrum.

If your eight-year-old foster daughter argues and whines until you give in, what do you think will happen the next time she wants something? Exactly. She will argue and whine.

If your teenage foster son yells and threatens you when you tell him he can't go out with his friends, and he eventually gets to go anyway, what do you think will happen the next time you tell him he can't go out? Yes. Yelling and threatening.

So when we ask, "Why teach self-control?", the answer is clear. You want your foster child to be able to respond to frustrating situations in healthy ways, not harmful ways. Maintaining self-control helps people get along with family members, do better in school, develop friendships, keep jobs, and take advantage of opportunities that would otherwise be lost.

When to Teach Self-Control

Treatment Parents report that they teach self-control in three types of situations:

- When a foster child comes to a home with a history of angry outbursts or physical aggression. Treatment Parents can use Preventive Teaching to teach a child self-control **before** he or she becomes uncooperative.

- When a foster child misbehaves and will not respond to Corrective Teaching. Instead, the foster child continues the misbehavior or the misbehavior worsens.

- When a foster child "blows up" – a sudden and intense emotional outburst during which the foster child refuses to do anything that the Treatment Parents ask.

Skills Taught in Follow-Up Teaching

As mentioned in earlier chapters, teaching specific skills helps foster children know what is expected of them. Here are some skills that Treatment Parents frequently find helpful to teach during Follow-Up Teaching:

Staying calm
Asking for help
Accepting criticism
Accepting "No" answers
Following instructions
Disagreeing with others
Appropriately expressing feelings (anger, sadness, disappointment, etc.)
Apologizing

Most often, these skills help foster children handle stressful situations in constructive ways. See Appendix D for detailed descriptions of these skills.

Helpful Hints

Staying calm. Staying calm is much easier when you stay on task. Implement all of the steps of Teaching Self-Control. Concentrating on your foster child's behavior is much easier when you have a framework to follow. Teaching Self-Control gives you a set of effective steps for responding to your foster children when you need it most. Those are the times when you are the most frustrated, upset, or exasperated. Your foster children may try to argue with what you say or call you names. They may say you don't care about them or tell you how unfair you are. They may say things to make you feel guilty or angry or useless. If you get caught up in all of these side issues, you lose sight of your original purpose – to teach your foster child self-control. And, you can lose sight of the original problem and how

you need to deal with it. If you find yourself responding to what your foster child is saying, remember to use a key phrase – **"We'll talk about that when you calm down."** Staying on task ensures that you won't start arguing or losing your temper.

Dealing with ongoing behavior. As previously mentioned, your foster child sometimes will not respond to your teaching right away. He or she may continue to be uncooperative by yelling, screaming, or being aggressive, or by simply ignoring you and not following instructions. These situations can be frustrating and tiring. Ideally, your spouse or support person will be available to help. Remember, you can **always** call your Consultant for advice or support. He or she will work with you during consultation meetings to develop strategies to deal with these types of behaviors and assist you in working with your foster child during the "crisis."

Physical actions. Throughout the process, be aware of your physical actions. Some Treatment Parents find that sitting helps calm the situation quickly. When they stand up – particularly fathers – they tend to appear more threatening. This only makes matters worse and makes it less likely that the foster child will calm down.

Pointing your index finger, putting your hands on your hips, scowling, leaning over your foster child, and raising a fist all are examples of physical actions that tend to increase tension in these emotionally charged situations. Try your best to avoid these gestures. Keep your hands in your pockets, cross them over your chest, or find something to do with them other than waving them at your foster child.

It is also important to pay attention to how close you are to your foster child. To ensure your safety and to avoid any physical aggression or need for restraint, it's important that you stay a safe distance away. Be aware of your surroundings and don't allow yourself to get backed into a corner, caught on the stairs, or blocked in a doorway. Remember that your foster child is not in control of his or her emotions and therefore is unpredictable. Your safety and that of your children and the foster child is most important. Any teaching or consequences can wait until the foster child has had a chance to cool down.

Planned consequences. It helps to have consequences set up in advance. For example, "Sarah, when I tell you 'No,' sometimes you want to argue with me. Then you get real mad and start yelling. From now on, if you do this, you will lose your phone privileges for two nights." Then explain to Sarah why she needs to accept decisions and why she shouldn't argue or scream. Planned consequences are consistent; if Sarah loses self-control, she is aware of the negative consequence she will receive. Also, planned consequences help you avoid giving unreasonable or harsh consequences that stem from your anger.

Earning back lost consequences. Remember that letting children earn back some of their lost privileges helps to keep them motivated to learn and role-play new skills. Children can earn back up to half of the privileges that are taken away.

The completion of Teaching Self-Control. As your foster child calms down and you complete the teaching sequence, numerous side issues can arise. For example, some situations may call for a problem-solving approach. Your foster child possibly doesn't have the knowledge or experience to deal with a certain situation. Take time to help find solutions.

Other situations may call for a firm, matter-of-fact ending to Teaching Self-Control – "Okay, we've practiced what to do. Now, go in your brother's room and pleasantly apologize to him."

Still other situations may call for an empathic, understanding approach. Some foster children cry after an intense situation. They just don't know how to handle what they're feeling inside. In such situations, you could say, "Let's sit down and talk about what's been going on to make you feel so angry. Maybe I can help. At least, I can listen."

Take the opportunity to help your foster child by using whatever you believe is the best approach. Sometimes, going through the rough times together forms the tightest emotional bonds.

Summary

Treatment Parents must have a bountiful supply of patience if their foster children have a problem with self-control. The wisest Treatment Parents are those who realize that learning self-control is an ongoing process. They are skeptical – as you should be – of anyone who claims that self-control can be taught immediately. They know it takes a long time. Don't try to rush the learning process; expecting too much too soon can create more problems than it solves. Be attentive to small accomplishments; praise even the smallest bit of progress your foster child makes. While you're at it, give yourself a big pat on the back. Teaching Self-Control is a tough job, and you wouldn't do it if you weren't committed to your foster child.

As you teach self-control, look for positive changes. Your foster child possibly will have fewer angry outbursts, or the outbursts won't last as long, or they won't have nearly the intensity they once had. Teaching Self-Control helps Treatment Parents and foster children break the painful argument cycle. When tension is greatest in the family, Teaching Self-Control gives everyone a constructive way to get problems resolved.

Finally, we'd like to say a few words about reporting a child's behaviors to your Consultant. Throughout this manual, frequent reference has been made to contacting your Consultant. Given that we are a **treatment** program, it is very important that you keep your Consultant informed of any unusual behaviors or incidents your foster children are involved in. The types of behaviors and incidents you need to report range from a simple bump on the knee to ongoing uncooperative behavior. Reporting behaviors quickly and accurately ensures that the foster child receives the best treatment possible. It also serves as a protection for the Treatment Parent. We like the approach of **no surprises**. During Preservice Training and consultation, staff will assist you in learning how and when to report events. Guidelines are further outlined in the Policy and Procedure Manual.

CHAPTER 17

Overview of Motivation Systems

One of the key ingredients to a successful treatment program for foster children is the teaching of skills and behaviors each and every day. When children learn different, better ways of behaving, they have more ways to solve problems and are better able to build relationships.

Many children who come into our program do not seem interested in learning and changing their behavior at first. Some may not respond to the kinds of consequences that we described in previous chapters. For example, losing TV time or getting hugs or praise from you may not be enough to make your foster children want to change their behavior. Until the child **does** begin to respond to the positive and negative consequences you can provide in your home, it is up to you and your Consultant to "dangle the carrot," to give your foster child extra motivation to learn new behaviors. This is why Motivation Systems are a part of the daily teaching of skills in the Boys Town program. In many ways, a Motivation System is like a plaster cast physicians use to help heal a broken leg. It is very important in the healing process, and its removal is a good sign that progress is being made.

Just as physicians use a variety of casts or splints to heal different kinds of breaks, you will use different tools within the Motivation Systems when changing your foster child's behaviors. The following are some of those basic tools.

Strategies Designed to Increase Behavior

Positive Reinforcement – "Giving something good." For example, a foster child earns a cookie or Effective Praise for making her bed.

Negative Reinforcement – "Taking away something bad." For example, the Treatment Parent "nags" the foster child until he follows her instruction and does the dishes. The Treatment Parent "takes away something bad" – the nagging – to reward the child for doing the dishes. As you can see, negative reinforcement needs to be used carefully or it will not produce positive results.

Strategies Designed to Decrease Behavior

Response Cost – "Taking away something good." For example, the foster child loses the privilege of riding his bike because he rode around the block without permission.

Punishment – "Giving something bad." For example, the foster child is required to clean the bathroom as a consequence for smearing toothpaste on the mirror. (Remember that spanking, which is a punishment, is NOT ALLOWED in our program.)

Treatment Parents will most often use positive reinforcement and response cost when dealing with a foster child's behaviors. The use of negative reinforcement and punishment should first be approved by your Consultant.

Differences Between Bribery and Motivation Systems

People sometimes mistake Motivation Systems for bribery. The two are very different. We know that bribery is giving a reward to someone to get him or her to **stop a negative behavior;** for example, giving your five-year-old a candy bar in the grocery check-out line so she will stop crying and arguing. A Motivation System, however, is a planned way to **reinforce positive (appropriate) behavior** with a meaningful reward; for example, giving a child a candy bar because she **isn't** whining or crying, and is cooperating when you tell her "No" to other things. Keeping your child motivated to use positive behaviors in a store and elsewhere makes your life and the child's life much more pleasant while helping him or her to learn new skills!

A Motivation System expands your ability to motivate, discipline, and monitor your foster child's behavior. In a way, it simply gives you more tools or options as a Treatment Parent. If one type of reward doesn't seem to be working with a child one day, the Motivation System you and your Consultant have worked out will give you other options to try. Motivation Systems can help, but they do not do the real work. They do not teach children; Treatment Parents teach children! Motivation Systems do not work by themselves. How well they work depends on the cooperation of the child and the skills of the Treatment Parents. Treatment Parents need to use the Motivation System as another tool with their own skills and abilities as they teach the child to become more successful. As the child learns more skills and learns to enjoy the natural benefits of appropriate behavior, he or she is faded off the Motivation System.

Contracts and Charts

Contracts and charts are an important part of Motivation Systems. Contracts specify exactly what is expected from the child, the Treatment Parents, and anyone else who is involved in the terms of the contract. Charts keep track of a child's progress toward goals and help the Treatment Parent measure the effectiveness of treatment methods.

Contracts and charts help Treatment Parents:

- **Focus on a particular problem behavior.** Behaviors that can be targeted include not completing homework, frequently complain-ing or whining when asked to do something, tantrums, or always being late for school in the morning.

- **Help the foster child achieve a therapeutic goal.** Common goals include getting involved in school activities, making friends, and remaining drug-free.

- **Help the foster child achieve a personal goal.** Common goals children set for themselves include making a sports team, earning money for a bike, and getting better grades.

Here are examples of things Treatment Parents have wanted their children to do:

1. Go to bed on time without a big fuss.
2. Finish their homework each night.
3. Ask permission before they play with others' toys.
4. Come home from school on time.
5. Get to school on time each day.
6. Get themselves ready for school each morning without having to be reminded.
7. Do their chores around the house.
8. Offer to help out.
9. Keep their room clean.
10. Knock before they enter a closed door.

Here are some of the things foster children have put on their list of things to do:

1. Have more allowance.
2. Have a later bed time.
3. Get to go more places.
4. Not have to do so many chores around the house.
5. Buy new clothes.
6. Have more play time with their Treatment Parents.
7. Pick a movie to rent.
8. Choose where to eat out.
9. Invite a friend over to play.
10. Earn more TV time.

These two lists are samples of what Treatment Parents want for their children and what foster children want for themselves. Now let's see how you can combine the two lists and put a contract together.

Writing Contracts

Contracts are often part of a child's Treatment Plan. Even though it is not a formal or legal document, it is still an agreement reached by you and the child. Contracts can be used when you want your foster child to be more involved in his or her treatment (e.g. he or she can help write the contract), when you want an extra bit of commitment from the foster child, or when you just want the agreement between you and your foster child to be "spelled out" in writing.

Here are the steps for writing effective contracts.

1. **Identify goals – yours and the child's**
2. **Write what you want your child to do**
3. **Write what your child wants to do**
4. **Set a time limit**
5. **Date and sign the contract**

Here's how you might write a contract with a school-age boy who wants to watch more TV when you want him to do his homework each night. Example 1 shows you how this contract might look.

1. Identify goals – yours and the child's

Treatment Parents' goal: The Treatment Parents want the child to be more responsible about completing his homework on time.

Child's goal: Child wants to watch more TV.

2. Write what you want your child to do

Treatment Parents' goal: Ronnie to study for at least 30 minutes every evening before asking to watch TV. He will start his homework before five o'clock and will work until he completes his assignments.

3. Write what your child wants to do

Earn an hour of TV each evening.

4. Set a time limit

Pick a specific time each evening when you and your child review progress. This continues for two weeks or until the contract is renegotiated.

5. Date and sign the contract

Signatures indicate that the contract is in effect. Signatures also indicate that you and your child feel this is a fair agreement.

Example 1
Ronnie's Read and Watch Agreement

I, Ronnie, will study for at least 30 minutes every evening (Sunday through Thursday) before asking to watch TV. I will start my homework assignments by five o'clock each day. If they take longer than 30 minutes, I will work on them until they're finished. I understand that if I don't do my homework, I don't get to watch TV.

We, Ronnie's Treatment Parents, will let Ronnie watch TV for one hour each night after he completes his homework as expected.

We will go over Ronnie's homework each night when he is finished. We will continue this contract for two weeks.

Ronnie's signature	Date
Treatment Parents' signatures	Date

Developing Charts

Charts make it easy for kids to see their progress. Charts are very helpful with younger children, who benefit from seeing visual, concrete examples, and with older children. Here are the steps for developing a chart.

1. **Identify goals – yours and the child's**
2. **Set a time limit**
3. **Draw a chart**

Example 2

Let's take a look at how this worked for 10-year-old Billy and his parents. Billy wanted to have a later bedtime, especially on weekends. His Treatment Parents wanted him to go to bed on time without arguing each night. They used a chart called "Billy's Bedtime Bonanza," shown on the next page, to help him get to bed on time.

Billy's bedtime on weeknights was nine o'clock. Each weeknight that Billy went to bed on time with-

billy's bedtime bonanza

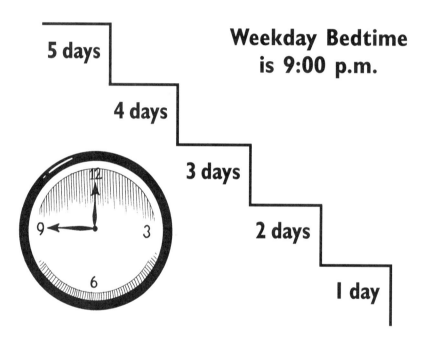

5 days

4 days

3 days

2 days

1 day

**Weekday Bedtime
is 9:00 p.m.**

Each school night that I get to bed on time, I draw a stick figure on my chart. The number of times I get to bed on time tells me how late I can stay up on Friday and Saturday nights.

**Friday and Saturday
Bedtimes**

1 day	9:15 p.m.
2 days	9:30 p.m.
3 days	9:45 p.m.
4 days	10:00 p.m.
5 days	10:30 p.m.

out arguing, he put a star on the corresponding stair. (A stick figure, happy face, or another symbol your child likes also can be used.) The number of times Billy reached the goal determined how late he got to stay up on Friday and Saturday. The more nights he went to bed on time, the later he got to stay up on the weekend. So, going to bed on time without arguing on three of five weeknights earned a 9:45 p.m. bedtime on Friday and Saturday. There was a built-in incentive for getting to bed every night on time.

While this arrangement was set up to help Billy get to bed on time, the same idea can be used for other goals, such as completing homework, being ready for school on time in the morning, helping others each day, keeping the bedroom clean, and so on. A similar chart could be used to help a child achieve any of these goals.

Many parents enjoy coming up with creative charts for their kids. Some of the most creative designs have come from the kids themselves. Young children in particular love to get out the crayons and make a colorful chart. This is a positive way to get your foster child involved in the process, and it gives you one more thing to praise.

At the end of this chapter are several examples of charts that can be adapted for your children. The first one (Reggie's Rebound) has been completed to show you how behaviors and rewards can be explained. The last three have been left blank so that you can photocopy and use them. Fill in your child's name at the top and list a desired behavior and positive consequences the child can earn in the blanks provided. Choose these consequences from the list you developed in Chapter 10.

Hints for Successful Contracts and Charts

State the goal positively. Say "When you finish your homework, you can watch TV" instead of, "If you don't finish your homework, you don't get to watch TV." Either of these statements can be true, but it's easier for a child to reach a goal if he or she is working toward something positive.

Follow through on the agreement. Be sure to review your foster child's progress each day and provide encouragement to keep going. When he or she reaches the goal, give what you promised. And pile on the praise!

Make the goals specific and measurable. A goal of "completing homework each night" is easier to measure than a goal of "doing better in school." Likewise, it's easier to determine if your foster child is "offering to help Mom once a day" than it is to determine if he or she is "being more responsible." Being specific and clear helps you know when your foster child has reached a goal.

Keep the goals reasonable. Setting reachable goals is especially important when you are first introducing the idea of a contract or chart. When you set a goal that your foster child can achieve, it sets up the child for success and helps build his or her confidence. The foster child is more likely to cooperate and follow through with the conditions of the contract or chart.

Provide the consequences. What the Treatment Parents agree to do when a child reaches a goal is the positive consequence. When the goal is reached, the consequence is given. If the goal isn't reached, the consequence isn't given. Remember Grandma's Rule.

Make it fun. Again, contracts and charts are used to help kids reach goals and experience success. This will be more enjoyable if it's fun for you and your foster child. Make a big deal out of each day's progress and use lots of praise during the day when your child is working toward the goal.

Contracts and charts are a great way to help children see that they can achieve success. Contracts and charts open lines of communication so that Treatment Parents and foster children can achieve goals together.

Token Economies

Why are charts and contracts so helpful for children? To answer that question, let's look at consequences again. Consequences can be natural or applied. **Natural consequences** are the typical or expected results of a behavior. For example, scrapes and bruises are often the natural consequences of falling down on a cement sidewalk. Losing weight is the natural consequence of cutting down on the number of calories you eat.

Applied consequences for behavior are results that are deliberately arranged. In our program, applied consequences take the form of "tokens" (for example, stars, stickers, poker chips, or points) that children earn for appropriate (positive) behavior and lose for inappropriate (negative) behavior. As an applied consequence, tokens are effective only because a foster child can exchange them for a wide variety of privileges – snacks, TV time, free time, allowance, etc. – that he or she wants.

In our program, tokens are like money. Children earn tokens and spend them on things they want. Privileges are the **real** reinforcers for the child; tokens are the medium of exchange. Having a list of available privileges helps ensure that a foster child can earn or lose only privileges, not basic rights. The Child Rights described in Chapter 2 should never be restricted, nor should they ever be earned or lost through a Motivation System.

For a variety of reasons, applied consequences like tokens are easier to use than direct privileges. Children continue to respond to tokens over long periods of time because they represent **many different** privileges. If you gave a foster child a candy bar every time she followed an instruction, she eventually would grow tired of eating candy, and she would no longer be motivated by candy bars. When you use tokens, children don't get tired of them because the tokens can be exchanged for a variety of privileges, not just candy bars.

Tokens are easily available. They can be given or taken away at any time or any place; this is not always true of privileges. For example, you may not always have a candy bar with you or be in a place where you can get one.

Because tokens are always available, they can be given or taken away **as soon as the behavior occurs.** This makes the consequence powerful, because the child can more easily see the connection between his or her behavior and the result of that behavior. It helps the child to better understand the

relationship between behavior and achieving goals or avoiding problems.

Because tokens are always available and can be delivered immediately, Treatment Parents can make them very predictable. **Every time** the behavior occurs, consequences follow. This consistency helps a child learn new skills and behavior more quickly.

Applied consequences such as tokens can be increased or decreased depending on the difficulty of the skill being learned. They can be used to reinforce small improvements as well as large achievements. This helps the foster child learn the new behavior and experience some immediate success for his or her efforts. Eventually, the skillful use of the new behavior will be followed by positive, natural consequences.

Applied consequences also can be used in a school setting. If your foster child has a history of difficulty in school, you and your Consultant may decide to have him or her use a school note. The school note is an easy, clear method for each child's teacher to provide regular feedback on social and academic behavior. A variety of school notes can be used to help a child get feedback on his or her behavior and to inform the Treatment Parents of the child's progress.

Privileges vs. Rights

The rights of children in our program were covered in detail in Chapter 2, "Creating a Safe Environment." The point here is to know the difference between rights and privileges. A **right** is something that is guaranteed; it's something you always have. For example, the Constitution of the United States and the Amendments to the Constitution specify a number of rights for all citizens. Freedom of speech, freedom from cruel and unusual punishment, and freedom from unwarranted searches are human rights guaranteed to all people in the United States. A **privilege** is a particular benefit that is granted to someone; it may or may not be earned.

Because not all programs for children have respected the rights of children, the courts have intervened and have begun to specify more clearly the rights of people in those programs. Each child in our program is guaranteed the rights described in Chapter 2. These basic rights are not privileges and are not part of any Motivation System in Treatment Foster Family Services.

Suggestions for Privileges

The children in our program should have a lot of privileges available to them so they are motivated to learn and change their behaviors. This is one of the advantages of living in a family's home during treatment instead of in a hospital or institution. Depending on the child, some privileges may be freely available (e.g. special time with a Treatment Parent, getting to choose what to have for dinner, playing with the dog, etc.), while others may have to be purchased with tokens the child earns. (Refer to Appendix E, "Positive Consequences that Cost No Money," for examples of things or activities that can be good privileges for children to earn.)

You also can take advantage of privileges that become available once in awhile or involve special activities or items. For example, your foster child may want to exchange 10 days worth of stickers (earned for good behavior at school) for a trip to the local circus. Access to these privileges is based on the child's individual needs, and the number of tokens needed to "buy" them is determined in advance.

Not everything should be "sold" or given to a foster child only because he or she does certain things. Treatment Parents should do many things for their foster children simply because it builds and maintains positive relationships. Treatment Parents, along with their Consultant, should develop a list of those privileges or activities that must be earned by a child on a regular basis, and other things that usually will be "free."

Keys to Effective Motivation Systems

To ensure that Motivation Systems are truly helping a child, Treatment Parents must pay careful attention to how they use them. When using the Motivation System you and your Consultant have developed, remember the following guidelines:

Treatment Parents should identify activities and material things that the child will work for. These are the things that will motivate the child to learn new behaviors and change old habits.

The child should earn privileges based on his or her behaviors. If a child can obtain privileges without earning them, the Motivation System is not as powerful because earning tokens is no longer the only way to get privileges. It also is important that you make sure that your foster children are earning their privileges most of the time. Otherwise, they are likely to get discouraged and misbehave because they think they can never be "good enough" to earn their privileges.

The Motivation System should be used when you are teaching the child. For example, if a child does something you asked him to do without arguing, you would praise him for following instructions and let him know that he earned a sticker on his chart. Later, the sticker can be added up with his other stickers and he can earn privileges based on how many stickers he has earned. Remember, Motivation Systems alone do not help children learn new ways to behave; teaching social skills is the most important element.

Treatment Parents should be in control of the Motivation System. The skills you are taught in Preservice Training, along with those your Consultant will help you learn, are to be used as tools. These tools help you provide the best treatment to the child and are designed to make your job as easy as possible. However, don't feel limited to using just these tools. Work in cooperation with your Consultant to come up with creative Motivation Systems. The possibilities are endless!

The child should be taught about his or her Motivation System. You and your Consultant should teach the child how to earn tokens and privileges, how tokens and privileges are lost, and how many tokens must be earned daily for certain privileges. Children also should participate in developing their Motivation Systems. They can tell the Treatment Parents and Consultants what they are motivated to earn and help in deciding what behaviors they need to work on. When foster children participate in their treatment planning, they are much more likely to work toward achieving their goals.

Although it's important for children to earn privileges regularly, they also should know what it's like to lose privileges. So, don't bend over backwards to help a child earn privileges if he's been behaving poorly all day. He needs to know that if he behaves poorly, life is not as fun as when he behaves well. Loss of privileges is a form of discipline.

In our program, the loss of tokens or privileges is paired with the opportunity for the foster child to "earn back" up to half of the privilege that was lost. For example, if your foster child loses the privilege of playing outside for one hour for not completing her chores, she can earn back up to 30 minutes of that time by following through and completing her chores. This has several advantages: 1) The foster child is given a chance to immediately practice the appropriate behavior (i.e. completing chores), which helps her learn the behavior more quickly; 2) Giving the foster child a chance to earn back part of the privilege keeps her from becoming too frustrated and keeps her interested in changing her behaviors; and 3) By giving the foster child the opportunity to earn back part of the privilege, you show that you want to help her learn, and this helps strengthen your relationship.

Treatment Parents should focus on using positive reinforcement. Remember to "catch 'em being good" and reinforce the child's appropriate behavior. This helps build positive relationships with children and helps to keep the focus on developing appropriate behavior. Without this, you can easily overemphasize the negatives and focus too much on inappropriate behavior. Using positive reinforcement helps to create a positive and effective home where children can learn and be happy.

Remember in the chapter on positive consequences when we talked about shaping? Shaping means reinforcing behaviors that are close to the behaviors you want to see. For instance, if you're working with the child on cleaning her room, you

will praise her a lot at first for just picking up things off the floor and making her bed. After she's done these two things several times in a row, you can start working on the mess **under** the bed! So, start small and work up to the big things, and remember: Praise, praise, praise!

Treatment Parents should remember the following:

- Always give consequences (both positive and negative) for behaviors.

- Provide them immediately.

- Have the size of the consequence fit the behavior.

For example, if a foster child doesn't make his bed, what kind of consequence should he earn? Should he lose 10 stickers or just one? Should you ground him for a week or just take away some TV time? You want to make the consequence large enough so that it means something to the child, but not so big that it's too punishing or discouraging. Using smaller consequences over and over is better than giving one big consequence one time.

It's important to remember that there is not one big consequence that is going to change a foster child's behavior. It's easy to get frustrated and think that maybe if you really "show 'em you mean business," the child won't ever repeat an inappropriate behavior. Unfortunately, this just doesn't work. Changes in behavior happen when the Treatment Parent gives the child a consequence every time a certain behavior occurs. Over time, the child learns to change the behavior so he or she won't earn a negative consequence. Also, inappropriate behavior **always** earns consequences. It's tempting to "let it slide, just this once." However, by letting it slide, you are actually increasing the chances that the child will do it again. So, for your sanity and the child's best interests, always provide consequences for inappropriate behavior. Remember that it took the child many years to learn his or her behaviors, and miracles don't happen overnight!

When you take a child into your home and begin teaching to his or her behaviors, you may see an increase in negative behaviors. Some might call this the "storm before the calm." Your foster child has not had consistent or firm limits and expectations set in the past, and chances are that his or her negative behaviors were sometimes ignored. But when the child moves into your home, he or she suddenly finds that you address every negative and positive behavior. The child probably will try to test you and see just what things will earn a consequence. Many children think that if they continue to "act up," the Treatment Parents will just give up and stop giving consequences. This can be a stressful time for Treatment Parents because they've been working hard and want to see fewer negative behaviors. However, as strange as it sounds, when you see an increase in negative behaviors, it can actually be a **good** sign – it means your teaching is working. Now, more than ever, it's important to be consistent and not give in. Soon, your foster child will realize that you aren't backing down and his or her negative behaviors will decrease and eventually mirror those of other children his age.

Punishment

A few words about punishment must be included. Punishment is **applying** a consequence after a behavior in order to decrease that behavior in the future. Spanking is an example of punishment. Punishment and losing privileges are not the same. As mentioned earlier, loss of privileges is "taking away something good" in response to inappropriate behavior. Punishment is "giving something bad" in response to inappropriate behavior.

Both loss of privileges and punishment can help decrease inappropriate behavior, but punishment is less effective, for several reasons: 1) When punishment (e.g. spanking, having a child clean the floor with a toothbrush) is used, the child may behave well around those who do the punishing and then behave poorly in other settings. For example, if a child is punished physically for being aggressive in the home, he may become well-behaved at home because he doesn't want to be hit. But he may become physically aggressive at school, where there is no physical punishment. Thus, the child will behave appropriately where physical punishment is used, but will not be motivated to behave appropri-

ately in other places; 2) The use of punishment may cause the child to simply substitute another inappropriate behavior for the behavior that has been punished. So instead of hitting, the child may simply yell, stomp his feet, or throw things; 3) As mentioned earlier, a child who loses tokens or privileges usually is given an opportunity to "earn back" up to half of the consequence that was lost in exchange for practicing appropriate behavior. This idea of "earning back" is not easily used with punishment; for example, how can you take part of a spanking? With loss of privileges, there is a consequence for inappropriate behavior (losing tokens and/or privileges), along with teaching and a chance for the child to earn a reward for appropriate behavior. The child learns more quickly and is less frustrated.

In our program, overcorrection and spanking (or other physical forms of punishment) are not allowed. **As a Treatment Parent, it is your responsibility to check with your Consultant before giving any consequences that have not been previously discussed.**

As we discussed in the chapter on negative consequences, adding work as a consequence can be an effective way of teaching responsibility. This is especially true if the work "chore" is related to the consequence (e.g. washing the dishes when a child has refused to help set the table). Sometimes, however, giving additional chores as a consequence can be misused. Here are a few cautions to consider before using chores as a consequence:

- The extra chores might not "fit the crime." Raking the yard has very little to do with hitting a brother unless raking was the brother's chore to begin with and the added chore is a form of apology.

- Doing chores may not offer the child opportunities to practice the alternative to the inappropriate behavior. It is hard to teach a child how to get along with a brother if the child who did the hitting is outside raking alone for an hour.

- If a child persists in a negative behavior, Treatment Parents may persist in "chore" punishment. They may reason: "If 30 minutes of pulling weeds didn't make him stop, maybe two hours of it will." Overusing the same chore or increasing chore time can quickly become harsh treatment and create a very angry and resentful child and terribly frustrated Treatment Parents. For these reasons, "chore punishment" should be used sparingly.

Summary

Motivation Systems are tools that you and your Consultant will develop together and refine over time. We provided examples of only a few Motivation Systems in this chapter; the possibilities are really limitless. So work with your Consultant and foster child, and be creative! Boys Town has learned that nothing can replace a Motivation System that respects the child's rights, teaches new skills, and helps the child experience success.

reggie's rebound

Each day that I finish my homework, I get to color a basketball. On weekends, I get to color a ball if I read for 30 minutes. Each day that I color a ball, I get to shoot baskets outside with Mom for 15 minutes.

End of the Week Bonus

On Saturday, I get a bonus for having 4 or more balls colored during the week.

4 balls colored = choose dessert for dinner on Saturday
5 balls colored = friends come over on Saturday
6 balls colored = bike ride on Sunday with Dad
7 balls colored = friends stay overnight on Saturday

morning stars

Each time I do one of the tasks, I get to put a star in that box.

	Get Dressed	Make Bed	Eat Breakfast	Brush Teeth	Ready for School on Time
Monday					
Tuesday					
Wednesday					
Thursday					
Friday					
Saturday					
Sunday					

Each day that I have 3 stars, I get to pick one of the following:

1.

2.

3.

Each day that I have 4 stars, I get to pick two from this list or the 3-star list.

1.

2.

3.

Each day that I have 5 stars, I get to pick three things to do from any list.

1.

2.

3.

"s" curve

Each time I _____,

I get to color in a circle. When three circles are colored, I get the reward.

Behavior:

Reward:

Reward:

Reward:

pool prize

Behavior _____

Every time I _____, I get to color a ball.

If I color _____ balls, I get to _____.

If I color _____ balls, I get to _____.

If I color _____ balls, I get to _____.

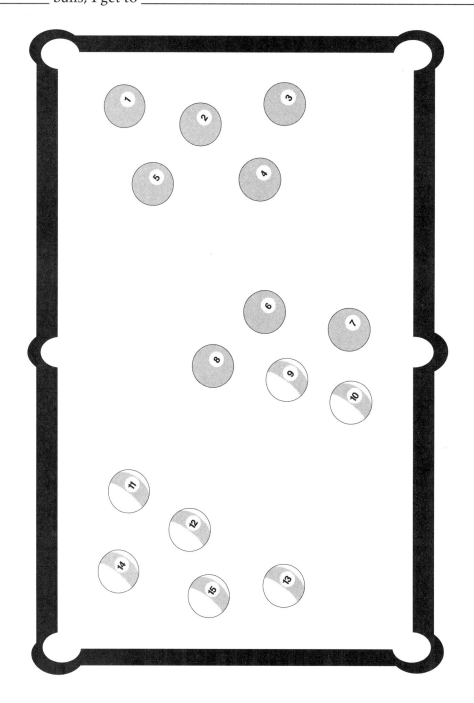

CHAPTER 18

Using Treatment Plans to Change Behavior

Michael is a nine-year-old boy who has been placed in the treatment foster home of Bob and Barbara Reed. The Reeds have a 15-year-old daughter at home as well. Michael has been "in the system" since he was three. The Reeds are Michael's fifth out-of-home placement. Michael's history includes a placement in two different psychiatric hospitals for a total of four months, placement in a regular foster home for two years, and a three-month stay at an emergency shelter. Michael has been placed back home several times in between these placements. Michael's referral behaviors include aggression toward peers, academic difficulties, and depression. He also has been sexually abused by his mother's boyfriend. The Reeds have observed that Michael has difficulty controlling his aggression. His aggressive behaviors include slamming doors, yelling and telling people to "shut up," and occasionally hitting other children. Michael also frequently forgets to close the door when he is in the bathroom. Furthermore, he makes sexual jokes, talks about sexually explicit movies he has seen, and stands too close to people when they are talking to him.

One of the key factors that sets Treatment Parents apart from other foster parents is that Treatment Parents don't provide just room and board, but actual treatment for the foster child. Your job as a Treatment Parent is to teach foster children the skills they will use, not only while they are living in your home, but for the rest of their lives.

How do you decide which skills your foster child needs to work on first? How do you know which skills to teach and the best ways to teach them? In the Boys Town program, these questions are clearly answered and a plan is set in place. So you are never expected to deal with a child's behavior "off the top of your head." Our job is to develop the best Treatment Plan possible to deal with a child's behavior and help you learn the best way to carry out that plan.

Treatment planning is an ongoing process in which Consultants and Treatment Parents create or update ways to change a child's behavior or attitudes. Treatment planning is done following the two-week assessment period, and the plan is reviewed and revised at regular intervals while the child remains in the home. Consultants document the treatment decisions that are made on the Treatment Plan form (next page).

Importance of Treatment Planning

The number one reason for doing treatment planning for foster children is to ensure that each one receives individualized treatment for his or her specific problems. This is a cornerstone of the program. To accomplish the plan's goals, Treatment Parents serve as the primary treatment providers, and the Consultant helps every step of the way by answering questions, addressing concerns, and helping the Treatment Parents sharpen their skills.

The second important reason for having a structured plan in place to deal with the child's behaviors is to help the Treatment Parents take a proactive, rather than a reactive, role in treatment. This means that when negative behaviors occur, the Treatment Parents have already planned ahead and are able to

TREATMENT PLAN

DATE:

NAME: SYSTEM:

PROBLEM AT ADMISSION:

TARGET BEHAVIOR:

BASELINE: FREQUENCY OF PROBLEM BEHAVIORS:

PROBLEM DEFINITION:

GOAL: FREQUENCY OF PROBLEM BEHAVIOR:

   __ PER DAY

GOAL: % OF TEACHING TO ALTERNATIVE BEHAVIOR:

   __ PER WEEK

STRATEGY:

   PREVENTIVE TEACHING:

   SPONTANEOUS TEACHING:

   FAMILY MEETING:

   RELATIONSHIP DEVELOPMENT:

   PROBLEM-SOLVING:

respond to the situation in a calm, fair way, rather than panicking and reacting to the child's behavior. When parents react by panicking, they are much more likely to violate a child's basic rights. This creates more problems and sometimes damages the relationship between the Treatment Parent and the child.

Finally, being prepared helps to make the Treatment Parents' teaching that much more effective. The foster child will benefit more from the teaching, which will help him or her learn the skills that are necessary for success much more quickly. So in the long run, this makes your job as a Treatment Parent easier.

Treatment Planning Pointers

Before reviewing in detail how to complete a Treatment Plan, here is some important information about how the process works.

1. Consultants have the primary responsibility for writing the Treatment Plan.
2. Treatment Parents have the primary responsibility for carrying out the Treatment Plan.
3. Treatment Parents are expected and encouraged to be actively involved in the treatment planning process. The Treatment Parents' observations of the child's behavior play an important part in deciding which areas the child needs to work on, how to motivate the child to change behaviors, and the best ways to teach new behaviors.
4. The Consultant and Treatment Parents work with other members of the treatment team who contribute information for the Treatment Plan. These other members include mental health professionals, caseworkers, the child's parents, and other Treatment Foster Family Services staff. We believe that it is important to seek input from many different individuals so that we can provide the best treatment possible to the children in our care.
5. It is very important that Treatment Parents follow through with the plan and teach the skills that are identified. If the Treatment

Parents begin using the plan and experience some problems or discover a better way to deal with the child's behavior, they must check with the Consultant before changing the plan in any way. The Consultant is a professional who is trained to work with troubled children and it is his or her job to work with the Treatment Parents to provide quality treatment.

6. Each child will have from two to four Treatment Plans at any one time to describe the individual target areas or skills that the Treatment Parents will be teaching. Target areas or skills refer to the behaviors that the Consultant and Treatment Parents decide are the most important for the child to learn.
7. Each Treatment Plan needs to be tailored to fit the child's specific needs. For example, if a child argues a lot, the Consultant is trained to determine if it would be most productive to target the skills of "Following Instructions," "Accepting 'No' Answers," or another skill. The Consultant will try to determine which skill will help the child improve the problem behavior the most quickly.
8. It is helpful to include the child in the treatment planning process. If the child is old enough to participate, he or she can develop a better understanding of his or her treatment goals. Furthermore, the child can suggest rewards that he or she would be willing to work for, and learn what the consequences will be for inappropriate behaviors.

Treatment Planning Process

Here are the five basic steps of the treatment planning process. An explanation of each one follows. The Consultant is responsible for completing these steps with the Treatment Parents' involvement.

1. **Identify the problems**
2. **Target specific skills**
3. **Develop a specific plan**
4. **Carry out the plan**
5. **Review the plan**

In order to illustrate how these steps are applied in the development of a child's Treatment Plan, a completed Treatment Plan is presented at the end of this chapter. The information included in the plan refers to Michael, the nine-year-old boy whose case was described at the beginning of the chapter. You will notice numbers like this #1 on Michael's completed plan. These numbers represent the first three steps of the treatment planning process, and show what type of information coincides with each of these steps. As you read the following explanations, refer to the Treatment Plan and the description of Michael's situation to see how the plan is created. Use this information to complete Exercise 1 at the end of the chapter.

Identify the Problems

The first task is to identify the problems the child needs to solve. When the child is placed in a treatment foster home, the Treatment Parents will be asked to complete the Assessment Sheet (next page). This information is then combined with other intake information about the child, such as presenting problems; psychological, psychiatric, and social history; behavioral strengths of the child; and treatment goals identified by the family and referring agency. Taken together, these data help the Consultant identify three or four conceptual target areas and the specific skills that are associated with them.

The Assessment System

The Assessment System is the beginning. Through observing and recording a child's behaviors over a two-week period, this system helps the Treatment Parents and the team develop a comprehensive and clear understanding of the child's current behavioral strengths and areas of development, and his or her actual social and behavioral skills.

The Assessment System can be used in combination with Brief Daily Summaries to observe and record the child's behavior in detail. For example, if you ask your foster son to carry out the trash, what does he do? He may roll his eyes, mumble, or complain that he "has to do everything." He may say he'll do it as soon as he finishes watching his TV program, and then only carry out the instruction

after you insist that he follow through. Or he may tell you that he'll take out the trash, and then do it immediately. By observing the child's current skills and willingness to please others, you can begin to identify behaviors you want the child to continue to use, and reward him with Effective Praise or extra privileges for those behaviors. You also begin to identify the skills the child needs to learn and how to motivate him to practice them and use them every day.

As Treatment Parents observe a child's behavior and try to decide what motivates him or her and what behaviors need to change, it still is important for them to teach to inappropriate behaviors and give consequences for those behaviors during the assessment period. Treatment Parents and their Consultant can discuss specific positive and negative consequences they can use with the child, and determine how well the child already responds to natural and logical consequences. This helps them get an idea of how much the child knows about the basic steps of self-control. Along with addressing those negative behaviors, Treatment Parents must remember to praise, praise, praise! This helps the child to feel more comfortable and welcome in the home and is the first step in building a strong relationship.

After the Assessment Sheet is completed, the Consultant organizes the information that the Treatment Parents and the other members of the team have compiled about the child. The Consultant suggests priorities regarding behaviors that the child needs to change right away, and organizes those observations into specific categories.

Next, the Consultant looks very closely at the child's behaviors and determines how often the behavior occurs, its duration, and its severity. Using information from observation and data from the Treatment Parents' daily reports (adapted from Chamberlain & Reid, 1987), the Consultant will count how many times a week on average a certain behavior or type of behavior occurs. This helps the team evaluate later in the treatment process whether the frequency of the behavior decreases after the Treatment Plan has been implemented.

The Consultant then fills in the "Problem at Admission," "Baseline: Frequency of Problem

BOYS TOWN
TREATMENT FOSTER FAMILY SERVICES
ASSESSMENT SYSTEM

NAME: _____   Assessment Period: _____

Please complete this Assessment System over 14 consecutive days for each skill listed below. Record a Y (yes) if the youth demonstrated the skill satisfactorily or an N (no) if the youth needs to learn or improve the skill.

SKILLS	M	T	W	T	F	S	S	M	T	W	T	F	S	S
FOLLOWS INSTRUCTIONS														
ACCEPTS "NO" ANSWERS														
ACCEPTS CONSEQUENCES														
ASKS PERMISSION														
DOES DAILY CHORES														
GOOD PERSONAL HYGIENE														
GOOD SCHOOL BEHAVIOR														
GOOD CHURCH BEHAVIOR														
GETS ALONG WITH PEERS														
TELLS THE TRUTH														
APPROPRIATE LANGUAGE														
APPROPRIATELY DISAGREES														
REPORTS WHEREABOUTS														

Behaviors" and "Problem Definition" categories on the Treatment Plan. (See the completed plan at the end of the chapter.)

In Michael's Treatment Plan, the "Problem at Admission" is "aggressive behavior," the frequency with which it occurs is five times per day, and the "Problem Definition" is a description of specific behaviors that occur when Michael becomes aggressive. These areas are designated with a #1 .

Not all Treatment Plans are this lengthy. This form is longer to give you an idea of what types of information and suggestions you may see.

Target Specific Skills

Once the conceptual target areas have been identified, the next step is to identify the specific skills the child needs to be taught. These skills are listed in Appendix D at the end of the manual. The skill or skills the Consultant selects are related to the conceptual target area, and will address the problems identified in the "Problem Definition" section of the Treatment Plan. The skills are selected to help change as many problem behaviors as possible.

Because Michael has problems with aggression, his conceptual target behavior is "Anger Control." The specific skill that will be taught is "Staying Calm." These are designated with a #2 .

Develop a Specific Plan

The third step in the treatment planning process is to develop a specific plan to change the child's behavior and improve his or her skills. This is done in two ways:

- The Treatment Parents, the Consultant, and the child set short- and long-term goals that will help measure the child's behavior. For instance, they may set a short-term goal of decreasing the child's problem behavior from five times a day to two times a day. The ultimate long-term goal would be to get the behavior to a level that is acceptable to both the Treatment Parents and the Consultant. In this example, the acceptable frequency of physical aggression is zero.

- The second way involves planning how to reach the goals using the specific teaching strategies outlined in previous chapters: Preventive Teaching, Spontaneous Teaching, Family Meetings (as needed), Relationship Development, and Problem-Solving. The Consultant also gives suggestions on how the Treatment Parents can encourage the child to develop a relationship with them as they teach this skill. Finally, any outside therapy that also addresses this problem behavior is described.

The percentage of teaching time a Treatment Parent spends on a particular behavior depends upon how quickly the Consultant and Treatment Parents would like that behavior to change. The process goes like this:

- The Consultant and Treatment Parents identify three to four target behaviors to address at any given time. On the completed Treatment Plan, Michael has "Anger Control" as his conceptual target area, and "Staying Calm" as the specific skill to be taught to address this target area. (See #2 on the plan.) Michael also would have from one to three other Treatment Plans to address different problem behaviors.

- These target behaviors are rated according to priority, and the most important or pressing target behavior receives the most teaching time. For example, Michael might have conceptual target areas that require three skills to be taught: "Staying Calm," "Setting Appropriate Boundaries," and "Following Instructions." The time to be spent teaching each of these skills could be broken down as shown on the chart on the next page. Please note that this is only a guideline for helping Treatment Parents focus their teaching. Treatment Parents should always take advantage of any opportunities to teach to inappropriate behaviors. (The sample Treatment Plan contains information only on Michael's first target skill, "Staying Calm.")

Target Behavior	% Teaching time	# interactions/day	# interactions/week
Staying Calm	50%	6	42
Setting Appropriate Personal Boundaries	33%	4	28
Following Instructions	17%	2	14
TOTAL	100%	12	84

The remaining information on the sample Treatment Plan for Michael is designated with a #3. When the plan is complete, it is signed by the child, Treatment Parents, and Consultant. The Treatment Parents and Consultant keep a copy.

Carry Out the Plan

The fourth step in the treatment planning process is to carry out the plan. As mentioned earlier, this is primarily the Treatment Parents' responsibility, with help from the Consultant. Carrying out the plan involves closely following the strategies that have been developed and reporting any concerns, problems, or changes in the child's behavior to the Consultant. Remember, it is very important to follow the plan and teach the skills that have been outlined. The plan is only as good as its implementation. The Consultant must approve any changes before they are implemented.

Each Treatment Plan is continuously monitored while a foster child lives in a home. Specifically, the Treatment Parents and their Consultant review the foster child's plan by looking at the child's weekly progress. This progress is "tracked" through the Daily Summaries, Parent Daily Report forms (adapted from Chamberlain & Reid, 1987), and motivation charts the Treatment Parents complete. (See Chapter 17 for sample forms.) The Consultant and the Treatment Parents review the information on a weekly basis during the consultation meeting. This is the time when Treatment Parents should bring up any concerns, questions, or problems they may be having in following through with the plan.

Review the Plan

The final step in the treatment planning process is updating the plan and changing it as needed. During weekly visits with the Consultant, the Treatment Parents and the child review the child's progress in improving behaviors and target areas in general. Once a month, they formally review each Treatment Plan. At this time, any changes can be discussed and put into practice, with the Consultant's approval.

Whenever Treatment Parents have concerns about the child's target areas, they should contact their Consultant and ask for a review of the Treatment Plan. In other words, Treatment Parents don't have to wait for the monthly review; they can talk to their Consultant any time they have questions or concerns about the foster child's treatment.

Summary

Treatment planning is the cornerstone of treatment foster care. Treatment Parents have a key role in the development of the plan and are the primary treatment providers for the child. Consultants and other members of the child's team contribute information and substantial support while the plan is being implemented in the home. Once children learn the initial skills described in the Treatment Plan, more advanced skills can be taught and ultimately mastered. Eventually, foster children will have the opportunity to return to their families or other settings with the confidence that they can make better, more mature choices in the way they interact with others and feel about themselves.

TREATMENT PLAN

DATE _____

(first Treatment Plan)

YOUTH: Michael   **#3** **SYSTEM**: Modified Motivation/Sticker Chart

#1 **PROBLEM AT ADMISSION**: Aggressive Behavior

#2 **TARGET BEHAVIOR**: (1) Anger Control: Staying Calm

#1 **BASELINE: FREQUENCY OF PROBLEM BEHAVIOR**
   5 per day (average)

#1 **PROBLEM DEFINITION**

When Michael is angry or frustrated he slams doors, throws things, and sometimes hits other children. He also swears, refuses to listen to adults, tells them to "shut up," and refuses to follow instructions.

#3 **GOAL**: Frequency of Problem Behavior: 2 per day (0 per day for physical aggression)

#3 **GOAL**: % of Teaching to Alternative Behaviors: 50% per week

#3 **STRATEGY** (Preventive Teaching, Spontaneous Teaching, Family Meeting, Relationship Development, Problem-Solving):

#3 **PREVENTIVE TEACHING**

Each day Michael will role-play the steps to "Staying Calm" before and after school, and every morning and afternoon on weekends. Michael will review the steps to "Staying Calm" which have been developed for him:

1. Take several deep breaths.
2. Relax my muscles (clench my fists and relax them, shake my arms for 10 seconds, roll head from side to side).
3. Tell myself to "chill out" or count to 10 slowly.
4. Tell someone I trust what is bothering me (appropriately expressing anger).
5. Try to solve the situation that made me upset.

Michael will be given an opportunity to review or practice the steps to "Staying Calm" prior to situations where he frequently loses control of this anger. Michael will earn a sticker each day for role-playing "Staying Calm" twice. He also will earn a sticker each day he is successful in controlling his anger. At the end of each week, Michael can exchange these stickers for:

- a candy bar (seven stickers).
- staying up an extra 30 minutes on a nonschool night (10 stickers).
- 30 minutes of playing with his Game Boy® (12 stickers).
- a video rental and eating popcorn during the movie (14 stickers).

#3 SPONTANEOUS TEACHING

Michael will earn stickers for using the steps of "Staying Calm" at home and at school. Michael will earn a time-out and/or lose privileges when he expresses his anger inappropriately. When this happens, Michael can earn back some of his privileges by role-playing "Staying Calm." Michael will lose from one to five stickers when he loses control of his anger at home (Corrective Teaching and Teaching Self-Control).

#3 FAMILY MEETING

The Reeds will hold a Family Meeting at least twice during the first week, and as often as needed each week after that. During these meetings, any problems that any of the children in the home are having with physical aggression will be discussed. (It is important not to "single out" Michael during these meetings, and not to discuss his private treatment issues in public.)

#3 RELATIONSHIP DEVELOPMENT

The Reeds will use Effective Praise to also help Michael notice when he is using the steps of "Staying Calm." The Reeds will look for opportunities to praise Michael for using the steps of "Staying Calm." Michael will be given reasons for how this skill will benefit him at home, at school, and during his visits with his family.

#3 PROBLEM-SOLVING

Michael will earn the privilege of spending $1 per day of allowance for completing **SODAS** on how to express anger appropriately and solve conflicts constructively. Michael will continue to see Dr. Lockhart once a month to monitor Michael's medication.

Exercise 1

This exercise requires you to think about how you would help a Consultant develop a Treatment Plan. If Michael were placed in your home, what suggestions would you make to the Consultant about a Treatment Plan to address the following behaviors?

TREATMENT PLAN

DATE _____

(first Treatment Plan)

YOUTH: Michael   **SYSTEM**: Modified Motivation/Sticker Chart

PROBLEM AT ADMISSION: Inappropriate Personal Boundaries

TARGET BEHAVIOR: Setting Appropriate Personal Boundaries: Following House Rules

BASELINE: FREQUENCY OF PROBLEM BEHAVIORS

Between 2 and 6 times per day

PROBLEM DEFINITION

When Michael is in the bathroom, he does not close the door. Michael also tells sexually inappropriate jokes, tries to wrestle with boys and girls at school, stands too close to people when they are talking to him, and talks to other children about sexually explicit films he has seen.

GOAL: FREQUENCY OF PROBLEM BEHAVIOR

__ PER DAY

GOAL: % OF TEACHING TO ALTERNATIVE BEHAVIOR

__ PER WEEK

STRATEGY:

PREVENTIVE TEACHING

What house rules would you develop to help Michael?

When would you teach and review them?

How would you reward Michael for participating in Preventive Teaching for this skill?

How could you role-play the skill of "Following House Rules?" (Hint: following bathroom rules, how far away you stand from others, telling inappropriate jokes, etc.)

SPONTANEOUS TEACHING

When would you use Effective Praise to help Michael continue to respect personal boundaries by following house rules?

When would you use Corrective Teaching to teach this skill? What consequences might you use?

FAMILY MEETING

How often would you hold Family Meetings? What would you review at the meetings?

RELATIONSHIP DEVELOPMENT

How could you strengthen your relationship with Michael while you are teaching him this skill? (Hint: What rationales would you give Michael for teaching this skill? How could you model this skill for him?)

PROBLEM-SOLVING

If Michael is looking for affection or opportunities to be close to other people, how could you teach him to get these needs met more appropriately?

Describe what you could do to help Michael participate in therapy for abuse victims.

CHAPTER 19

Making Decisions

Reggie tells you that some children at school have asked why he is in foster care and he doesn't know what to say. How do you help him?

Michelle discloses that her mother's boyfriend has been at Michelle's home during her last few home visits. The court has ordered her mother not to let the boyfriend see Michelle. Michelle says she is worried that her mother will be mad if she tells someone, but she also doesn't feel safe going home when he is there. What do you say to Michelle?

In both situations, these children must make decisions. Children frequently make decisions on the spur of the moment, sometimes without thinking. They tend to look at solutions to problems as black or white, all or nothing, yes or no, do it or don't do it. Children also focus on the situation at hand and have difficulty looking ahead to see how a decision could affect them later.

So, how can Treatment Parents prepare foster children to make the best decisions?

The SODAS Method

At Boys Town, we use a five-step problem-solving method called **SODAS®.** The principles are simple, yet this method is adaptable to many situations. The **SODAS** method accomplishes two goals.

- First, it gives Treatment Parents and foster children a process for solving problems and making decisions together.
- Second, it helps Treatment Parents teach children how to solve problems and make decisions on their own.

The **SODAS** method helps both foster children and adults think more clearly and make a decision based on sound reasoning.

SODAS stands for:

1. Define the **S**ITUATION
2. Identify **O**PTIONS
3. Discuss **D**ISADVANTAGES
4. Discuss **A**DVANTAGES
5. Choose a **S**OLUTION

Let's look at each step of the **SODAS** process.

Define the SITUATION

Before you can solve a problem, you need to know what the problem is. Defining the situation sometimes takes the greatest amount of time because foster children often use vague or emotional descriptions. Also, children aren't always aware that a certain situation can cause problems. A four-year-old may think that running into the street isn't a problem; he's only thinking about getting his ball back. He doesn't realize the dangers of his actions.

Other decisions may not contain obvious dangers, but they still may cause problems. Regardless, these are opportunities for your foster child to make a choice. Children will have to decide how to spend their allowance, who to hang around with, or how to respond to the unique challenges of being a foster child. Children and Treatment Parents can use the **SODAS** process to help make these daily decisions.

Tips for defining the Situation:

- **Ask specific, open-ended questions to determine the situation**. Avoid asking questions that your foster child can answer with a one-word answer ("Yes," "No," "Fine," "Good," etc.). Instead, ask questions such as, "What did you do then?" or "What happened after you said that?" These questions help you piece together what occurred.

- **Teach your foster child to focus on the entire situation, not just part of it**. For example, questions that identify who, what, when, and where help you get a clear picture of the whole situation.

- **Summarize the information**. Sometimes, children get so overwhelmed by the emotions surrounding a problem that they lose sight of what the actual problem is. State the problem in the simplest, most specific form. Ask your foster child if your summary of the situation is correct.

Exercise 1

Describe a current situation where your child or foster child needs to make a decision. It could concern school, friends, playtime, or any other area of the child's life. Use this situation as you complete the exercises that follow the explanation of each step of the **SODAS** method.

Situation:

Identify OPTIONS

Once you have a complete description of the situation, you can begin discussing options – the choices your foster child has. There usually are several options to each problem.

Children, however, frequently think of solutions in the form of "all-or-nothing" options. For example, a student gets a bad grade on a test and immediately wants to change classes since everything is "ruined." It's common for children to only see one solution to a problem, or take the first one that pops into their heads. Other times, they may see no options at all.

Your role as a Treatment Parent is to get your foster child to think. Say things like, "Try to think of something else you could do" or "What else could solve the problem?" Consistently asking these questions helps the child eventually learn how to make decisions without your guidance.

Tips for identifying Options:

- **Let your foster child list good and bad options.** Don't express your approval or disapproval at this time. It's a common tendency for Treatment Parents to jump right in and immediately tell their children what they think. But remember that you're trying to get your foster child to think of ways **to make a decision on his or her own.**

- **Limit the options to four or fewer**. Any more than that tends to get confusing. (Also, make sure at least one of the options has a chance for success.)

- **Suggest options if your foster child is having trouble coming up with them**. This way, children learn that in many situations, there is more than one option.

Exercise 2

Using the situation you described earlier, identify three or four possible options for resolving the problem. Write down what you think your child or foster child would come up with, as well as options you might pick.

Options

1.

2.

3.

4.

Discuss DISADVANTAGES/ADVANTAGES

In this step, you help your foster child look at the pros and cons of each option. This helps your foster child see the connection between each option and what could happen if that option is chosen.

Tips for discussing Disadvantages/ Advantages:

- **Ask your foster child for his or her thoughts about each option.** What's good about the option? What's bad about the option? Why would the option work? Why wouldn't the option work?

- **Help your foster child come up with both disadvantages and advantages for every option.** This will be easier with certain options; the child may not have the experience or knowledge to know possible outcomes for all options.

Exercise 3

List a possible disadvantage and advantage for each option that you listed in Exercise 2.

Disadvantages

1.

2.

3.

4.

Advantages

1.

2.

3.

4.

Choose a SOLUTION

At this point, it's time to determine which option will work best. Quickly summarize the disadvantages and advantages of each option and ask your foster child to choose the best one.

Tips for choosing a Solution:

- **Make sure that your foster child knows the options and the possible outcomes of each one.** You're trying to help your foster child make an informed decision and establish a pattern for making future decisions.

133

- **Some decisions are hard to make**. If a decision doesn't need to be made immediately, let your foster child think it over.

Additional Thoughts

Treatment Parents usually have a lot of questions about **SODAS** and the types of situations in which it can be used. Here are some things to think about when using the **SODAS** method.

- Children sometimes pick options that don't sit too well with their Treatment Parents. In general, if the decision won't hurt anyone and isn't illegal or contrary to your moral or religious beliefs, then let them make the choice and learn from their decision. For example, your foster son might insist that he wants to spend most of his money on a very expensive video game. You may not agree with his choice but it won't harm anyone if he decides to buy the game. Let him buy it and learn from the consequences. Perhaps he will enjoy the game so much he won't mind not having money for other activities. Or he might wish later that he had not bought such an expensive game. Either way, he'll learn from his decision.

- Occasionally, children face situations that are illegal or immoral, or that will harm them or others. This is the case in the earlier example where Michelle reports that her mother has allowed someone to participate in visits in violation of the court order. You **must** report this to your Consultant; Michelle has no control over this option. But **SODAS** still can be used to help Michelle think through her options for dealing with the "secret" being disclosed. This structured, problem-solving process may help her see that she still has some choices. She will learn that she can think through an emotionally troubling situation without impulsively acting out and feeling even more overwhelmed.

- Sometimes, foster children may choose options that are not good for them. In these cases, Treatment Parents have found it helpful to clearly state their disapproval, repeat the disadvantages to that solution, and let their foster child know the consequences of making that choice. For example, if your 14-year-old foster daughter decides that she is going to fight another girl who has been bullying her, you can let her know that you don't want her to fight and tell her why. You can explain what consequences she will earn if she decides to fight and how it may affect her continued placement in treatment foster care. Sometimes, despite all of your efforts, children still make wrong decisions. When that occurs, it is necessary to follow through with the consequences you described. If possible, help your foster child go back through the **SODAS** process and come up with more acceptable solutions.

- While we want to encourage children to make decisions on their own, we need to let them know that we'll be there to help at any time. This includes supporting them as they implement the solution. If the solution does not work out the way the foster child planned, you must be there to offer support and empathy. You and your foster child can then return to the **SODAS** format to find another solution to the problem.

- Practice putting the solution into effect. The most you can do is help your foster child reach a reasonable solution and practice implementing it. The purpose of practice is to help your foster child feel confident about the solution that's chosen.

- Check with your foster child to see how the solution worked. Set a specific time to talk about this. This is an excellent opportunity for you to praise your foster child on following through with the decision. You also can look for additional solutions, if necessary.

In the next exercise, we have applied the first four steps of **SODAS** to the situations that were described at the beginning of the chapter. Which option would you choose if the child in the example were your foster child?

Exercise 4

Situation – Reggie tells you that some children at school have asked why he is in foster care and he doesn't know what to say.

Options	Disadvantages	Advantages
1. Reggie can tell the children that his family is having some problems and nothing more.	1. Others will know his family is having trouble; maybe they won't like him as much.	1. It is the truth. Most families have troubles sometimes, so most children will understand that and leave him alone about it.
2. Reggie can refuse to answer their questions.	2. Children may keep bugging him, make stuff up about him, or ignore him.	2. Reggie won't have to tell them anything; it isn't their business anyway.
3. Reggie can tell them all about his problems and many placements.	3. Some children may think he is too "weird" for them, and may shun him.	3. Some children may think it's "cool" and want to be his friend.

Solution – Which option do you think Reggie will pick? Which option would you pick?

Situation – Michelle discloses that her mother's boyfriend has been at home during her last few home visits. The court has ordered the mother not to let him see Michelle. Michelle is worried that her mother will be mad if she tells someone but she doesn't feel safe going home when he is there. What can Michelle do?

Options	Disadvantages	Advantages
1. Michelle can deny that the boyfriend was at the visits.	1. Michelle will feel bad about not telling the truth, and she still will be worried about her safety on visits home.	1. Michelle's caseworker may decide to let Michelle continue to have visits in the home since Michelle changed her original report.
2. Michelle can write her mother a letter explaining why she told her Treatment Parents about the boyfriend.	2. Michelle's mother may not understand and will still be mad at Michelle.	2. Michelle's mother can hear directly from Michelle how she felt and may be more willing to protect Michelle in the future.
3. Michelle can refuse to go on any more visits with her mother.	3. Michelle would miss her mother and they won't get this problem worked out.	3. Michelle can avoid dealing with the whole problem so she won't have to face her mom being angry. Also, Michelle will be able to avoid her mother's boyfriend.

Solution – Which option do you think Michelle would pick? Which option would you pick?

As mentioned earlier, there are some situations in which the foster child does not have complete control over the situation or options. In the second situation in Exercise 4, it is your obligation as a Treatment Parent to tell your Consultant about the violation of the court order. Michelle may not understand that you have that obligation when she tells you about this problem. She may think that you can keep her "secret" until she decides what to do. But you can't keep her secret and you need to be up front with her about this. She may be very unhappy with you for disclosing this problem to your Consultant, who will then notify the caseworker. What you can do is help Michelle think through options for dealing with this situation now that it will be addressed by the caseworker. The situation can be redefined by asking: What are Michelle's options now that the caseworker knows that her mom has ignored the judge's order?

Summary

We've looked at just a few of the many possible situations where children need to learn how to solve problems. **SODAS** is an excellent process for teaching your foster child how to make decisions. It is practical and can be applied in many different situations your foster child will face. You can feel confident that you have given your foster child an effective, easy-to-use method for solving problems.

CHAPTER 20

Building Relationships Through Communication

As you know by now, emphasizing skill development and treatment technology is a distinguishing hallmark of Boys Town Treatment Foster Family Services. So by practicing and using the skills necessary to implement the treatment technology, you will become effective Treatment Parents, right? Not necessarily. There is another key element to helping children – a relationship. Perfection of skills and brilliant treatment planning are not sufficient. Both need to take place in the context of a caring relationship in order to be effective. Can we teach caring relationships? Yes and no. We hope that the caring is something you bring with you; we hope that your commitment to helping children is based on caring because we cannot teach you how to care. However, we can teach you how to build relationships because relationship-building is a skill, or rather a set of skills.

Like everything else in life, these skills come more naturally to some people than others. But they can be learned and they are essential to our work in changing children's behaviors. Why? Because modeling is important to behavior change. Aren't you more likely to try to be like someone you not only respect and admire, but also care about? Social reinforcers for the foster child, such as spending time with a Treatment Parent, are important to behavior change. How can time spent with a Treatment Parent be rewarding if there is no relationship?

Even if you are comfortable with your ability to build relationships, it will be important to focus on how you go about that process. Usually we build relationships with others who also want a relationship with us. Unfortunately, some of the children who need our help have no idea that relationships with adults can be mutually satisfying. Because their primary relationships may have been with adults who were critical and uncaring, they may respond to our efforts to build relationships in ways we don't expect. For instance, they may push us away, or at the other extreme, they may expect too much. Therefore, it is important to take a look at the qualities that will increase a foster child's desire to build a relationship with you.

The following personal qualities that enhance relationships will be discussed in this chapter:

1. **Empathy**
2. **Openness**
3. **Encouragement**
4. **Composure**
5. **Respect**
6. **Genuineness (sincerity)**
7. **Specificity**

Empathy

Empathy means understanding how someone feels and being able to communicate that understanding (Saccuzzo & Kaplan, 1984). It does not mean identifying with a child's feelings so much that you take them on as your own. To communicate empathy, you should try to put yourself in the child's shoes; determine how the child must have felt, then try to describe what the child's feelings and reactions seemed to be.

All Treatment Parents can use active listening to express empathy to the child. This means that you respond by identifying and verbally reflecting the feelings that you see or hear the foster child express. For example, if a foster child comes home and says he hates school, you could say, "You look really mad" or "You have tears in your eyes." You then can help the foster child explore his feelings and find out what's really bothering him. You don't tell him how he feels; you only describe how he looks or sounds to you. The foster child can agree or disagree with you, but either way, you are communicating without judging the child.

It is helpful to use active listening when:

- The foster child is thinking about something and you want to encourage him or her to talk about it.
- The foster child says one thing but his or her behavior is saying something else.
- The foster child is talking about sensitive topics, like his or her own family or friends, or things that happened before he or she came into foster care.

Active listening allows you to provide understanding without passing judgment. When you use active listening with children, they learn to identify their feelings and express them more effectively. This is extremely important with foster children who have not had adults teach or model this for them. When they learn to talk about their feelings, they don't have to act them out.

It does take time and patience when you are helping foster children who may rarely have discussed their feelings with other people; they may have many pent-up feelings and be confused about to how they really feel.

Sometimes it is helpful to begin by asking the foster child open-ended questions. This can help you understand the situation, or help the foster child confirm his or her thoughts or explain areas that are confusing. Open-ended questions work best when you need more information because they:

- Require foster children to answer with more than a "Yes" or "No," or a one-word answer.

- Typically start with "how," "what," "where," "when," "who," "why," or "which." Starting a question with these words does not guarantee that it is open-ended. Asking "Who told you that?" won't exactly encourage a foster child to talk.
- Encourage a foster child to share information, thoughts, feelings, and opinions. Asking a question like, "How did you feel when that happened?" will encourage a foster child to talk.

When you are helping foster children work through a problem, they should do most of the talking. Asking open-ended questions allows this to happen. Communicating through active listening shows the foster child that you understand what he or she is telling you, that you care about his or her feelings, and that you will try to help.

Treatment Parents also can show concern and empathy through passive listening. This means listening to the child without speaking, but doing things like nodding your head or saying "Okay" to let the child know you are paying attention.

Openness

Openness expresses your willingness to discuss sensitive subjects with the child without being judgmental. As an open Treatment Parent, you are showing that you understand that the child has the right to his or her own feelings. Foster parents who do **not** express openness say things like, "You shouldn't feel that way," or "Don't be upset." We encourage our Treatment Parents to accept a child's feelings whether they seem correct or not. (This does not mean that Treatment Parents accept inappropriate behaviors. Such behaviors should be addressed through teaching.)

Openness also involves having the ability to tolerate differences in values and lifestyles. For example, while you may not agree with the lifestyle of a child's parents, you should communicate a desire to get to know them as individuals and focus on their strengths.

Encouragement

Encouragement means being an active supporter of and an advocate for the child (Saccuzzo & Kaplan, 1984). You express encouragement by giving the child hope and confidence that things will improve. Encouragement communicates that you believe the child can overcome fears and anxiety, and meet the challenges of life. Effective Praise helps express these messages to the child by specifically describing his or her strengths and abilities.

Composure

Composure means remaining calm regardless of the child's behavior. Although no parent is perfect, a child gains confidence and can deal better with his or her own feelings when the child knows a parent is composed. This is another reason for Treatment Parents to practice staying calm (as discussed in Chapter 14).

Respect

Treatment Parents show respect for their foster children by showing genuine concern for their well-being. This means taking a real interest in a child and liking him or her. As a Treatment Parent, you can reject certain behaviors of a child, but still see and treat him or her as a person who is worthy of respect (Patterson, 1985). This concept should be extended to the child's family of origin, as well as the family's cultural, religious, and ethnic background.

Genuineness

Genuineness is a rather hard concept to define. In a therapeutic relationship, a Treatment Parent must relate to the child in a real and honest way. At the same time, he or she should not express hurtful or threatening thoughts or feelings to the child. "I statements" are an effective way for Treatment Parents to communicate their feelings. "I statements" allow them to express concern, worry, or any other feeling to the child. "I statements" usually include this information:

Examples of Feeling Words:

angry	happy	fearful
grouchy	afraid	helpless
annoyed	numb	scared
mad	delighted	relieved
hurt	vulnerable	embarrassed
tricked	pressured	tense
used	responsible	nervous
ignored	moved	guilty
displeased	thankful	relaxed
jealous	loving	calm
upset	satisfied	drowsy
insulted	excited	confused
frustrated	foolish	depressed
anxious	hopeful	sorry
lost	torn	proud
restless	silly	needed
discouraged	curious	crushed
miserable	lonely	disappointed
exhausted	ashamed	

"I feel (feeling word) when (describe the situation) because (provide a reason)."

For example, you might tell your foster child, "I feel worried when you are late coming home from school because I don't know if something has happened to you."

A helpful way to know that you are using "feeling" words rather than "thinking" words is that feelings always can be stated in one word.

Exercise 1

Can you think of several examples of an "I" statement you could use with your family?

I feel _____ when _____

because _____.

I feel _____ when _____

because _____.

Specificity

Specificity is expressed in a relationship by focusing on the concrete and specific concerns of the child. This means not smoothing over the child's concerns or problems with statements such as "Everything will be all right," or "You need to change your attitude." When you teach to a child's specific behaviors and teach specific skills, you actually are helping to strengthen the relationship. Children learn that you are fair and that you care enough to help them. They also learn what is expected of them and see that the skills they are learning really work.

Summary

A caring relationship between a foster child and his or her Treatment Parents is one of the keys to successful treatment in a foster home. Such relationships can be created and developed only through open, honest, and sincere communication. As a Treatment Parent, you have a unique opportunity to develop a therapeutic relationship with the foster child in your home. By implementing the concepts described in this chapter, you can increase the child's ability to make the changes necessary to improve his or her emotional and social functioning.

CHAPTER 21

The Family as a Member of the Team

Like most families, families with children in foster care can be defined in many different ways. Children become attached to their own parents or other parent figures – stepparents, grandparents, boyfriends or girlfriends of their parents, etc. Children do not need to have a biological relationship with someone to feel attached to that person. In this chapter, we'll refer to the person or people a child is attached to as his or her "family." It is our belief that it is very important to invite people the child defines as "family" to be members of the treatment team.

Why are the children of these families in foster care? Many studies have tried to answer this question. One study (Jenkins & Sauber, 1966) found five major reasons why parents have to place their children in foster care. These are:

1. Physical illness or incapacity of the child-caring person, including confinement.

2. Mental illness of the mother.

3. Personality or emotional problems of the child.

4. Severe neglect or abuse.

5. Other family problems, including unwillingness or inability to continue care, desertion, parental incompetence, alcoholism or other addiction, marital conflicts, or arrest.

In addition, poverty and a landslide effect of one problem on top of another force many families to place children in foster care. Usually, children who are placed in Boys Town Treatment Foster Family Services come from families that have experienced one or more of these problems. As a result, a court places the child in the custody of the state department that is responsible for child welfare services (e.g. the Department of Human Services, Department of Social Services).

Professionals who work with children who have been neglected or sexually or physically abused often have strong reactions of shock, anger, or revulsion when they hear about mistreatment of a child. It is easy to understand that someone would have a strong reaction to a person who is identified as the abuser. In spite of these feelings, it is important to remember that you are a member of a professional team and cannot do good therapeutic work if you listen only to your emotions.

We must remember that just as there is no such thing as a "perfect parent," no parent **wants** to be a poor parent. In fact, the great majority of these parents love their children. But frequently they don't have the skills or enough motivation to develop the skills necessary to be a successful parent at the time their children are placed in foster care. Every parent has strengths and weaknesses. It is our obligation not only to recognize the family's weaknesses, but also to identify its strengths. A more productive way of working with families, then, is to think about them having a range of skills and skill deficits. For example, one set of parents may make sure that the child has expensive athletic shoes, which helps him feel confident at school. At the same time, they may ignore his need for a winter coat or forget to pay the utility bills. If we concentrate only on what they did "wrong," then we miss opportunities to build on the parents' commitment and concern for their child.

Why Parents Should Be Part of the Treatment Team

Our main goal is to help the foster child have the best possible relationship with his or her family. When the child is placed in Treatment Foster Family Services, the court and the agency responsible for the placement will establish a plan that sets a goal for the family and the foster child. This plan is reviewed periodically to determine if progress has been made.

What does it mean if the court approves reunification as the plan for the family? Family reunification is the planned process of helping the foster child and his or her family work toward living together again. A variety of services may be offered to help them accomplish this goal. These services may help the family meet basic needs (housing, food, etc.), improve parenting skills, provide psychological services, etc. Boys Town or other agencies can provide these services.

One of the first steps in helping a foster child return home is to help the child maintain ties to his or her family of origin while in placement. It is important that parents not become so discouraged about getting their child back that they begin to "count this child out" of their family. This may be happening if a family gives the child's bedroom to someone else, doesn't visit the child while he or she is in foster care, or plans future events without considering the child's needs.

At Boys Town, we believe it is important to work with the child and his or her family for two very important reasons:

Attachment significance. Our families are for life. As we will discuss in the next chapter ("Separation and Attachment"), foster children often develop their primary attachment to one or both of their parents, and this profoundly affects the way they view themselves. If a child is attached to parents who feel good about themselves, the child

learns to respect himself or herself. If a child is attached to parents who don't feel good about themselves, the child may feel like he or she has no value. So, when we help a child's parents become more confident and positive about their ability to care for themselves and their children, the children benefit by having opportunities to attach to positive role models instead of negative ones who make them question their own value.

Reunification. Many foster children return to their own family or the home of another relative. Boys Town's Treatment Foster Family Services research has shown that the average length of stay for a child in Boys Town foster care is about one year; some foster children stay longer, while others leave our program sooner. About 4 out of 10 foster children are discharged to live with their parents or other relatives (Mott et al., 1995). Therefore, in order to best help the child, we have a duty to help make the environment to which the child will be returning as supportive and helpful as possible. We can do this, in part, by working with the family to teach members the parenting skills they don't have. Additionally, by including the parents on the treatment team, the team benefits from the parents' knowledge of the child. Finally, the parent learns about the services and service providers that are currently helping the child, and will have more knowledge about what the child will need when he or she eventually returns home.

The Treatment Parents' Role in the Reunification Process

As Treatment Parents, you can make several important contributions to helping your foster child's family. The remainder of this chapter will discuss these contributions.

Provide support and understanding to the biological family and build relationships. Treatment Parents can be very positive role models for the child's parents. Can you think of people in your life who are positive role models for you? Before you decided that these were people you wanted to be like, you probably developed a relationship with them that allowed you to learn more about their values, abilities, and personalities. As a result of this relationship, you learned to value the way they lived their lives. You may have consulted them when you had a problem or decision to make because you knew they made sound decisions.

This is also true for the families of foster children. Before they decide to accept some of your suggestions for parenting the child during visits or when he or she returns home, they need to get to know you. When they develop a relationship with you, to the extent that is possible, they will be more likely to trust your judgment and suggestions about how to parent.

You can encourage parents to develop this relationship with you by listening to their suggestions and explanations about the child's unique needs and personality. By doing this, you help affirm the parents' ability to understand and desire to help their own child. Although you may not agree with all of the parents' values or personal decisions, it is very important to look for positive attempts on their part to help and stay involved with the foster child. Many parents are quite isolated and have a small support system. They may seem cautious when you initially meet them because they feel that they have been labeled "bad parents" and you are the "good parents." But if you persist in being pleasant and offering them common courtesies, they will probably decide to trust you more and eventually may want to listen to your suggestions.

Be empathetic with the parent's feelings of temporary loss of the child from the family. Listen, make eye contact, smile. What you do is as important as what you say. Some parents will remain angry that the foster child was placed against their wishes. You don't have to defend or explain why the foster child was placed. Listening in general is an important tool in developing a relationship with anyone and will help you get to know the child's parents. Expressing understanding of their sense of loss may help them feel that you are there not to judge them, but to support them.

Imagine that a parent comes home from visiting her children and writes this in her diary:

I've just got back from visiting my kids in the foster home. Those foster parents are taking care of my kids now. They are doing what I should be doing for my own kids. I feel like a real failure, I don't even have my own kids with me. I don't know how to describe what it felt like to hear Jason and Matt calling the foster parents "Mommy and Daddy." My feelings don't make any sense because I want my kids to be treated right if they can't be with me. But at the same time, I don't want them to start thinking of this other home as theirs. I don't want them to forget that I'm their real Mom.

So, I was thinking all this when I went for THE VISIT. My stomach was in a knot and I ran out of cigarettes. But I walked up to the house anyway. Before I could ring the doorbell, the kids came running out and they both ran up and gave me a big hug. Jason is getting so big, he nearly knocked me over. I was so relieved that they were glad to see me. But I couldn't really relax because I was expecting the foster mother to come over and watch me with the kids like I was some criminal. But I was wrong. I couldn't believe the foster mother. She wasn't anything like I expected. I thought she'd be fancy and looking down her nose at me – but it wasn't like that at all.

She came over and said "Hello" and asked me to come into the kitchen for some coffee. The phone rang as we walked in so she told me to pour my own coffee and I sat at the table. Her house looked like kids lived in it with pictures on the fridge and dishes in the sink. She came back and poured herself some coffee. My kids were kinda wound up about seeing me and running around to get things to show me. The foster mother, Maria, seemed to understand and didn't get too weird about it. When Matt pushed Jason, Maria seemed comfortable letting me tell him to stop it.

Someday I think I might tell Maria that it really would have spooked me if she had been all dressed up and every hair just in place. She just seemed like a regular person who hadn't already decided that I was a dangerous character. We might even be friends someday.

Give the parents opportunities to parent their own kids. This can be hard to do. If you know the parents have abused or neglected the child in the past, it is hard not to worry about how they will treat the child now. But even if the visits are completely supervised, the parent should still have the opportunity to do some parenting. This could include simple activities like brushing the child's hair, giving a snack, or stopping an argument. This gives parents an opportunity to "practice" new skills they are learning or to use skills they already have.

Most of the time, parents will feel like they're "playing second fiddle" to you. Most of their power or respect as a parent has been taken away and they often will feel intimidated, in competition, or inadequate next to you. They may not attempt to do much parenting when you are around because they don't want to have their decisions or actions compared to yours. However, if you express confidence in them and praise them for things they do for their child, the parents can develop more confidence and will be more likely to continue to take on the parenting role when they are with the child.

This is good for the parent as well as for the child. No matter how well you take care of your foster children, you are not their "real" parent. Although you will care for and love your foster children, this will not replace their desire to be loved by their own parents. Kids express this longing differently at different ages, but it is never completely gone. You hope that someday a child's parents can love him or her the way the child wants them to, and part of your job is to encourage and strengthen the love between them. It is important to remember that foster children have membership in another family by birth and will at times prefer that family over yours.

What can you do to give parents an opportunity to parent their children during visits?

Be approachable. Because you provide care for the foster child, the parents may begin to see you as the "expert" who really knows how to parent or set limits with their child. You will start to figure out what works and what doesn't work with this particular foster child. This will become especially clear when you begin to have some success in helping the foster child change his or her negative behaviors. Parents may ask you for advice about how to respond to certain behaviors the child displays during visits. You can tell them how you would handle it and ask them if they think it would work for them. You also can reinforce the parents' belief that they too have some valuable parenting skills by identifying some of the child's strengths that the parents have already taught. For instance, you could say, "John always gets up when his alarm clock rings. How did you teach him to do that?" Or you could find out more about the family's way of responding to a certain behavior and let the parents know that it worked in the foster home, too.

Also, if your cultural or ethnic background is similar to that of the parents, the foster child's family may feel more comfortable. This can be extremely important if they begin to view you as a role model for parenting.

In the diary entry you read earlier, what did Maria do to help the foster children's mother feel less threatened about visiting her children in someone else's home?

Teach effective parenting skills. Modeling is a very powerful teaching tool. When the foster child's parents see you handle misbehavior without hitting, screaming, or withdrawing, they may begin to think you know something that they may want to learn. Not all parents will get on the bandwagon, but some will. Those parents who are ready and willing to learn better parenting skills will watch you carefully and, with support, will want to try to do what they see works in your family. As mentioned earlier, parents will be more likely to accept your suggestions if they feel they have a sincere and honest relationship with you.

While modeling and teaching are important, you must exercise some caution here. As we said earlier, parents must have opportunities to parent their own children. Use your judgment to determine whether a child's parents are receptive to what you are teaching, and whether or not you are taking away their opportunity to interact with their children.

Anyone who is a parent can appreciate that we all need some help from time to time. Most of us know that using resources in the community makes our job a lot easier and makes us more successful. You can model for the foster child's parents how to use community resources. Sometimes, what we take for granted may be new information for another person. You can show parents how to call the doctor for an appointment, how to give medicine appropriately, how to advocate for the foster child to get the help he or she needs at school, or how to choose a daycare. The list is endless. As you get to know the foster child better, you will learn which resources have helped you and you can transfer that knowledge to the foster child's parents.

How would you feel most comfortable suggesting a resource to a parent?

Develop the foster child's skills. By implementing the foster child's Treatment Plan, you will help the foster child have a better chance of being successful when he or she returns home. For instance, when your foster daughter improves her ability to accept "No" answers or use the **SODAS** method of problem-solving, she is more likely to respond to her parents' instructions and handle stress appropriately.

Working with foster children ahead of time on new social skills they can use during home visits will help them have the best visit possible. By supporting the children and helping them have positive visits with their parents, they will feel your support of their families as a whole. This in turn will help the children feel better about themselves.

What would you say if the parent asked you, "Why are you always telling my child that what she just did was so good?"

What are some skills that you could remind the foster child to use during the next visit with his or her parents?

Help preserve the foster child's ethnic identity. We know that a child's positive self-identity and sense of belonging are essential to eventually growing up to feel positive about his or her place in the family and community. This is particularly true for foster children. Helping foster children learn

145

about their ethnic identity can strengthen their connection to their family. Ignoring a foster child's ethnic roots may communicate to the foster child that his or her background isn't important or valued.

Celebrating cultural and religious holidays that are significant in the child's culture can be an important way for the child to affirm self-identify and a connection to his or her family and community. If the parents cannot visit a child on certain holidays, find out from them how they celebrate those holidays and try to include some of those traditions in your family's regular traditions.

Can you think of some ways that you could help a foster child with a similar cultural background celebrate holidays and learn more about his or her culture? What about a child with a different cultural background?

Don't take criticism too personally. It is hard not to take personally a parent's jealousy of you or your role as the foster child's primary caretaker. It's important to realize, though, that many parents would feel defensive if someone else – a stranger – was chosen to parent their child. Try to remember that parents are very aware that you are doing the job that they should be doing. They may undercut you by suggesting that you should have sent a coat with the foster child during a visit, or that you should have taken a child with a cold to the doctor. Don't let this get under your skin. Parents may feel jealous of **whomever** was chosen to care for their children, whether it was you or someone else. Most of us would feel much the same way if we were in those parents' shoes.

If a parent's criticism is an ongoing problem, you may mention to him or her that you are doing the best job you can. Do this only when the foster child is not around. The message you are sending may not help the parent change but may begin to help him or her see that you aren't a saint and you are doing your best to help the child. And, as always, feel free to talk to your Consultant about your concerns.

What would you do if parents criticized your care of their child?

Keep the family and the child "connected." Treatment Parents can encourage parents to keep the child involved with the family by arranging visits (when possible), and helping the family continue to celebrate holidays, birthdays, and other important events together. Having the parents meet all of the treatment providers before the child is actually placed is extremely important. This tells the parents that their information and relationship is valuable and needed by the rest of the team and that no one is "counting them out."

Other ways to support families include: teaching children social skills that will help them have pleasant visits with their parents; suggesting that the parents visit when the child is rested or doesn't have to get up early for school the next morning after an evening visit; praising the parents for being on time for visits or reporting information to you about how a visit went; and thanking parents for making suggestions about the child's care (e.g. food allergies, hobbies, or ways to comfort the child when he or she is upset). As the foster child gets ready to move home, it is especially important for parents to attend school conferences, doctor appointments, and other meetings, so that the transition is as smooth as possible for the child. A successful reunification is most likely if the child's family and the child feel that the foster family is willing to help them work toward this goal and supports reunification.

146

Summary

While foster parents might think it seems easier to have little or no contact with the foster child's family, there are actually many short- and long-term benefits of working together. Not only do both families benefit from exchanging information, but the child also experiences more continuity in his or her life. If the child returns to live with his or her parents, the parents may be willing to use many of the parenting techniques the foster parents have found helpful. Everyone wins!

CHAPTER 22

Separation and Attachment

When adults temporarily cared for foster children in the past, the adults and the children were discouraged from getting "too attached" to each other. In some cases, a foster child was moved from a foster family's home because someone was worried that the child was beginning to feel like a member of that family or because the foster parents were beginning to feel "too close" to that child. After many decades of experience and research, however, we now understand that it is vital for foster children to learn to attach to their parents or caretakers. Why is this so important? Should foster children become attached to their Treatment Parents even if the plan calls for them to return to their own parents? Before we address those questions, let's first talk about what attachment is and why it is important for children to learn to attach to someone.

Attachment has been defined as "an affectionate bond between two individuals that endures through space and time and serves to join them emotionally" (Klaus & Kennell, 1976). Parents and children begin this attachment cycle at birth. The cycle begins with the child expressing a need. Babies express a need by crying or fussing to let someone know they are uncomfortable. When the parent or caretaker meets the child's need for food, warmth, or comfort, the child becomes calm and relaxed. The cycle begins again when the child has a new need. Repeated successful completion of this cycle helps the child to develop trust and security and to become attached to his or her primary caregiver. The cycle, called the Arousal-Relaxation Cycle, is illustrated here.

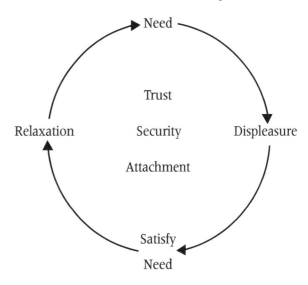

The Arousal-Relaxation Cycle

Need

Trust
Security
Attachment

Relaxation

Displeasure

Satisfy
Need

Adapted from V. Fahlberg, 1991. Reprinted with permission.

The Importance of Attachment

According to Vera Fahlberg (1991), having a strong attachment to a parent allows children to develop both trust in others and trust in themselves. They begin to have confidence that the world is a safe place where they can explore and have their basic needs met. These earliest relationships with parents influence the child's physical and intellectual development, and form the foundation for psychological development. The child's earliest attachments become the example or blueprint for future interpersonal relationships. The following list highlights the many positive long-range effects of a child's strong, healthy attachment to parents. Many children who enter foster care are in jeopardy of losing some or all of these strengths because the child's basic attachments are not well formed initially, and are therefore weakened.

Attachment helps the child:

- Attain full intellectual potential.
- Sort out perceptions.
- Think logically.
- Develop social emotions.
- Develop a conscience.
- Trust others.
- Become self-reliant.
- Cope better with stress and frustration.
- Reduce feelings of jealousy.
- Overcome common fears and worries.
- Increase feelings of self-worth.

Adapted from V. Fahlberg, 1991. Reprinted with permission.

Studies of children raised in institutions have shown that adequate physical care alone is not enough to lead to the development of a physically and psychologically healthy child with optimum intellectual functioning. For normal development to occur, children need at least one person they can trust to always care for them. This person, who responds to the child's needs and initiates positive activities with him or her, seems to be indispensable for healthy human development. Those infants whose emotional needs have not been consistently met respond to the world either by shrinking from it or doing battle with it (Bowlby, 1973).

Absence of Healthy Attachments

By the time most children enter treatment foster care, they have had many people care for them. In addition to their parents, they may have been cared for by stepparents, relatives, and/or baby-sitters; further, they may have lived in many out-of-home settings such as shelters, hospitals, and other foster homes. Needless to say, these children might have difficulty knowing who they can trust to care for

them over a long period of time. Some of these foster children will display the symptoms of attachment problems. (See chart on Pages 154–158.) These attachment problems are the result of the way this foster child was parented, the child's current and past environment, and his or her particular personality traits.

Bourguignon and Watson (1987) identify three forms of attachment disorders:

- **The traumatized child**, who has been seriously traumatized in an earlier relationship and is reluctant to trust or hope again. Children who have been physically or sexually abused frequently fit into this group. Children who have seen a parent killed or abused also can become traumatized.
- **The inadequately attached child**, who had primary attachments that were interrupted, unhealthy, and undependable. These children have difficulty re-establishing new attachments. Children who had chaotic or undependable caregivers – particularly when they were infants or toddlers – frequently fall into this group. Any child who has had his or her primary caregiver change frequently and abruptly may experience problems with attachment.
- **The nonattached child**, who has the most severe disorder. This generally occurs when a child has been deprived of the earliest opportunities to make a primary attachment. Children who were raised in impersonal situations as infants and toddlers or who were severely abused or neglected as small children may fit into this category.

If children have a weak bond with a parent because they received poor care in their family, problems with attachment usually increase when the child enters the child welfare system. The foster child who has been moved several times will have greater problems dealing with issues of trust and attachment. This contradicts old theories that recommended moving a child from stable foster care if he or she was "getting too close" to the foster family.

We now understand that a child who has had an opportunity to develop a strong positive attachment will be more likely to develop other positive attachments in the future. Teaching a child how to securely attach is the central therapeutic value of treatment foster care. When children are able to attach, they are more likely to benefit from teaching and to make up some of the developmental and social delays that brought them into treatment foster care in the first place. For example, take a foster child who is impulsive and who physically hits others or threatens to hurt himself when he feels overwhelmed. With secure attachments to a caregiver, this child may be more willing to trust an adult to help him find other solutions to his problems. Another child may not be able to relate to the feelings of other people or pets. She might treat animals cruelly or tease younger children with no feelings of guilt. When the child learns to attach, she will begin to feel some empathy for others and will want to please the parent by showing concern for others.

One of the difficult realities about being a Treatment Parent is that if you do your job well, the foster child will probably leave your home for a more permanent family. But just as you teach a child how to attach, you can teach him or her that it is okay to leave and attach to other people. Children may feel disloyal to you as they start to develop stronger attachments to their own parents or to a new permanent parent. That's why they need permission to attach to other caregivers; this teaches them that they can care for many people instead of only one.

Separation and Loss

Many of us have faced unwanted separations from people to whom we were attached. We have experienced grief. Unfortunately, the foster children in our care have experienced repeated separations and losses early in their life, and have had to face them alone in many cases. One of the greatest challenges in child welfare work is to help foster children cope with these traumatic separations and losses.

Factors Influencing the Reaction to Separation

Foster children respond to being separated from their parents in many different ways. Responses vary from severe depression in children who are well-attached to their parents and then abruptly separated from them, to almost no reactions in children who have been emotionally neglected and have little connection to their parents. The reactions of most foster children entering the child welfare system fall between those two extremes. The two primary factors that influence an individual's reaction to loss are the strength of the relationship being broken and the abruptness of the separation.

Stages of Grieving

Young children do not have the power to decide where or with whom they will live. As Exercise 1 at the end of this chapter clearly shows, children can be removed from their home with little or no warning or explanation. Besides, a child's sense of time is much different than an adult's. Several weeks can seem like a year to a child. When a child has been in a foster home for weeks, months, or years with little guarantee that he or she will ever live at home again, the child frequently experiences the classic stages of grief because it is such an important loss.

Elisabeth Kubler-Ross (1975) has identified the common stages of grieving, which can help us understand what a child goes through after being separated from an important person in his or her life. Most parents also experience a mourning process when their child is removed from their home.

Here are the stages of grieving:

1. Shock. This is most severe when the separation is abrupt. The foster child wants to shut down emotionally, and possibly physically, in order to cope with the overwhelming insult of the separation. He or she may appear to be numb, show little emotion, and even act mechanical.

2. Denial. Many children at first refuse to accept that they've been separated from their parents. Because they are thinking they will be going home any time, they may not adjust well to your home at first. Foster children may have problems regulating their sleep and eating patterns. Nightmares are common. They may seem "spacy" or forgetful; they're expending so much energy denying their loss that they may be out of touch with their environment.

3. Anger. Stages 3, 4, and 5 (anger, bargaining, and sadness and despair) can occur in any order and may recycle. Anger is frequently taken out on others, including Treatment Parents and other children. In trying to get a feeling of control over their own lives, foster children may turn ordinary requests into control issues. So the next time your foster child engages in a control struggle, he or she may be experiencing this stage of grief.

4. Bargaining. Foster children will make promises to get back what they feel they have lost: "If only I had been better and hadn't fought with my sister..." or "I promise...."

5. Sadness and despair. Foster children may look very sad and cry easily. They also may have problems with eating or sleeping. They may not be interested in doing things other children their age enjoy. Children in this stage may need more physical comforting than other children their age.

6. Resolution. The foster child begins to accept emotionally that he or she has two sets of parents. The child may not like being placed in foster care, but accepts it.

Exercise 1 on the next page examines the sense of loss and separation that children experience just before they enter a foster home. Read the story and answer the questions at the end.

Developing Healthy Attachments

Treatment Parents have two tasks in this area when a foster child enters their home. The first is to help the child develop healthy attachments, so that continued growth and development can occur. The second is to help the child extend the attachments that are developed and behavioral gains that are achieved while in foster care to future caregivers, who may be birth parents, adoptive parents, or new Treatment Parents.

Suggestions for helping children adjust to your home include:

- Work with your Consultant to choose one behavior that the foster child needs to change and identify what you think is the underlying need that the foster child is trying to meet. Based on the Arousal-Relaxation Cycle you read about earlier, choose a need (behavior) that you think you can help change in a short time (several weeks). By picking an "easy" behavior, you and the foster child can experience success early in the placement. For example, helping the foster child learn to be kind to the dog (instead of teasing it) will help him enjoy a new "friend" and feel less lonesome in this new home. You also might teach him to take his frustrations out on the basketball court with you rather than on the family pet.

- Identify activities and behaviors that represent your family, and include the foster child in those activities. For example, if each member of your family has a special place at the table and seat in the family room, then help the foster child to feel like part of your family by giving him or her a special place at the table (Bayless & Love, 1990).

At the end of this chapter is a chart containing some of the common behaviors displayed by foster children with attachment problems, possible explanations for why they act that way, and some suggestions for ways Treatment Parents can help a foster child with those behaviors. (The eight behaviors listed in this chart are adapted from *Assessing Attachment, Separation and Loss* by Linda Bayless and Lillie Love.)

Summary

Children who are placed in a Treatment Foster home frequently have had many obstacles to overcome in order to experience a healthy parent-child relationship. Treatment Parents are encouraged to understand these obstacles and to help children learn that they can trust the foster parents to act in a child's best interests. By providing a safe, trusting home for your foster children, you're helping them learn to attach and best preparing them for the future.

Exercise 1

Imagine yourself in a situation like this:

You are eight years old. Your parents have left you and your younger brother and sister home alone. They have done this a lot so it doesn't seem unusual to you.

All of you are in bed; everything is quiet, and you are sound asleep.

Suddenly there is a knock on the door, quickly followed by heavy footsteps. You hear unfamiliar voices downstairs. Someone in uniform enters your bedroom and announces, "You're coming with me." He takes you and the other children outside. You all get into a car. It's cold, and your brother and sister are crying. You fight back tears. You didn't get a chance to grab your favorite stuffed animal or even to change out of your pajamas.

Another uniformed man drives the three of you to a strange neighborhood, far from your home. The car stops in front of a house. You stay in the car as your baby brother is taken to the front door. The man knocks, someone answers the door, and your brother is handed over to this person. The man returns to the car, and he drives on. Then he stops at a second strange house and takes your sister inside.

He drives farther. He stops again. You are taken to the door of a house. The man knocks and when a person answers, he says, "Here you go." You are handed over to the person in this house and left there.

Answer the following questions:

How did you feel when the person came into the house?

How did you feel when you left your neighborhood?

How did you feel as you were separated from your brother and sister?

How did you feel as you were handed over to a stranger?

How would you want to change things?

Adapted from V. Fahlberg, 1991. Reprinted with permission.

BEHAVIOR	EMOTIONAL NEEDS UNMET AND FUNCTION OF THE BEHAVIOR	TREATMENT PARENT CAN HELP MEET THAT NEED BY:
Aggression • hitting, breaking objects, name-calling, teasing, or hurting pets	• keeping adults and others from getting close • repeating what he has seen adults do • inability to handle fears, frustration, and anger, resulting in "taking it out" on others • gaining control over an unpredictable environment • expressing anger about being separated from parents	• providing consequences for negative behaviors immediately to help teach cause-effect relationship for hurting others • teaching "Asking for Help," "Staying Calm," "Appropriately Disagreeing," "Appropriately Expressing Feelings," etc. • helping the child develop impulse control by gradually learning to wait a little longer each time for what he wants • expressing empathy and helping the child talk about his feelings
Control Battles • arguing, cannot accept "No," does exactly what he is told not to do	• having difficulty trusting others to act in his best interest • anxiety may make it difficult for the foster child to understand and respect limits • "testing limits" to see if foster parents will be consistent, and to determine "rules" of new home (what will and will not be tolerated) • trying to assert control over the Treatment Parents to compensate for feelings of powerlessness over previous abusive parent • refusing to be "parented" by anyone other than his own parents	• using Effective Praise to help the foster child feel successful and in control of himself and his environment in a positive way • being consistent in delivering consequences so the child knows what to expect and what is expected of him • giving the foster child choices when possible (e.g. what clothes to wear) • teaching the foster child to identify feelings of frustration, sadness, etc. • using foster child's ideas in treatment planning • role-playing "Accepting 'No' Answers"

BEHAVIOR	EMOTIONAL NEEDS UNMET AND FUNCTION OF THE BEHAVIOR	TREATMENT PARENT CAN HELP MEET THAT NEED BY:
Chronic Anxiety • expresses many fears and will cling on others • night terrors or other sleep problems • tries so hard to please that he seems insincere • finds security by reverting to earlier developmental stage (sucking thumb, baby talk, mood swings)	• feeling insecure about having basic needs met; questioning self-worth • has probably experienced traumatic losses including moving with little or no planning	• providing consistent parenting and daily schedule; physically comforting foster child if he will allow you to • making a Life Book together to help foster child understand family and moves • helping foster child learn to talk about his feelings • not punishing foster child for acting younger than his age
Delayed Conscience Development • does not understand consequences of his actions and projects blame on others • does not understand how his actions affect others • has difficulty expressing remorse when caught doing something he has been told not to do	• may believe that it is okay to hurt others in ways he has been mistreated himself • difficulty knowing the difference between what has really happened and what he has imagined • may believe whatever he has to do to survive is okay • may believe no one will take care of him so he can lie, steal, or trick others out of what he thinks he needs	• giving consequences consistently for positive and negative behaviors • teaching "Accepting Consequences" and not blaming others for his actions • teaching how to apologize for negative behaviors and express remorse • role-modeling when to apologize • helping him identify feelings when he or someone else is physically or emotionally hurt • providing frequent assurance that you care about the foster child • not taking it personally if the foster child does not appreciate what you do for him

155

BEHAVIOR	EMOTIONAL NEEDS UNMET AND FUNCTION OF THE BEHAVIOR	TREATMENT PARENT CAN HELP MEET THAT NEED BY:
Indiscriminate Affection/Poor Personal Boundaries • calling every caregiver "Mom" or "Dad" • hugging or kissing people the foster child hardly knows • affection may come across as being seductive • trying to please everyone • willingly going off with strangers or allowing an adult to take advantage of his desire to please	• by expressing affection for everyone, the behavior proves that no one adult is more important than another to the child • seductive behavior may have been encouraged by an abuser and may have resulted in some reward (e.g. affection, money, etc.) • foster child believes that he must meet the adult's emotional or sexual needs before the adult will meet the foster child's emotional, social, or physical needs • foster child believes his sexuality is the only good quality he has	• reinforcing foster child for only calling specific people "mom" and "dad" • monitoring foster child closely to ensure he does not wander away with others, or engage in sexual behavior with other foster children or adults • modeling how to provide nonsexual affection to other foster children, spouse, etc. • praising foster child for his attempts to provide appropriate affection to selected family members • not taking it personally if the foster child does not appreciate what you do for him

156

BEHAVIOR	EMOTIONAL NEEDS UNMET AND FUNCTION OF THE BEHAVIOR	TREATMENT PARENT CAN HELP MEET THAT NEED BY:
Lack of Self-Awareness • foster child may be out of touch with his own body • he may stuff himself with food or water, or not realize when he is hungry • he may fail to recognize pain and extremes in temperature • inability to express needs clearly; this is confusing to the adults that care for the child • wetting the bed, soiling his pants, etc., because he has not learned to recognize those body functions	• the parent may not have met the child's basic needs in infancy • the child has not consistently experienced the pattern of cause and effect; for example, feeling hungry (cause), eating, and feeling full (effect) • the child does not expect relief following feelings of discomfort; for example, being surprised that going to the bathroom makes him feel better	• praising foster child for recognizing need to eat, sleep, and eliminate • helping foster child recognize feelings of being tired or feeling full after a meal ("Your eyes are hardly open, you look very tired; Your tummy must feel good because you have eaten quite a bit") • reinforcing foster child for dressing appropriately for the weather, resting when he gets tired, etc. • talking to the foster child about why he needs to eat, sleep, or take a bath
Overcompetency • foster child prefers to take care of himself and doesn't think you need to take care of him • foster child acts like a parent and will try to take over your role, including taking care of younger children in the house	• the foster child may have been encouraged by parents to take care of himself or to parent younger children • the foster child is afraid to rely on others to take care of him since he has been disappointed in the past	• praising the foster child for his willingness to help himself or younger children • gradually encouraging and reinforcing the foster child to participate in more age-appropriate behaviors • reassuring the foster child that **you** can parent the younger children in the home • talking with your Consultant, spouse, etc., about your own feelings of rejection as a result of the foster child not letting you "parent" them

BEHAVIOR	EMOTIONAL NEEDS UNMET AND FUNCTION OF THE BEHAVIOR	TREATMENT PARENT CAN HELP MEET THAT NEED BY:
Poor Eye Contact • the child avoids eye contact with others • a sideways glance is common with foster children who have been abused. The child may appear to be "sneaky" or dishonest because he refuses to look at adults, especially when being confronted with an inappropriate behavior	• in abusive situations, the foster child may have been punished for making eye contact • avoiding eye contact may have helped the foster child avoid contact with an abusive or disturbed parent, or may have been an attempt to "dissociate" or disappear from the abusive environment • in some cultures, not making eye contact may be a sign of respect for adults, especially when the foster child is being disciplined	• not expecting the foster child to immediately change • using shaping to help the child make eye contact with others: praising the foster child's efforts to look you in the face (vs. the eyes), reinforcing the foster child for making brief eye contact; teaching this skill when you both feel relaxed and the eye contact is more natural and enjoyable

CHAPTER 23

Transitions:
A New Child Enters Your Home

In the last chapter, we talked about the problems foster children have when they do not experience healthy attachments to their biological parents and how separations are even more traumatic for them. In this chapter, we will discuss more about what we can do to help lessen the trauma that foster children experience when they move in and out of homes.

The opportunity to plan ahead and make some preparations would make a transition like this easier. Most foster children have gone through this experience many times before they come to live with you. Children rarely are placed in treatment foster care directly from their parents' home on an emergency or unplanned basis like this. However, the child may have had this experience in the past. The goal of Exercise 1 is to help you understand how profound a change it is for a child to move from one home to another when there is little or no chance to prepare for it.

In our program, a set procedure is used to help make such moves smoother and less traumatic for the child and his or her family. The chart on Page 161 outlines the steps in this process.

Exercise 1

Imagine that you are one of the foster children in Exercise 1 from Chapter 22. Read this "next-day" scenario and answer the questions that follow.

It's morning. As you awaken, you look around. You're in an unfamiliar room. You slept little last night. You've always been warned about strangers and here you are, with no one else you know, in the midst of them. You hear people up and about. What are you supposed to do? Lie in bed until someone comes and tells you to get up? Get up, get dressed, and go downstairs on your own? Did anyone tell you last night what was expected? Your memory is fuzzy.

Where are your parents? When will you see them? Do they know where you are? One question after another engulfs you. Pulling the covers over your head, you try to block them out.

What could be done to make this transition easier?

How would you feel if you knew the adults you were with?

How would you feel if your brother or sister was at the same house?

How would you feel if you had your own teddy bear to hug?

Adapted from V. Fahlberg, 1991. Reprinted with permission.

Preplacement and Placement Process

The first part of the plan is called the Preplacement Process. This occurs **before** the child is moved to the foster home, and involves Preplacement Visits between the foster child and the treatment foster family. These visits allow the child and the family to decide if they are right for each other.

Preplacement Visits help the foster child turn the unknown into the known. The stronger the foster child's attachment is to his or her parent or other caretaker, the more important the process of transferring the attachment will be. The younger the foster child, the more important it will be to have direct contact between the past and future caregivers.

The second part of the plan is the Placement Meeting, which is a meeting of the entire team (caseworker, therapist, child's parents, child, etc.) that occurs after the Treatment Family and the foster child have decided they want to live together. This meeting also takes place before the child moves into the Treatment Home, and helps everyone understand what is expected of them and how they can work together to help the foster child.

The Placement Meeting is a very important opportunity to gather together everyone who is involved in the child's care or therapy to discuss how those services can be provided while the child is in Treatment Foster Family Services. Many times, this is the first time that Treatment Parents meet the child's caseworker, parents, therapist, and other professionals involved with the child.

The following topics are discussed during the Placement Meeting:

1. **Permanency plan**
   - Estimated length of child's placement
   - Family issues that must be addressed before the child can return home
2. **Other services the child's family will be receiving**
3. **Visitation schedule** for child and family (frequency, location, supervised or unsupervised, transportation, length of visit)
4. **Child's medical history and providers**
5. **Other services** the child may receive
   - Therapy, what type, who will provide it

6. **Educational or vocational services**
   - Who will provide them, where
7. **Statement of the child's commitment to treatment goals** (if appropriate)

A Placement Meeting form containing this information is completed during this meeting. A sample form is included at the end of the chapter.

At this meeting, it is important to discuss how the child's placement goals can be achieved. If the court has decided that the child is to be reunified with his or her family after leaving treatment foster care, planning for that should begin. So from the very beginning, the child's eventual departure is already being discussed and planned.

Life Books

For most of us, our family's photo albums are some of our most precious possessions. When most people are asked, "If you had a fire in your home, what possession would you want to take out first?", they say, "My family album!" Many children in foster care have lived with so many different families, have gone to so many different schools, and have had so many friends, pets, etc., that their family history becomes very confusing to them. Their memory of their own parents may become quite vague. Wouldn't it be awful to grow up with the feeling that you don't know your own history?

Life Books are a way to make sure this doesn't happen. Life Books help children keep track of what their parents look like, how they celebrated holidays, what their foster parents looked like and where they lived, the schools the children attended, and so on. But Life Books are more than photo albums. They're **therapeutic** photo albums. They're therapeutic because the child's life story also is written in the book in order to tell about the people or events in the pictures. The "story" explains why a child was placed in foster care, why he or she didn't live with his or her parents, or why the child is being placed for adoption. As you can imagine, it takes careful thought and sensitivity to explain these events so that the child retains a feeling of self-worth and hope for the future.

Preplacement and Placement Process

The organization or program receives a referral and determines that the foster child could be helped through participation in Treatment Foster Family Services.

A staff member identifies a specific Treatment Family as a good "match" to care for the child, based on the child's needs and the strengths of the Treatment Family. Family members are asked to review the file and discuss whether they would consider caring for this child.

The Treatment Parents decide whether they might be willing to care for the child. They may ask the staff member additional questions about the child to help them make their decision.

A Preplacement Visit is set up. The Consultant prepares the child for the visit by telling him or her that this is a chance for the child and the Treatment Family to get to know each other and make a decision about whether they want to live together. The Consultant tells the child that Treatment Families sometimes decide not to have a foster child live with them because of things that have nothing to do with the child. For example, a family member may become seriously ill, or the parents might learn that they are expecting a new baby. The Preplacement Visit gives the foster child and the Treatment Parents an opportunity to meet and find out a little bit more about each other. This first meeting usually lasts one to three hours and may take place in a neutral setting (a park or restaurant, or the place where the foster child is currently living) or in the Treatment Parents' home. The Treatment Parents may ask their own children to be present during this visit.

If the Treatment Parents and child are interested in learning more about each other after the first visit, a one-day or overnight visit is scheduled. After the second or third meeting, a final decision is made about whether the child and the Treatment Family want to make a commitment to the placement.

If these visits go well, a staff person will notify the referring agency that the foster child has been accepted for placement and arrangements are made for a Placement Meeting.

Treatment Parents can make an important contribution to the child's Life Book by taking pictures of the child shortly after he or she moves into the home. This helps children remember how old they were when they came to live in the home, what their hobbies or interests were, the names of the other children in the family, etc. During the placement, report cards, certificates of achievement, drawings, and other important documents can be included in the book. When children are ready to leave your home, they can look back in their books and see how much they've changed, their success in making friends, their improvement in school, or how they've developed new talents. This helps put a child's life in a context that is real and positive. Your Consultant or a child's therapist can help you write the child's life story.

If the child does not have pictures of his or her family, home, or pets to put in the book, you can ask the child to draw pictures of them or find similar-looking people in magazines to represent them. Some children also like to have pictures of their Consultant, therapists, or other helpers that they have grown to care about and respect.

Summary

Although the "real world" is not perfect, it is helpful to set goals that will help foster children manage the transition from their current placement to your home. When the foster child's concerns can be addressed before the move, it can lessen how upset they become and there is less "old business" to take care of once the child is in your home. The Placement Meeting helps the team begin to plan for and coordinate the child's treatment and eventual departure from the Treatment Home.

BOYS TOWN
TREATMENT FOSTER FAMILY SERVICES
PLACEMENT MEETING

Youth: _____   Date: _____

Attended by: _____

1. Reason(s) for Placement

2. Treatment Goals

3. Permanency Plan

_____ Reunification

Estimated Length of Stay _____

Family Issues Needed to be Addressed _____

_____

Ancillary Family Services:

_____ Currently in Family Therapy (Provide Details)

_____ Therapist to Be Assigned (Provide Details)

Visitation (Frequency, Location, Supervised, Unsupervised, Length)

Phone/Written Contact (Define)

4. Pertinent Medical History:

Family Physician _____

Address _____

Psychiatrist _____

Address/Phone _____

Medications _____

5. Ancillary Youth Therapy Services
   Currently in Therapy _____
   Assigned Therapist _____
   Frequency of Therapy _____
   Location _____

   Treatment Goals:

   Therapist to Be Assigned _____
   Address/Phone Number _____
   Frequency of Therapy _____

   Treatment Goals:

   Follow-up Contact:

6. Educational/Vocational:

   Previous School _____

   Grade _____

   Type of Classroom _____

   Special Needs _____

   School to Be Attended/Phone Number _____

   Contact Person/Teacher _____

   Type of Follow-Up _____

   Grade _____

   Transportation _____

   Directions to School _____

7. Youth Commitment to Treatment Goals:

   _____   _____   _____
   Treatment Parent   Caseworker   Boys Town Consultant

   _____   _____   _____
   Treatment Parent   Parent   Boys Town Coordinator

   _____   _____   _____
   Youth   School Representative   Therapist

Caring for the Sexually Abused Child

Child sexual abuse can be a very emotionally upsetting subject. For people who love children, talking about any type of child abuse produces very strong negative feelings. Thinking of child sexual abuse makes most of us feel anger, disgust, and the desire to get revenge on the person who hurt the child. As professionals who provide services to children who have been victims of sexual abuse, it is important that we acknowledge that we have these very strong feelings. Treatment Parents must express these feelings with other professionals so that emotions do not get in the way of providing good treatment for the victims.

This chapter will try to answer some of the most frequently asked questions about child sexual abuse and explain how Treatment Parents may have to modify their treatment strategies when caring for these children. We'll also discuss rules that should be implemented to ensure a safe environment for children in your home.

What Is Child Sexual Abuse?

Child sexual abuse is defined as any form of touching, kissing, fondling, touching of the genitals of either the victim or the perpetrator, and/or anal/genital intercourse between an adult and a child (or between an older child and one who is at least three years younger). During these contacts, the child victim is used for the sexual stimulation and/or gratification of the older person (Bagley & Ramsey, 1986; Finkelhor, 1979, 1984; MacFarlane & Waterman, 1986; and Russell, 1986).

Incest is a form of sexual abuse in which the perpetrator or abuser is a relative of the victim. The abuser might be a parent, stepparent, grandparent, older brother or sister, or an uncle or aunt (Collins & Collins, 1989).

Myths

There are many myths about child sexual abuse and incest. These often lead to misunderstandings that can allow abuse to occur or continue, or can hinder treatment of victims. Finkelhor (1986) and Stovall (1981) identified some of these most common myths.

1. **MYTH:** Sexual abuse is rare.
   FACT: It is estimated that one in four female children are sexually abused before the age of 18. For boys, estimates range from one in seven to one in ten. These figures include incest as well as sexual abuse by someone other than a family member.

2. **MYTH:** Children usually are sexually abused by strangers.
   FACT: Estimates are that 80 percent of all sexual abuse cases involve someone the child knows, such as a family member, neighbor, baby-sitter, relative, or friend.

3. **MYTH:** Sex offenders are dirty old men.
   FACT: Sex offenders can be young or old, rich or poor, educated or uneducated, men or women, good-looking or unattractive. In other words, anyone can be a sex offender.

4. MYTH: Most children who are sexually abused do something to cause the abuse.
FACT: The responsibility for the abuse lies solely with the abuser. The notion of the sexually provocative child is a myth that lays the blame for the assault on the victim. The child's behavior is neither an excuse nor an explanation for the abusive actions of offenders.

5. MYTH: The sexual abuse victim is usually an adolescent female.
FACT: Children between the ages of 8 and 12 years report sexual abuse more often than any other age group. Both boys and girls are sexually abused. Even toddlers and infants have been sexually abused.

6. MYTH: Sexual abuse of children usually involves violence.
FACT: A reasonable estimate is that only five percent of child sexual abuse incidents involve violence. Offenders frequently gain the child's cooperation through deception or bribes, or by taking advantage of their adult authority or a child's trust in adults.

7. MYTH: If a child exhibits any of the symptoms of sexual abuse, the child has suffered sexual abuse.
FACT: Many children occasionally exhibit some of the behavioral symptoms associated with sexual abuse: sleeping problems, soiling pants, withdrawal, or unusual fears. If these occur consistently, they often are signs that the child is experiencing some stress. Sexual abuse is one possible source of that stress.

Gender Differences in Child Sexual Abuse

While boys and girls who have been sexually abused experience many similar problems, there are some unique differences. Some research (Finkelhor, 1979) has shown that 43 percent of the sexual abuse of girls occurs within the family, while this is true for only 17 percent of boys who are sexually abused. As a result, boys face some unique obstacles in reporting their abuse and some therapy issues that are different from those of girls. Yet an important similarity of the abuse of boys and girls is that they both are most commonly victimized by men. Research (Finkelhor, 1984; Russell, 1986) has revealed that men are the perpetrators in 95 percent of the cases involving female victims, and in 80 percent of the cases involving males.

These are the most common gender-related differences:

● As noted above, boys are more likely than girls to be abused by someone outside the family. Most of these abusers are individuals who come into contact with children in the community – teachers, coaches, mothers' boyfriends, or baby-sitters.

● Boys are more likely than girls to be abused along with other children. For example, the abuse may be part of a "sex ring" where the same adult has contact with many children through a group or recreational activity. The adult trades favors, such as special privileges or presents, for the sexual involvement.

● Boys who have been abused over a long period of time are more likely than girls to have emotional problems, especially depression and suicidal behaviors (Bagley, Wood, & Young, 1994.)

● Researchers (Finkelhor, 1984; Bagley et al., 1994) have demonstrated that girls report incest more often than boys because male victims have many fears about reporting abuse (James & Nasjleti, 1983). Boys are taught to take care of themselves. They are taught to "fight their own battles," so they don't ask for help as soon or as often as girls, even when they should. Boys worry about the additional stigma of homosexuality. In most groups of boys, the stigma of being labeled a "queer" can make a boy totally unacceptable to the group. A boy who has been sexually abused by a man may have serious doubts about his own sexuality. If his parents learn about the abuse, they may also worry about this and they may decide it is better not to report it to the police and further stigmatize the boy in the community. Unfortunately, this means the boy probably will not receive therapy, and will continue to have self-doubts about his sexual orientation. The abuser also is more likely to abuse more children.

- Boys have more privileges to lose if they report being a victim. In general, boys are given more freedom from supervision than girls. A boy may believe that he will lose some of his freedom if he reports the abuse so he chooses not to report it.

- If a boy has been abused by a woman, he may be afraid that no one will believe that this type of abuse could happen. He also may worry that others will not view the incident as abusive.

What Behaviors Indicate a Child May Have Been Sexually Abused?

When children enter Treatment Foster Family Services, we have a lot of information about them. If a child has been sexually abused, many times he or she has already disclosed this to another professional and it is documented in the child's file. However, never assume that the file tells you everything you need to know about a child. Children may have been sexually abused, but never reported it to the police or an adult. As a Treatment Parent, you should be able to recognize some of the behaviors that sexually abused children exhibit. Here is a list of some of those behaviors (Collins & Collins, 1989).

Overt sexual acting out toward adults. Adults who molest children often tell their victims that sex between adults and children is okay and is an accepted way of showing love. Sexual abuse victims, not surprisingly, may often make sexual advances toward adults they like because they have been taught that such behavior is appropriate. They have come to link affection with sexual behavior through their molestation experience. They also may believe that they must provide sexual gratification for adults in order to receive care and love. Some of these children do not understand the difference between sexual and nonsexual touch. They may think that all hugs are meant to be sexual, not affectionate, or that kisses between children and adults are only sexual in nature.

Fear of being alone with an adult, either male or female. Children who have been sexually abused often have been told by the abuser that they are physically irresistible to adults. The child may then come to believe that all adults will be unable to control their sexual impulses and are just waiting for a chance to molest them.

Fear or repulsion when touched by an adult of either sex. Children who have been abused frequently do not associate a nurturing touch with pleasure or safety. They often have linked touching, such as hugs, to foreplay before sex. It's unlikely that the child will view being touched affectionately by an adult as pleasurable. It may make them feel confused, anxious, or sexually aroused. When you are getting to know children, it is best to limit your physical contact with them or to ask them if it is okay before you give them a hug.

Violence against younger children. Sexual abuse victims may not be able to express the anger and frustration they feel toward the abuser(s) and may displace their feelings onto "safer" objects, such as younger children. They also may act out this anger with adults.

Self-mutilation. Child victims often develop feelings of self-hatred that stem from their feelings of being powerless to defend themselves from sexual abuse. This loss of self-respect may be expressed in self-abusive behaviors, such as tattoos, putting cigarette burns on their arms, or "cutting" themselves.

Fear of bathrooms and showers. Many times, bathrooms and showers are the places where victims were molested. Under the pretense of helping the child with his or her bath, the abuser may have used such opportunities to molest the child.

Knowledge of sexual matters and details of adult sexual activity that are inappropriate to the child's age or stage of development. Children who are being molested are not aware of the uniqueness of their experience, often because the molester has convinced them that it is "normal." A child learns details of sophisticated adult sexual activity by experiencing it. A young child "French kissing" or rubbing an adult's genitals are examples of such inappropriate knowledge and behavior.

Simulation of sophisticated sexual activity with younger children, animals, or toys. Some children will act out the sexual abuse they have experienced on younger or less capable children, animals, or toys. They may "hump" other children, animals, or toys, or ask other children to perform behaviors that are clearly sexual in nature on or with them. Although male and female children may not admit that their molestation of younger children is result of their own victimization, this often is true.

Combination of violence and sexuality in artwork, written schoolwork, language, and play. Children experience being molested as a violation of themselves even when they are not physically injured. They may express a great deal of anger and pain in describing their abuse, whether it is in artwork (e.g. drawing genitals on their pictures) or play (re-enacting sexual intercourse with dolls). Molested youth frequently report attempting to communicate their problem to adults through their schoolwork.

Refusal to undress for physical education at school or extreme concern that someone may see them when they undress in your home. Some victims of sexual abuse believe people can tell just by looking at their bodies that they have been abused; as a result, they don't want to be seen nude or in a bathing suit. They may have been convinced by the abuser that their bodies are irresistible, and concluded that other people will lose control and molest them. Other children feel unable to protect themselves, and are worried that if someone sees them undressed, they will not be able to protect themselves from further abuse.

Excessive or public masturbation. Excessive masturbation may be a symptom of extraordinary interest in the child's own sexuality. It also may be a subconscious practice aimed at calling others' attention to an abusive situation. Although masturbation is a common and developmentally normal activity for both boys and girls, excessive and/or public masturbation are signals that there is something wrong in the child's development. It also may be true that constant masturbation is done to relieve the itch and discomfort of a venereal disease.

Other behaviors. Other behaviors that are frequently associated with sexual abuse include:

- Running away or finding other ways to avoid dealing with overwhelming feelings.
- Difficulty in going to sleep or staying asleep; nightmares.
- Frequently feeling depressed, having thoughts about committing suicide, or attempting suicide.
- Alcohol and other drug abuse.
- Being a "loner" or having trouble making friends.
- Either poor hygiene or efforts to look "perfect."

Keep in mind that just because your foster child exhibits one or more of these behaviors, it doesn't mean that he or she has been sexually abused. However, if you suspect that a child has been sexually abused, you should contact your Consultant so a professional assessment can be conducted.

Responding to a Child's Disclosure of Sexual Abuse

Sexual abuse is most often detected when the child confides in a caretaker, teacher, friend, or another person as a way of asking for help or emotional support. It is important to realize that many times the child does not know that police and social service officials must then be contacted. Frequently, the child may feel betrayed because he or she thought that the person would keep the disclosure confidential. The child may become angry that the person who was trusted to "just listen" revealed the "secret" to other people. Even children old enough to understand that police and social workers will become involved probably do not anticipate the multiple responses that will occur within the next few days. The child has lost control of who knows "the secret" and what those people will do with the information, and feels threatened by his or her loss of personal control.

Most children in Treatment Foster Family Services have been out of their homes long enough to have already been interviewed about whether they have been sexually abused. However, never assume that you know everything about a child. If a child discloses to you that he or she has been sexually abused, or if he or she adds significant information to an earlier disclosure (the names of previously unknown abusers, for instance), it is absolutely mandatory that you contact your Consultant. This information cannot be kept confidential. If you're not sure, tell your Consultant about any new information you receive from the child about his or her abuse. All states have mandatory reporting laws that require caretakers to report suspected child abuse to the state or law enforcement authorities.

While your role as a Treatment Parent is to listen to and support the child, you should **not** attempt to interview a child or ask leading questions. The child will very likely meet with someone who is experienced in conducting sexual abuse investigations. Sometimes, a sexual abuse investigation begins when physical signs of abuse are observed, such as physical injuries, venereal diseases, and/or pregnancy. It should be pointed out, however, that physical injuries are not common in sexual abuse situations, especially with younger children (Sgroi, 1978). Sexual abuse also is occasionally disclosed because another child, who is being victimized by the same individual, asks for help.

During the first 48 hours following a sexual abuse report, a number of significant events will occur in the child's life. When the symptoms of sexual abuse are detected, an interview should be conducted, preferably by a specially trained police investigator who is sensitive to the child's distress. The child may be interviewed individually in a neutral setting, or with a person the child trusts who is willing to cooperate in the investigation. Interviewing the child alone reduces the pressure a child might feel. The one-to-one interview also may provide the child with a sense of relief as he or she discloses the "secret" in detail. If a child is unwilling to be interviewed by an investigator alone or is extremely uncomfortable with that arrangement, having another trusted adult present may help ease the child's anxiety.

Most children need to be convinced that they are believed (Sgroi, 1982). The child may feel uncomfortable or guilty about what has already happened, and may be fearful that he or she has been damaged or that no one will ever like him or her again. The child may wonder what other family members think of him or her. The secret that was kept at a high emotional cost is now public. It may become known that police have interviewed and possibly arrested the abuser. The victim may be told that he or she cannot return home, and must live with unfamiliar people, at least temporarily. A child may worry that friends and teachers feel that he or she was somehow responsible for the sexual behavior, and may fear being labeled as "bad" (James & Nasjleti, 1983).

A complete physical examination by a physician often is necessary. This medical interview requires privacy and time. It includes a review of all information surrounding the nature of the assault and the adult who abused the child. As you can imagine, this is a very stressful time for many victims.

The "Grooming Process" and Children's Relationships

"Grooming process" is the term used to describe how an abuser sets the stage for sexual abuse to occur. As you read in the section on myths about sexual abuse, most children are molested by someone who is in a caretaking role. Very often, an adult does not have to resort to violence to get a child to submit to sexual contact. In most cases of sexual abuse of children, coercion or trickery are the main ways the abuser convinces the child to allow a sexual relationship to develop. The abuser starts by encouraging the child to trust him or her. This is done by giving the child presents of candy, food, money, and clothing, or by spending time with the child and assuring the child of the "rightness" of what they are doing (Christiansen & Blake, 1990).

In cases of incest, the child begins to feel like the abuser's "favorite" child and eventually, the other children and spouse feel left out or emotionally distant from the victim. As this process continues, the abuser begins to ask the child to keep secrets; the abuser might tell the child these secrets are necessary because other people wouldn't understand their "special kind of love." The relationship becomes more and more sexual, eventually leading to intercourse for some children. By then, the child usually feels that the sexual contact is something he or she has agreed to voluntarily. Children in this situation also may feel responsible and guilty because they may have physically enjoyed the sexual experience – at least in the beginning – and they worry that they will "break up the family" if they tell anyone about the sexual abuse.

A very damaging part of the this type of abuse is the betrayal of trust the child feels deep inside. That's why it is essential to the healing process for Treatment Parents to develop healthy relationships with children who have been "groomed" by their abusers. Adults also need to understand that in many cases, the child doesn't know what a "normal" parent-child relationship should be like.

Building Relationships with Sexually Abused Children

Children who have lived in families with unhealthy boundaries tend to either "overdo" or hide from new relationships. Children who "overdo" developing relationships may want physical contact with you right away. During your first meeting with them, they may want to hug you, sit on your lap, put their face close to yours, or constantly invade your personal space. Children who do this have probably been encouraged to act like this with other adults, and were rewarded when they did. They are emotionally starved and think it is their job

to meet the adult's sexual needs in order to receive attention or affection. It is important that you trust your own feelings and begin setting limits on the child's contact with you during your first visit. You could say, "I usually don't hug people I have just met, but how about if we sit together while I tell you about our family."

If the child is overly physically expressive, you might try some of the following practices once the child is in your home:

- Suggest that the child can give you three hugs a day (rather than 20).
- Teach the child how to ask before he or she hugs you.
- Teach the child to stand an arm's length away when you are talking together.
- Praise the child whenever possible for appropriate behaviors.
- Model and teach healthy boundaries so the child will be more successful in other social relationships and will be less likely to be abused again.
- If the child tries to engage other children in sexual play, monitor them very closely and teach the other children to report any sexual behaviors that occur.

For children who seem distant or hide from new relationships, you will want to take a different approach. It is very understandable that they will not trust adults and older children. For them, getting close to someone initially carries the threat of being sexually abused again. Because of this, you will have to be extra careful about physically touching the child.

Here is a suggestion for determining if it is okay to comfort a child physically. Ask if you can give the child a hug. By being asked, the child will know that you care about and respect his or her feelings. If the child says "Yes," give a hug around the shoulder, not a big frontal hug. A strong frontal hug may be too much for a child who is scared of physical contact with an adult. If the child says "No," you can say that you are glad he or she can tell you what feels right.

This demonstrates that you respect the child's right to set personal boundaries. You may want to develop a less-threatening way to show the child approval and affection, such as giving "high fives" or "pinkie shakes" (connecting your little finger with the child's little finger) instead of hugs. You also may tell the child that he or she can ask for a hug anytime.

Treatment Parents also must be sensitive to secrets and lies. Since many children were exposed to a "grooming process" prior to the actual sexual abuse, they may be trying to see if that "grooming" will begin in your home. "Little secrets" between adults and children are especially dangerous. If an adult asks a sexually abused child to keep a secret, the child may wonder if the adult is testing her. The child may worry that by keeping a small secret, the adult will begin to expect her to keep sexual secrets between the two of them. Treatment Parents should never ask foster children to keep secrets. It is okay to ask a foster child to participate in a "surprise." A surprise, for example, is when you buy a birthday present together, and the child promises not to tell what the gift is until the party. This type of secret is time-limited and everyone will know about it in a fairly short period of time.

Here are a few more tips on developing a relationship with a sexually abused child:

- Don't focus on the abuse. Many children feel like they are "damaged goods" and focusing on the abuse only reinforces the notion that this is the most important thing about them.

- Praise them for positive behaviors and talents. This helps them to feel good about themselves and to begin to recognize their natural talents and strengths.

- Be sensitive to the child's feelings. Help the child learn to identify his or her feelings; for example, say things like, "You look sad," or "Are you feeling disappointed?" This helps give the child a language to express inner emotions.

- Remind the child that the abuse was not his or her fault. Treatment Parents can't say this often enough. The abuser has probably told the child repeatedly that no one will believe him or her, and that the child is responsible for the sexual abuse because he or she was seductive, helped keep the secret, and is "crazy."

- Be understanding of the child's desire to go home with the abuser or unprotective parent. Do not criticize the parent. Although it seems hard to imagine, many children report that they feel that the abuser is the person who has actually cared for them the most. The child may view the abuser as someone who spent time with her doing fun activities and cared about her when many other people didn't. Further, the child may remember the sexual contact as pleasurable and not abusive. If a child says she wants to see or go home to live with the abuser, you can reflect those feelings back to the child. For instance, you could say, "I bet you miss him a lot." Most children begin to get a more realistic picture of the family after they are in a safe home, receive therapy, and begin to feel better about themselves. Ask your Consultant for support if you are frustrated by the child continuing to deny the abuse or wanting to see the abuser.

- Do not use the sexual abuse as an excuse for inappropriate behavior. Children still must take responsibility for their own behavior.

Helpful Treatment Parent behaviors:

1. Use a calm, pleasant tone of voice.
2. Be helpful by telling the child about your family, answering questions, or predicting the next activities the child will encounter.
3. Be a pleasant, positive person for the child to spend time around. Use appropriate humor to build your relationship.
4. If the child seems to be trying to avoid developing a relationship with you, allow him or her to "take the lead" in deciding how much physical contact he or she will have with you. If the child is overly physical, be gentle yet firm in setting limits.
5. Be fair when giving consequences.
6. Tell the child what he or she does well.

171

7. Model being polite to others and expressing concern for others.
8. Explain to the child what you want him or her to do.
9. Get to the point quickly.
10. Encourage the child to express his or her feelings.

Harmful Treatment Parent behaviors:

1. Having a short temper and blaming others for problems.
2. Being grumpy or unpleasant to be around. Expecting things not to work out.
3. Always pointing out what other people do wrong.
4. Using profanity.
5. Having little insight or concern for others.
6. Not giving children a chance to express their opinions.

Setting House Rules to Create a Safe Environment

(Adapted from Collins & Collins, 1989)

By setting rules and outlining expectations early, you can avoid future problems with sexual behaviors of the foster children in your care. This should be done with all the foster children in placement regardless of whether they have been sexually abused. You should take the care and safety of your own children into consideration when developing these rules. In fact, these rules may be applied in your own home, regardless of whether you have foster children in your care. You should set firm but reasonable guidelines concerning appropriate behavior and privacy in the home and then see that they are enforced. Children who have been sexually abused need a safe home environment where they feel comfortable. Children who are trying to heal from their sexual abuse should not be burdened with additional worries as to whether they are safe in their new home.

Sexually abused children have not yet learned how to successfully develop relationships. They sometimes push themselves onto other children, usually those who are younger or weaker. They

have not learned how to express their affection for others in socially acceptable ways. Some children who have been victims of sexual abuse may try to abuse someone else to avoid feelings of being a victim. This way, a child can be in control instead of being controlled. For Treatment Parents who live with sexually abused children and have children of their own, this can be an area of concern. Parents instinctively want to protect their children from harm. There are preventive measures that you can take to create a safe environment in the home.

An effective and logical way to protect children from potentially abusive situations is to monitor the activities of all children in the home. Randomly checking on foster children has proven to be a good preventive tool. In other words, Treatment Parents should know the whereabouts of their own children, as well as the whereabouts of their foster children at all times. Treatment Parents should not leave their own children unsupervised or allow the foster children to baby-sit their children.

When reviewing the rules in your home, remember to clearly state them in terms that the children can understand. Be sure to state what, if any, exceptions there are to each rule. Then enforce the rules right away. It is important to consider the following issues when establishing rules in your home:

Privacy. Everyone has a right to privacy. Making sure that all family members have privacy doesn't necessarily mean locking doors. Locked doors can be a safety hazard should a foster child need help. Family members should always knock and receive permission before going into someone's room when the door is closed.

Bedrooms. Boys and girls should not share bedrooms. Foster children should not sleep in the Treatment Parents' bedroom or be allowed in the parents' bed at night. Treatment Parents should not take a foster child into their bedroom to do teaching; the child may become confused and think that he or she is going to be asked to engage in sexual acts with the adult. Limiting the foster child's access to the Treatment Parents' bedroom in general will help prevent questions or criticism about their care of the foster child.

Foster children and the Treatment Parents' children should not play in a bedroom together with the door closed. Treatment Parents should regularly supervise children who are playing together in bedrooms to ensure that the play does not become sexual in nature.

Clothing. No family member should be outside the bedroom or bathroom in underwear or pajamas without wearing a bathrobe. Bathing suits should be worn only at the pool and the beach. Bathing suits should not be worn in the house unless a robe is also worn, and suits should easily cover all genitals. Treatment Parents should allow children to help choose their own clothing, but children should not wear clothing that is particularly seductive or inappropriate for their age. Treatment Parents should model modesty in their choice of clothing.

Touching. No one should be allowed to touch another person without permission. No one should touch another person's private parts except while administering a necessary and professional medical examination or appropriately assisting with using the toilet or bathing. The foster children should be taught to care for and clean themselves. All children should be taught to report behavior that makes them feel uncomfortable. Parents should support and respect a child's desire to not be touched. An example is a child who doesn't want to be hugged by a relative who always hugs too tightly.

The right to say "No." All of us are born with an ability to sense what is comfortable or uncomfortable. We know when we like being hugged and kissed and when we don't. Sexually abused children have had this "internal radar" confused. They have been tricked or shamed into accepting physical and sexual touching even after they may have asked the abuser to stop. The child trusted the abuser who said that the sexual touching was okay and "won't hurt." As a result, many sexually abused children have lost the confidence to trust their instincts about what feels right and what doesn't.

A very important part of the healing process is giving the child back the ability to trust and to determine what type of touching and relationships feels right for them. Children learn by example, so modeling the ability to set these limits in your own life is important. Also, if children say they feel uncomfortable with a certain type of touch (hugs that are too tight, kisses on the lips, sitting on an adult's lap), then you should help them set this limit. Some adults don't believe in a child's right to say "No." You may hear them say, "Oh, come on. Let me give you a hug. I don't see you that often," or "We always kiss good-bye," or "Come sit on my lap for just a minute." When this happens, you may need to step in and tell the adult that the child has the right to say "No," even if the adult is offended. It is much more important to help children learn that they can trust their own feelings and protect themselves from unwanted touching than it is for an adult to meet his or her own needs for a few minutes.

Sex education. Learning about sexuality is important for children as they grow up. The information and how much they are told should match their age and stage of development. Children should know that sexual feelings are normal, but that doesn't mean those feelings should be acted out. One part of sex education is teaching children the proper words for sexual organs and behaviors. All children need to know the correct terms for penis, buttocks, rectum, breasts, and vagina. If children don't know the words for these body parts, they will have trouble describing what has happened to them sexually. Some children in treatment foster care who have been sexually abused have extensive knowledge of explicit sexual acts. You should tell these children that you, your Consultant, or their therapists can answer their questions about sexual matters. They also should be told that it is inappropriate to share their story of sexual abuse with other children because it would probably confuse and scare them.

Language. Children should learn early that suggestive and obscene language is not acceptable in your home and will not be allowed. Encourage them to use correct terms when asking questions or talking about sexuality.

Secrets. While all family members have a right to their privacy, no one should keep secrets that cause physical or emotional harm to the child or someone else. As mentioned earlier, Treatment Parents should never ask foster children to keep secrets.

Being alone with one other person. Foster children and your own children should never be allowed to go off alone together or stay alone at home without being monitored. Children who are significantly different in age should be carefully watched. Older, stronger children may test the personal boundaries of younger, weaker ones. Treatment Parents cannot assume that all children will report inappropriate behavior even when they have been taught to do so. That is why monitoring is so important.

Treatment Parents should be careful about going off alone with a foster child in their care; they could be vulnerable to allegations of abuse if a foster child would misinterpret their behavior. Taking a foster child to the dentist is okay, but spending long periods of time alone in the basement with the child may be misunderstood. When Treatment Parents must spend a lot of time alone with a child, they should always give specific information to another adult about where they are going, how long they will be gone, and what they will be doing. This helps protect the Treatment Parent from someone suggesting that the foster child was not cared for properly. You and your Consultant will talk more about this during the foster child's placement to help you feel confident that you are setting appropriate boundaries.

As mentioned before, Treatment Parents should avoid talking with a foster child in either the child's or adult's bedroom. If it is necessary to talk in a bedroom, leaving a door partially open is an option. Try to have serious conversations in the main part of the house where others will know where you are. When possible, doing things in threesomes or with more people is advisable because a witness is present should any questions arise about the foster child's care. A high-risk foster child who is behaving seductively or aggressively should be watched even more carefully.

Wrestling and tickling. Wrestling and tickling are considered normal childhood behaviors. They can take on sexual overtones, however. Wrestling

and tickling can be painful, humiliating, or uncomfortable for the weaker person who is on the receiving end when mutual respect or sensitivity is ignored. For sexually abused children, wrestling, tickling, and roughhousing can be sexually stimulating and can lead to more explicit sexual activities. Therefore, these activities should be strictly limited for children or allowed only under close adult supervision. Treatment Parents should not wrestle with or tickle foster children because these behaviors can be misunderstood by the foster child or others.

If you enjoy wrestling with or tickling your own children, you can continue to do so. Explain to the foster child that you do not know him or her well enough to play this way, and that you don't want to hurt the child's feelings or cause any misunderstandings. Try to find other activities you can do with the foster child to make him or her feel special and liked.

Sitting under blankets and towels together. It is a good idea to discourage this type of behavior. There will be times when foster children or your own children will want to snuggle up together under a blanket, towel, or coat because they're cold. However, this can be sexually stimulating for a foster child who has been sexually abused. Also, it is very difficult for adults to monitor where each foster child's hands are when they are covered up.

Role models. Treatment Parents must be good role models. Foster children watch their behavior and use it as the example of appropriate adult behavior. Treatment Parents should avoid sexually suggestive jokes, behavior, clothing, or entertainment when children are around. Sexually abused children may find such provocative behavior frightening, stimulating, and confusing.

Creating a Safe Environment for Treatment Parents' Children

When children who behave in an aggressive or sexually inappropriate manner move into a Treatment Family, the Treatment Parents want to create a home that is safe not only for the foster children but also for their own children. They want to keep the foster children's behaviors from negatively affecting or influencing their own children. This section will discuss ways to create a safe environment in the home for all children who live there.

The best way to prevent possible harm to the children is to carefully monitor the children's interactions with each other. Check on them frequently and at unpredictable intervals. Children should not play behind closed doors, or in sheds or garages where it is difficult to provide close supervision.

Another way to help make sure all the children are likely to be safe is to encourage children of similar ages to play together, if possible. This makes is less likely that age and power differences will give one child an unfair advantage over another.

Teaching all the children to report inappropriate behavior to you will help you stop problems before they get out of hand. Children need to learn to work out some of their own problems, and you can't settle every little dispute. But clearly stating the house rules will help children know when they need to report behaviors that are definitely prohibited.

Be cautious about allowing mildly abusive behaviors. For instance, no child should be allowed to bully, trick, or threaten another child into doing something. All children should have the right to tell each other "No" regarding any type of touching. Examples of mildly abusive behaviors include snapping someone with a towel, tickling someone even after that person has said to stop, and wrestling when one child clearly has an advantage. When mildly abusive behaviors are allowed, a child may use them to establish his or her power or control over another child. The more powerful child may then try to see what he or she can get away with when you are not around. The "Right to Say 'No' Rule" should apply to every child in the home.

It is important that you spend time alone with your own children on a regular basis. Your children are more likely to tell you about their problems in adjusting to a new child in the home if they have opportunities to talk with you alone. Most Treatment Parents are very busy people and it may not seem easy to spend time alone with your children. But the amount of time you spend alone is not as important as simply making some time. Ask your

children to ride with you to the store or walk to the mailbox, or talk with them before they go to sleep at night. Ask them how they think things are going and if there is anything you can do to help them adjust to having a new child in the home. This will give your children an opportunity to talk to you about things that may be troubling to them. Be sure to report to your Consultant any concerns you may have about how your children and the foster children are adjusting to each other. This is very important. By discussing problems or concerns when they are small or less serious, it is easier to prevent or solve them before they become serious.

One final note about boundaries and children. Many Treatment Parents ask if they can have different boundaries for physical contact with their own children and their foster children. Yes! When you have a long history of a secure attachment with your own children, you can touch and love them in ways you wouldn't use with an abused child you haven't known long. For example, many parents allow their own children to climb in bed with them on Saturday morning or during a thunderstorm. In some families, members tickle each other while playing or kiss each other on the lips. You don't have to change any of these behaviors unless you want to.

When you explain your house rules to the new foster child, tell him or her that some of the rules about touching are different for your own children. You can say something like, "I want you to feel safe in this home and know that no one will touch you in ways that make you feel uncomfortable. Since we are just getting to know each other, I won't hug and kiss you like I do my own kids. Sometimes I tickle or kiss them to let them know I love them. But since we don't know each other very well, I won't kiss you and we won't tickle each other. Is that okay with you? I'm sure you miss your family a lot and a hug sometimes might help. I think all kids need a hug from time to time. If I think you need one, I'll ask before I give you one just to make sure. Is that okay? You are always welcome to come up and ask for a hug. Does this make sense to you?" This will help the child understand why some rules are different for your own children. It also lets the child know how he or she can receive or give affection within your family.

Exercise 1

Describe the House Rules you plan to use. When this form is completed, post a copy in your home.

Privacy: _____
_____
_____

Bedrooms: _____
_____
_____

Clothing: _____
_____
_____

Touching: _____
_____
_____

The Right to Say "No": _____
_____
_____

Sex Education: _____
_____
_____

Language: _____
_____
_____

Secrets: _____
_____
_____

Being Alone with One Other Person: _____
_____
_____

Wrestling and Tickling: _____
_____
_____

Sitting Under Blankets and Towels Together: _____
_____
_____

Summary

Working with foster children who have been sexually abused requires Treatment Parents to implement additional elements into the care and treatment they provide. Foremost among these is sensitivity to the child's emotional pain and ensuring that all the children in the home are safe.

Our goal is to remember that these are children and that we want to try and give them back as much of their childhood as possible. By implementing the suggestions in this chapter, you will help create a safe environment for every child in the house. This will help ensure that your own children continue to be happy and safe and that foster children will receive the best possible treatment in a family setting. Again, you are encouraged to discuss with your Consultant any concerns you may have about the relationship between your children and the foster children. This clearly is an issue that affects the foster child's placement and one that your Consultant is prepared to help you with if necessary.

CHAPTER 25

Respecting Cultural Differences in Children and Families

What do you think of when you hear the word "culture?" Oftentimes, "culture" brings to mind brightly colored costumes, folk dances, unfamiliar languages, and unusual food. While it's true that culture involves these things, cultural differences oftentimes are not obvious.

The *Oxford American Dictionary* defines culture as **"the customs and civilization of a particular people or group."** Every family is influenced by its culture, and these influences shape the family's attitudes, beliefs, values, traditions, rituals, preferences, and rules. Just how your foster child and his or her family's culture differs from your own will vary.

Exercise 1

Remember when you first began dating your wife/husband? What was it like to go to your spouse's parents' house for a meal or family gathering? Did you feel uncomfortable being around people you didn't know very well? In the space provided below, describe three things about your spouse's family that were unexpected or made you feel different from them.

Differences between individuals and families are everywhere in our society. However, the impact of these differences is often minimized, misunderstood, and even ignored. When Treatment Parents and their Consultants don't understand the differences between families, the results can be very harmful to both the foster child and the relationship between the Treatment Parents and the child's family.

The philosophy of Boys Town Treatment Foster Family Services is to respect the family and its cultural differences. We believe that all families have a right to be respected. Our goal in this chapter is to help you understand how your cultural background may be different from those of families you will meet and work with. We will explore the role culture plays within a family and the strengths it provides so that you can incorporate these differences and strengths when helping the foster child and his or her family.

How can you do this? The first step is to understand your own values and beliefs. It helps to realize that the way you live, how you were brought up, your values, and so on, is only one way of living. It is helpful to remember that people live in other ways – not necessarily better or worse, just different (Kadushin, 1983).

When you understand your own family's customs and traditions, you are better able to appreciate the customs and traditions of your foster child and his or her family. Respecting family differences can also help you build better relationships with family members. As they see you trying to be sensitive to their preferences and traditions, they may realize you aren't out to change their value systems and traditions. As a result, the family will probably fear you less, trust you more, and sense your acceptance of them as individuals. In turn, the family will be more open to your suggestions.

Origins of Differences

Family differences originate both in the past and the present. Childhood experiences and patterns of behavior form the basis for these differences. In the present, many influences create differences in families. Together, these influences shape a family's belief, self-image, and view of the world. Some basic factors that can influence family differences are:

1. Environment
2. Family of origin
3. Religion
4. Ethnicity

An explanation of each of these factors is presented on the following pages. At the end of each explanation is a scenario and some questions. Read the scenario and answer the questions in the space provided.

1. Environment. Where a family lives greatly influences the family's lifestyle. Does the foster child's family live in a large metropolitan area, an average-size city, or a small town or rural area? Is the family's home large or small, well-kept or cluttered, in good shape or in need of repair? In some large cities where housing costs are high, you may find several generations of a family living together. In a farming community, you may find that children miss a great deal of school to help their families harvest a crop. In areas with few resources, you may find families that have difficulty meeting their medical or financial needs. All these things contribute to children's environments and the way they interact and feel comfortable in their foster home.

Your foster child's parents live on a farm several miles from the nearest town. Although their house is in need of repair and they often have difficulty paying their utility bills, their children wear "designer" tennis shoes, own several video games, and are given a substantial allowance on a weekly basis. What does this environment say about the parents' values and beliefs? What strength can you see in these values?

2. Family of Origin. Parents in every family have rules, values, and traditions that originated in their upbringing and the rules, values, and traditions of their parents. In other words, how a person was treated by his or her parents while growing up often has a great impact on how that person treats his or her own children. The parents of the children you will work with may have styles of rearing children that are similar to or different from your own style. These similarities or differences could include attitudes about discipline, the definition of success and failure, competition and achievement, and desirable lifestyles.

Your foster child's parents are very strict disciplinarians. They frequently yell, curse, and physically discipline their children. They comment that this is the way they were brought up and "we turned out okay." What does the way they discipline their children say about their family values? How could this be seen as a strength? What is your reaction to their methods of discipline?

3. Religion. Religion can be culturally, ethnically, or individually defined. Religious beliefs can strongly influence a family's value system. Families could participate in a number of religious rituals and events to which you must be sensitive. Some pray at certain times, some dress in a particular manner, and some decorate their homes in accordance with religious practice. Other families may not have a religion that they practice and will be cautious about how much their child is expected to participate in religious activities such as attending church.

Your foster child comes from a family that does not belong to a church or participate in religious activities. In the past, the parents have strongly objected to any help from a local church. In order to have the child accepted into Treatment Foster Family Services, they have agreed to let him go to church with you while he lives in your home. How can this be seen as a strength? How can you help the family feel comfortable with this decision?

4. Ethnicity. Differences in this area can come from many cultural sources such as nationality, religion, and race. Some cultures believe that several generations of a family should live together in the same household – parents, grandparents, aunts, uncles, and cousins. In some cultures it may be unacceptable to discuss family problems with the children unless the parents are present. Some ethnic groups have a strong group affiliation and interpret life events in racial terms, especially if these events involve someone who is not part of the culture.

It is important to say a few words here about cross-racial placements in Boys Town. There is no universal agreement among mental health professionals as to whether it is beneficial for children of one race to be placed with families of a different race. Some people feel cross-racial placements should never occur because the family cannot teach the child about his or her culture, and indeed may not even understand it. People who adopt this perspective may further point out the lack of belonging and alienation the foster child is likely to feel because he or she is visibly different from the rest of the family.

Other professionals argue, however, that a variety of factors – including race – should be considered when matching a foster child with a family. This is Boys Town's position. We look at the "big picture" – family make-up, resources in the community, Treatment Parent skills, willingness and ability to work with the child's family, etc. – when deciding to place a child. Certainly race is a factor, and we try to place foster children in families of the same race whenever possible. However, if a child and a Treatment Family are a good match in other areas (including speaking the same language), we will consider cross-racial or cross-cultural placements.

Your foster child is Native American. In his culture, it is a sign of disrespect to look you in the eye when he is being corrected. How could you change or modify your expectations of him in order to respect his ethnicity?

Can you think of other changes you can make to help a child feel comfortable in your home with regard to other nonverbal behaviors and language differences?

Contrasts in Family Differences

Now that we've looked at some examples of factors that can influence a family's differences, let's look at several areas in which these differences are generally seen in everyday family life. To varying degrees, you will find family differences in the following areas:

1. **Parenting styles or tolerances**
2. **How families relax and spend free time**
3. **Educational and vocational choices**
4. **Holiday celebrations and rituals**
5. **Food preferences**

An explanation of each area is presented on the following pages. At the end of each explanation is a scenario and some questions. Read the scenario and answer the questions in the space provided.

1. Parenting styles or tolerances. Every family develops its own parenting styles and tolerances. In fact, no two individuals have identical parenting styles or tolerances, whether they're in the same family or not. Many family traditions and values regarding raising children have been handed down through generations and are well-established. A family's choice of discipline or tolerances may have been learned from past generations and is respected by family members. That's why you may hear parents say, "My parents raised me that way and I turned out pretty good." Or parents may reject the parenting style of their parents, saying, "My parents made me do that and punished me for every little mistake. I'll never do that to my kids."

Your foster child's parents don't closely monitor their children. They allow their children to roam the neighborhood all day in search of playmates and the children don't have to be home until dark. What do their tolerance levels say about their values and beliefs? What strength can be seen in these values?

2. How families relax and spend free time. Families relax and spend free time in different ways. These can include involvement in church group activities, outdoor recreation, social clubs or bars, and various hobbies and pastimes. One family's relaxation time may revolve around being outside while another family's free time may be spent at bingo halls and flea markets. Some pastimes are more active than others. The level of involvement in family activities also may vary for individual family members. While being together or doing something is a priority for one family, the members of another family may be so actively involved in outside interests that they spend little time together.

Your foster child's family spends a majority of its free time watching TV. The children very rarely spend any time outside doing anything physical. What strengths can you see in this? How would you work with the foster child and family to be sensitive to their values regarding free time? How would you explain your emphasis on other activities, and the foster child's introduction to them?

3. Educational and vocational choices. Educational choices often are influenced by how much value a family places on education. Families that place a high value on education stress the importance of school attendance, achieving good grades, selecting challenging subjects, earning a high school diploma, and going on to college or trade school. When parents don't stress the importance of school (or when parents, their children, and the school have conflicting values), the children often have problems in school (i.e. truancy, failing grades, illiteracy, suspension, and dropping out). Family differences also may be evident in the vocations and socioeconomic status of the family. In some situations, parents even model their occupational choices. Many occupations, such as farming, mining, or practicing medicine or law, tend to be passed on this way from generation to generation.

Your foster daughter's parents have good blue-collar jobs. They did not graduate from high school and are not encouraging their daughter to go to college. Their daughter excels in school and talks about being a social worker, psychologist, or teacher. Her parents reject her ideas about these careers and are proud of the simple fact that she will be the first in the family to graduate from high school. They believe that blue-collar work is honest, hard work, and that having their daughter attend college so she can enter a profession would be a waste of time and money. What does this family value in regard to educational and vocational choices? How can the parents' values be viewed as a strength? How could you help the family see the foster daughter's career interests as a strength?

4. Holiday celebrations and rituals. Family differences can be clearly seen in a family's holiday celebrations and rituals. The family's culture influences not only whether a holiday or ritual is celebrated, but also how it is celebrated. The way families celebrate national holidays and family birthdays also reveal their traditions. It is important for Treatment Parents to know which holidays, if any, are important to the family. As a Treatment Parent, you need to be sensitive to a family's traditions, and encourage and respect their uniqueness without interfering with their beliefs.

Your foster child's family does not believe in celebrating holidays or birthdays. Your family places great emphasis on holiday and birthday celebrations. How would you work with the family and the foster child to be sensitive to their beliefs regarding family celebrations? How can you view their differences as strengths?

5. Food preferences. Food choices can be influenced by cultural differences. The variety of foods and ways meals are prepared can differ greatly depending on the family, its ethnicity and upbringing. Some religions determine food preferences and prohibit certain foods. For example, Orthodox Jewish families do not eat pork or combine meat products with milk products. At times, a parent's vocation will determine food preferences. Many farm families prefer their largest meal at breakfast or lunch while urban families usually have their biggest meal in the evening. As a Treatment Parent, you need to be sensitive to the foster child's food preferences and respect the family's differences.

Your foster child's family does not eat red meat. You and your spouse come from farming backgrounds and eat red meat at least once a day. How can you work with the foster child and her family to ensure that her nutritional needs are met without interfering with her family's food preferences?

Summary

Every family is unique in how it is affected by changes and challenges. Every family adopts specific values and beliefs that are influenced by past experiences and culture. Every family has differences. As Treatment Parents, your goal is to respect the foster child's family and its cultural differences, and, as much as possible, view those differences as strengths.

Appendix A

NOTICE TO TREATMENT PARENTS
WHO ARE THE SUBJECT
OF A FACT-FINDING INQUIRY

Purpose:

The purpose of this document is to outline a consistent set of rules and procedures for conducting fact-finding investigations into an incident or situation regarding a Treatment Parent's behavior. This notification sheet shall be given to each Treatment Parent who is the subject of a Treatment Parent Inquiry that involves either a violation of child rights or a general investigation into the Treatment Parent's conduct. In order to promote a safe environment for both foster children and Treatment Parents, Father Flanagan's Boys' Home thoroughly investigates all allegations to protect the rights of all parties involved.

Rules and Procedures:

The investigation is guided by the following procedures:

1. You are the subject of an inquiry. It is to your best advantage to actively participate in this inquiry and provide relevant testimony and evidence.

2. All information provided as a result of this fact-finding investigation will be kept confidential and shared only with those Boys Town supervisory personnel who have an appropriate need to know.

3. At the onset of the investigation, you will be notified of the general nature of the allegation(s). During the interview you should:

    a. Answer all the questions asked of you. Your failure to answer questions will jeopardize the inquiry.
    b. Provide information that supports your testimony, including the names of individuals whom you think should be contacted to provide information relevant to the inquiry.

4. During the investigation you are required to:

    a. Cooperate fully with the fact-finder or auditor conducting the investigation.
    b. Be truthful and forthright when responding to the allegations and answering questions.
    c. Have no contact about this inquiry with anyone, including children, Boys Town employees, or third parties who may have information regarding this inquiry. Such contact will, in itself, constitute tampering with the inquiry.

5. At the conclusion of the inquiry, you will be informed of the outcome. You will not be entitled to see the investigative file in order to protect the rights of others who have provided information. This file is confidential and privileged.

6. You may take notes and may take time to review any documents provided to you during the inquiry. You do not have a right to find out the source of these documents or the information about which questions are asked.

7. At the end of the interview, you may make any kind of statement that you want to make.

8. Portions of the inquiry will be tape-recorded. It is a standard practice in these types of inquiries. Should a transcript be made of your interview, a copy will be made available to you.

These steps ensure that the inquiry is accurate, complete, and objective. Failure to comply with these directives is grounds for discontinuing you as a Boys Town Treatment Parent.

I hereby acknowledge that I received these rules and procedures.

_____

Treatment Parent   Date

_____

Treatment Parent   Date

_____

Witness   Date

NOTICE TO A TREATMENT PARENT
WHO IS A WITNESS IN A
FACT–FINDING INVESTIGATION

Purpose:

The purpose of this document is twofold: to provide information and to describe Father Flanagan's Boys' Home's expectations of any individual who is not covered by a collective bargaining agreement and who is interviewed during a fact-finding inquiry into an incident or situation regarding another individual's behavior.

Information and Expectations:

1. You are not the subject of the inquiry. You have been identified as a person who may have witnessed or have information related to the incident or situation being investigated. As a result, you are expected to participate in this inquiry and provide relevant testimony and evidence.

2. All information provided as a result of this fact-finding inquiry will be kept confidential and shared only with those Boys Town supervisory personnel who have an appropriate need to know.

3. During the investigation you are expected to:

    a. Cooperate fully with the fact-finder or auditor conducting the inquiry.
    b. Be truthful and forthright when answering questions.
    c. Have no contact about this inquiry with anyone, including children, Treatment Parents, employees, or third parties who may have information regarding this inquiry. Such contact will, in itself, constitute tampering with the investigation.

4. You can take notes and can take time to review any documents about which you are questioned during the investigation. The source of documents or the information on which a question is asked will, however, remain confidential.

5. At the end of the interview, you can make any kind of statement that you want to make.

6. Portions of the inquiry will be tape-recorded. It is a standard practice in these types of inquiries. Should a transcript be made of your interview, a copy will be made available to you.

These steps ensure that the inquiry is accurate, complete, and objective. Failure to comply with these directives constitutes insubordination and is grounds for discontinuing you as a Boys Town Treatment Parent.

I hereby acknowledge that I received this information and expectations.

_____   _____
Treatment Parent   Date

_____   _____
Treatment Parent   Date

_____   _____
Witness   Date

Appendix B

TREATMENT PARENT EVALUATION

All members of the Boys Town treatment team (Treatment Parents, Consultant, Coordinator, Site Director, etc.) participate in the yearly review of a Treatment Parent couple's performance. This helps us learn, individually and as an agency, where our strengths are, and where we need to improve. By learning more about our strengths, we will know what we must continue to do to be successful. Also, it is gratifying to learn how and where we are making a difference in children's lives. By collecting information about areas that need to be improved, we can change and be more effective in meeting children's needs and working with consumers. The following is a step-by-step description for all Boys Town Treatment Parent evaluations.

Treatment Parents are evaluated (twice during the first year and annually thereafter) on information from two primary sources: In–Home Observations and Consumer Questionnaires.

In-Home Observation

Consultants will regularly visit the Treatment Parents' home to discuss the child's progress, develop and assess the child's Treatment Plan, and answer questions. While the Consultant is in the home, he or she also will observe how the rest of the family is adjusting to the child's presence in the home and observe the teaching the child receives.

As part of the six-month and 12-month evaluation, two Boys Town staff members (other than the family's Consultant) will visit the Treatment Parents' home. During these visits, the staff members will formally and informally evaluate the following:

1. **Youth Happiness**. This does not mean that the child will always be happy with the Treatment Parents' decisions or will always get his or her way. It does mean that most of the time, the child will feel that the parents are concerned about him or her and are trying to make living in the home a positive experience.

2. **Youth Skills**. Through observation, the evaluators determine whether or not the child's social skills are improving while the child is in the Treatment Parents' home. Have the child's general social skills, such as conversation skills, improved? Have the child's Treatment Plan and Motivation System been implemented? Is the child closer to achieving his or her goal of moving into a permanent home?

3. **Treatment Parent Skills**. We do not expect anyone to be a perfect parent, but we do look at the Treatment Parents' ability to model the skills they are teaching the child to use. For example, do the Treatment Parents express their frustrations appropriately? Can they accept compliments? Do they ask for help when they need it? The Treatment Parents' commitment to the child also is considered. Do the Treatment Parents keep trying when the child is having trouble changing or do they ask the child to be removed without trying new ideas? The Treatment Parents' ability to teach social skills is a critical component that is evaluated. Questions that are considered include: Do the Treatment Parents recognize opportunities to teach? Is the teaching effective? Do the Treatment Parents use praise? Do they develop positive relationships with their foster child? Do the Treatment Parents implement the Treatment Plan?

4. Family-Style Living. In general, do the Treatment Parents provide a physical environment that is warm and inviting? Does the home provide a real family atmosphere? Is it a place where children have toys and other age-appropriate activities available? Are mealtimes pleasant, a time for family members to enjoy visiting with each other?

5. Professionalism. When the Treatment Parents are evaluated, their records also are reviewed. The records are examined to determine if they are organized, accessible, easy to read, and complete. Again, perfection is not expected, but the records need to be in reasonable order and Treatment Plans must be implemented.

6. Licensure. The Treatment Parents are expected to maintain their compliance with state regulations so that they remain licensed foster parents.

Consumer Questionnaires

Questionnaires are sent to the treatment team members to determine how well the Treatment Parents work with them. The questionnaires are usually sent to the child's parents, therapist (if he or she has one), school, Treatment Family staff, caseworker, etc. The questionnaires ask if the Treatment Parents are correcting the child's problems, cooperating with members of the team, communicating about the child's needs, and are pleasant to work with. The Consultant discusses this process more fully with the Treatment Parents and addresses unique issues that can arise with some consumers.

Time Line for Evaluations

The time line for evaluations is based on the number of days Treatment Parents have had a foster child in their home. Due to the nature of placements in foster care, "windows" have been established to provide flexibility in conducting evaluations.

Day 1	A child is placed in a Treatment Home.
90 – 120 Days (3 – 4 months)	A pre-evaluation conference is arranged for the Consultant and Treatment Parents to discuss how the couple is doing overall.
120 Days (4 months)	The Consultant sends a list of the Treatment Parents' consumers to the Home Campus office at Boys Town, Nebraska. Consumers are people from outside the treatment foster care program who are members of the child's treatment team. Teachers, probation officers, or family members are examples of consumers.
135 Days (4 1/2 months)	The Home Campus office at Boys Town mails the Consumer Questionnaires to consumers. The questionnaire asks individuals to rate the Treatment Parents' progress in areas such as cooperation, communication, effectiveness, and pleasantness.

150 — 210 Days **6-Month Review**	Two Boys Town staff members visit the Treatment Parents and the child in their home. Staff members look at the quality of care the child is receiving, review the logs the Treatment Parents keep, and talk with the foster child alone about his or her overall care. A written summary of this evaluation visit is sent to the Home Campus office.
3 weeks later (from the in-home evaluation)	The Consultant schedules a meeting with the Treatment Parents to formally discuss the results of the evaluation. The Consultant reviews the Treatment Parents' strengths and areas that need improvement, and a plan is developed to help the Treatment Parents accomplish their professional goals. The Consultant shares the Consumer Questionnaire data with the Treatment Parents.
9 – 10 Months	The Consultant sends an updated list of the Treatment Parents' consumers to the Home Campus office. During the tenth month, the office sends the Consumer Questionnaires directly to the consumers.
11 – 13 Months **Annual Certification**	The certification in-home visit occurs. The in-home visit may be made by the Site Director, the Coordinator, or another Consultant. The family's own Consultant does not perform the actual in-home visit; this helps ensure that the evaluation is fair and impartial. The process that is used in the six-month review is followed for this visit.
2 weeks later	The Treatment Foster Family Services Evaluation Review Committee reviews all the evaluation materials and makes a recommendation as to whether the couple should be certified.
4 weeks later	The written evaluation is completed.
1 week after the the Consultant receives the written evaluation	The Consultant meets with the Treatment Parents, reviews the evaluation materials, and gives them a copy of the written evaluation.

From the beginning of the child's placement, your Consultant will begin to discuss the evaluation process with you so that you feel prepared and confident to participate in this review.

Appendix C

RECORD-KEEPING AND RECORDING EVENTS

The following documents are included in this appendix along with brief explanations and descriptions.

I. Initial Documentation
Service Agreement
Confidentiality Policy
Inventory of Belongings
Assessment System

II. Documentation During Treatment
Brief Daily Summary/Weekly Summary
Medication Log
Parent Daily Reports
Contact Log
Appointment Record (Medical, Dental, and Mental Health)
Morning Report
Incident - Post Crisis Report
Monthly Clothing & Allowance Log
Reimbursement Form
Respite Information Sheet & Respite Checklist

III. Documentation Completed by Consultants
Treatment Plan
Treatment Plan Review
Consultation/Observation Feedback
Weekly Consultation Agenda
Teaching/Treatment Progress Report

I. Initial Documentation

Service Agreement: This agreement outlines the primary responsibilities and duties of the Treatment Parents. Exhibit "A" of this agreement specifies the rate of reimbursement the Treatment Parents will receive from Boys Town Treatment Foster Family Services. The Service Agreement is signed by both Treatment Parents and the Consultant on the date of placement and then each year on the anniversary of the same child's placement.

Confidentiality Policy: This form is signed by the Treatment Parents and outlines the policy for maintaining and protecting a child's privacy regarding the dissemination of information about the child's history, family, and treatment. A complete description of this policy can be found in the Boys Town Treatment Foster Family Services Policy and Procedure Manual.

Inventory of Belongings: On the date of placement, the Treatment Parents are expected to complete an inventory of the youth's clothing and belongings. This form is completed and signed by the child, the Treatment Parents, and the child's guardian in order to protect the child and the Treatment Parents. It also can be used throughout the placement to keep track of belongings that are brought in or removed from the foster home by the child or guardian. Having complete and accurate records of the child's belongings will avoid any misunderstandings that may arise when the child leaves the Treatment Home.

Assessment System: The Assessment System is typically used during the first two weeks of placement and allows the Treatment Parents an opportunity to learn a child's strengths and needs. The Assessment System also is helpful in treatment planning. This form is discussed in Chapter 18, "Using Treatment Plans to Change Behavior."

II. Documentation During Treatment

Brief Daily Summary/Weekly Summary: The Brief Daily Summary (BDS) form is used as a daily diary of the child's activities and behaviors. Treatment Parents comment on the youth's positive and negative behaviors, as well as the consequences and privileges earned for each. The Weekly Summary may be substituted for the Daily Summary once the child has stabilized and the Treatment Parents are experienced in the format of documenting daily behaviors. The Weekly Summary documents the same information as the BDS, only in a shorter format. Both summary forms can be used by the treatment team to track the child's patterns of behavior and response to consequences or privileges.

Inventory of Belongings: See description under "Initial Documentation."

Medication Log: This log serves as documentation of any and all medications that a child takes while in the foster home. The Treatment Parents must document the date and time medication is given to the youth. If the medication is a psychotropic drug used for mental health purposes, the Treatment Parents also must initial the entry as described in the Boys Town Treatment Foster Family Services Policy and Procedure Manual.

Parent Daily Reports (PDR): Throughout the child's placement, the Treatment Parents will complete this daily checklist of behaviors. At the end of each week, the Consultant collects the PDRs and the information is entered into a computer program. The Treatment Parents and Consultant may request a printout of the PDR in graph format, which will show the child's progress and general patterns of behavior.

Contact Log: Treatment Parents use the Contact Log to document any and all contacts they or the child have with anyone concerning the child. These contacts include caseworkers, school personnel, the child's parents, therapists, and doctors.

Appointment Log: This form is used to document all medical, dental, and therapeutic appointments for the child. Record the date, location, phone number, and name of the person providing the service on the first line and in the appropriate boxes. The second line is for notes and follow-up information about interactions Treatment Parents have with the service provider.

Morning Report: Many events and activities must be reported to the Consultant immediately, and then reported to the TFFS office by 10 a.m. the following business day. Each event is coded and reported in a consistent manner. The Boys Town TFFS Policy and Procedure Manual clearly defines Morning Events and reporting procedures. Treatment Parents must read this policy and should ask their Consultant for guidance on writing Morning Reports.

Incident - Post Crisis Report: This form is used to document the details of a crisis or certain Morning Reports as outlined in the Boys Town TFFS Policy and Procedure Manual. The form is initially completed by the Treatment Parents and then given to the Consultant for approval and follow-up. All Incident Reports must be completed in a timely manner (within 24 hours of the incident) and signed by the Program Coordinator or Site Director. Completing this form will help the treatment team process the antecedents and outcomes of an event so that similar incidents can be avoided in the future. In the event that a child makes allegations against a Treatment Parent, this form will serve as immediate documentation of the incident.

Monthly Clothing & Allowance Log: This form serves two functions. First, it shows how much money Treatment Parents spend for a foster child's clothing. The Clothing Log section should document the date, item purchased, the store where the purchase was made, and the amount. Use the remaining column to keep a current balance of money spent. The second part of this form documents how much allowance the child earned and how it was spent. These expenses are included as part of the Treatment Parents' monthly stipend. How much you spend on these items will vary from child to child. As outlined in the Boys Town TFFS Policy and Procedure Manual, the suggested monthly amount for clothing is $45, and the suggested allowance each foster child can earn is from $24 to $30.

Reimbursement Form: This form is completed by the Treatment Parents and sent to the TFFS office on a monthly basis. A completed form contains all required information, and all necessary receipts are attached. For further information on reimbursements, read the Boys Town TFFS Policy and Procedure Manual.

Respite Information Sheet & Respite Checklist: The Respite Information Sheet is a summary and guide for respite parents. Treatment Parents complete this form by documenting any special needs of the foster child (e.g. medications, diet, biological family contact), as well as effective reinforcers and consequences. The beginning and end dates of the respite also are recorded on this form. The Respite Checklist is a checklist of items that are to be packed and given to the respite parents.

III. Documentation Completed by Consultants

Treatment Plan: The Treatment Plan form is discussed at length in Chapter 18, "Using Treatment Plans to Change Behavior."

Treatment Plan Review: Treatment Plans are formally reviewed once each month by the Treatment Parents, Consultant, and foster child. The Consultant uses this form to document progress and any changes to the treatment strategy. The Treatment Plan Review form is signed by the Treatment Parents, Consultant, and child, and each receive a copy of the completed document.

Consultation/Observation Feedback: This form is used by the Consultant to document in-home observations of the Treatment Parents' interactions with the foster child. Noncertified Consultants are required to conduct an observation a minimum of two times per month; certified Consultants must conduct an observation at least once a month. The experience and skill level of Treatment Parents also determine the frequency of in-home observations. The Consultant will document strengths and progress areas and suggest target areas and/or skills that need further development. This feedback is intended to offer support and information that will make the Treatment Parents' job easier. If the Consultant suggests a target area for improvement, he or she also will offer suggestions and a plan for making the improvements.

Weekly Consultation Agenda: The Consultant uses this form to document what is discussed during each in-home consultation with the Treatment Parents. The Consultant gives a copy to the Treatment Parents. The Weekly Consultation Agenda then can be used as a reminder for tasks that are to be completed and treatment issues that have been discussed.

Teaching/Treatment Progress Report: Using Treatment Parent input, Weekly Consultation Agenda information, Morning Reports, Contact Logs, and other documentation, the Consultant summarizes a child's behavior and activities in a quarterly Progress Report. A Progress Report is completed after the first month of placement, after the third month of placement, and every three months thereafter. Once the Progress Report is completed, it is signed by the Treatment Parents, foster child, and the Consultant. It is then mailed to the child's caseworker, biological parents, guardian ad litem, and other members of the child's treatment team.

I. Initial Documentation

BOYS TOWN
TREATMENT FOSTER FAMILY SERVICES
TREATMENT PARENT SERVICE AGREEMENT

Father Flanagan's Boys' Home Treatment Foster Family Services (hereinafter referred to as Boys Town Treatment Foster Family Services) has established this Service Agreement beginning _____ (date). We _____ (names) have read the Policy and Procedure Manual for Boys Town Treatment Parents and we agree that:

1. Our reimbursement for expenses related to child treatment and care will follow the schedule shown in the Policy and Procedure Manual, beginning at the current contracted daily rate (as identified in Exhibit "A" hereto and incorporated herein by reference). Reimbursement will be initiated on the day the child is placed under our care and supervision. Because Treatment Foster Family Services is a treatment program, specialized services are provided by Boys Town Treatment Parents.

   Boys Town Treatment Foster Family Services has contracted to serve a population of youth who require treatment for behavioral, emotional, academic, and other problems. On occasion youth requiring less-intensive treatment services may be referred to the Program. Should we agree to accept such a youth for placement in our home, we understand the current contract rate will not apply and the reimbursement we receive will be less than the current contracted rate (as identified in Exhibit "A").

2. We will comply with all laws, policies, and regulations of the State and Father Flanagan's Boys' Home.

3. We must attend inservice training sessions regularly. To continue our involvement in Treatment Foster Family Services, we must attend 80% of all these sessions.

4. We will cooperate fully with Treatment Foster Family Services Staff by informing them about any problems that may arise, sharing important information about youth, and trying to implement their suggestions. We will also allow Program Staff to speak with the youth whenever necessary.

5. We will allow the Consultant and/or designated Treatment Foster Family Services Staff to visit our home in conjunction with licensing procedures and youth treatment planning and placement.

6. We will similarly cooperate with the Boys Town Home Evaluator when it is time to formally evaluate our treatment parenting at 6 months, 12 months, and yearly thereafter.

7. In treating and parenting youth, we will employ the procedures taught in the Boys Town Preservice Training (along with the many other positive parenting skills we have) to the best of our ability and within the bounds of good judgment. We also agree to document our interactions with youth by completing all required daily records.

8. We will adhere to the Boys Town Confidentiality Policy, which we have read and signed.

9. We are responsible for providing daily necessities for the youth, which include, but are not limited to: a balanced diet, adequate (in quality, style, quantity) clothing in good condition, transportation, ample recreation, adequate allowance (when youth's behavior is appropriate), appropriate medical care, and any prescribed medications.

10. We will treat the child(ren) placed in our care as a member of our family, and when recommended by Boys Town Treatment Foster Family Services, will make every effort to support, encourage, and enhance the child(ren)'s relationship with his/her biological family.

11. We understand that Boys Town Treatment Foster Family Services has the authority to make and carry out program plans for the child(ren), such as a transfer to another home, temporary respite care, or the return to biological parents or relatives.

12. We will administer only medications prescribed by a physician and previously authorized by Boys Town, and document times and dosage.

13. We will keep one or more (2 or 3 is desirable) smoke detectors in good operating condition at all times in our home and located in appropriate places (such as at the head of the stairs, outside bedrooms, etc).

14. We will ensure that all medications are locked up, and any weapons we possess are dismantled and locked up.

15. We will carry a homeowner's policy of $100,000 to $300,000 comprehensive liability and auto liability insurance of at least $100,000 (you may already have these common amounts), and provide Boys Town with a copy of these policies. These policies insure us for damages or loss caused by a youth to persons or property, either ours or others'. We understand that Boys Town is responsible for damage or loss only if caused by negligence of Boys Town. Boys Town staff will provide us with information, prior to accepting a youth, that will help us judge whether there is significant risk of such damage or loss and decide whether we will accept placement of the youth.

16. We will conduct at least one fire drill for the whole family each time a new youth moves into our home, and at least one annually thereafter, with the youth being located in his/her bedroom at the time, as though sleeping.

17. We must be examined by a physician and tested for communicable diseases, if we have not already done so, and must provide Boys Town with the physician's statement that we are free from such disease.

18. When we are ready for a youth, there may not be an appropriate youth ready to be placed in our home. Much time can go by before a youth for whom our home is the most appropriate and who is acceptable to us is available. Boys Town has no obligation to keep homes "filled" with youth.

19. We will confer with the Consultant before taking the child out of our home for an overnight period or out of the state for any time.

20. We will report to the Consultant any changes in the composition of our household, change of address, and any change in the employment status of either adult member of the household.

21. We will give a child a fair chance to adjust to our home, and in the event we feel that such an adjustment is not possible, will give the Consultant and the Boys Town Treatment Foster Family Services Program fair notice (30 days) before asking for removal of the child.

22. We will provide the child with responsible supervision appropriate to the child's age and emotional stability and will not leave the child unsupervised or in the charge of inappropriate or unapproved persons.

23. We will accept into our home only those children referred by Boys Town Treatment Foster Family Services.

24. We will, at all times, provide safe and humane care and treatment for the youth placed in our home by adhering to the youth rights and accompanying rules and guidelines as taught in the Preservice Training as well as the State Foster Care Regulations.

_____   _____
Signature/Date   S.S.#

_____   _____
Signature/Date   S.S.#

_____   _____
Witness   Date

BOYS TOWN TREATMENT PARENT SERVICE AGREEMENT
EXHIBIT "A"

On this day, _____, we agree to provide the care and treatment for _____ as defined by the Boys Town Treatment Foster Family Services Program. In so doing, we will be reimbursed at the rate of $. per day. We are fully aware of our responsibilities and obligations to this child and Boys Town Treatment Foster Family Services and will work in cooperation with all policies and procedures.

_____   _____
Signature/Date   S.S.#

_____   _____
Signature/Date   S.S.#

_____   _____
Witness   Date

BOYS TOWN
TREATMENT FOSTER FAMILY SERVICES
CONFIDENTIALITY POLICY

Due to the nature of the services provided by Boys Town Treatment Foster Family Services, all Boys Town Treatment Parents must be very careful about the information they give others. Even accidental disclosure of personal information about youth or their families is a violation of confidence. Good judgment and respect for the rights of youth and their families is required.

Boys Town Treatment Parents will be given a substantial amount of information about a youth and his/her family for treatment purposes. They are not to be given information that is unnecessary for treatment, and they must not share personal, sensitive bits of information with others who have no treatment role (e.g. that a youth's parent may be an alcoholic, that a youth was once hospitalized for certain behavior, or that the youth has been adjudicated delinquent, etc.).

When someone else does have a role in the youth's treatment, such as a teacher or visiting relative, the only personal information that should be shared is what the other person needs or has a right to know to help in the youth's treatment/development; even that information must be shared in a confidential, professional manner.

Discussion of treatment procedures and such should not take place in public; you would be surprised how many mental health professionals have found that a waitress, passenger on a bus, or other stranger knew one of their clients. If procedures are discussed at an inservice workshop, meeting, or semi-public place, the name of the youth and his/her family should not be used.

We have read the above confidentiality statement and understand that any violation of this policy is adequate grounds for immediate termination of our involvement with Boys Town Treatment Foster Family Services.

_____   _____
Signature   Date

_____   _____
Signature   Date

_____   _____
Witness   Date

BOYS TOWN
TREATMENT FOSTER FAMILY SERVICES
INVENTORY OF BELONGINGS

YOUTH'S NAME: _____ DATE: _____

BOYS TOWN TREATMENT PARENTS: _____

The articles under the letter **A** are by no means a "must." The number behind the items only serves as a suggestion for a basic wardrobe. Please use the line in front of the article to put down the number of items of particular clothing the youth brings with him/her that are acceptable for wear and in good condition.

The items under **B** are the additional possessions the youth brings to Boys Town. Again, fill out the number of items that are in good condition. Give a good description of the luggage at the bottom of the list.

	A		**B**
Number:	*Description:*	*Number:*	*Description:*
_____	Light Jacket (1)	_____	Raincoat
_____	Heavy Jacket (1)	_____	Sweaters
_____	Belt (1)	_____	Sweatshirts
_____	Sport or suit or dress coat (1)	_____	Short pants/sundress (summer wear)
_____	Dress pants/dress (2)	_____	Gym shoes
_____	School pants (4)	_____	Sports articles (glove, ball, etc.)
_____	Jeans (3)	_____	Radio, record player
_____	Everyday shirts (7)	_____	Camera
_____	Dress shirts (2)	_____	Games (checkers, etc.)
_____	Shoes (leather) (2)	_____	Watches
_____	Socks (12)	_____	Jewelry (tie clasps, rings, etc.)
_____	Pajamas (2)	_____	Wallet
_____	Shorts (underwear) (9)	_____	Books
_____	T-shirts (underwear) (9)	_____	Rubber boots
_____	Bathrobe (1)	_____	Houseshoes (slippers)
_____	_____	_____	Eyeglasses
_____	_____	_____	Medication
_____	_____	_____	Luggage (describe):
_____	_____	_____	_____
_____	_____	_____	_____

IMPORTANT - READ THIS CAREFULLY, PLEASE: BOYS TOWN CANNOT BE HELD RESPONSIBLE FOR ANY ARTICLES THAT ARE LOST, GIVEN AWAY BY THE YOUTH, OR TAKEN WHEN HE/SHE IS ABSENT WITHOUT OFFICIAL LEAVE. BY SIGNING THIS FORM YOU WILL GIVE EVIDENCE THAT YOU HAVE UNDERSTOOD THIS STATEMENT AND THAT YOU ARE IN AGREEMENT. THE YOUTH WILL ALSO READ THIS AND WILL SIGN THE INVENTORY (IF AGE-APPROPRIATE) UPON HIS/HER PLACEMENT IN BOYS TOWN TREATMENT FOSTER FAMILY SERVICES.

_____
Legal Guardian

_____
(Person taking inventory)

_____
Youth

BOYS TOWN
TREATMENT FOSTER FAMILY SERVICES
ASSESSMENT SYSTEM

NAME: _____ Assessment Period: _____

Please complete this assessment system over 14 consecutive days for each skill listed below. Record a Y (yes) if the youth demonstrated the skill satisfactorily or an N (no) if the youth needs to learn or improve the skill.

SKILLS	M	T	W	T	F	S	S	M	T	W	T	F	S	S
FOLLOWS INSTRUCTIONS														
ACCEPTS "NO" ANSWERS														
ACCEPTS CONSEQUENCES														
ASKS PERMISSION														
DOES DAILY CHORES														
GOOD PERSONAL HYGIENE														
GOOD SCHOOL BEHAVIOR														
GOOD CHURCH BEHAVIOR														
GETS ALONG WITH PEERS														
TELLS THE TRUTH														
APPROPRIATE LANGUAGE														
APPROPRIATELY DISAGREES														
REPORTS WHEREABOUTS														

II. Documentation During Treatment

BOYS TOWN
TREATMENT FOSTER FAMILY SERVICES
BRIEF DAILY SUMMARY

YOUTH: _____   DATE: _____

Completed By: _____

What did the youth do well today?

What did you do?

_____ Praise the youth   _____ Youth earned reward/privilege

_____ Hug   _____ Other (please explain)

Comments:

What behavior was the most difficult to deal with today?

How did you deal with it?

_____ Talk with the youth   _____ Youth lost privilege

_____ Other (please explain)

Comments:

BOYS TOWN TREATMENT FOSTER FAMILY SERVICES
MEDICATION LOG

Boys Town Treatment Parent:

Youth:

MONTH	MEDICATION	MEDICATION	MEDICATION	MEDICATION
1.				
2.				
3.				
4.				
5.				
6.				
7.				
8.				
9.				
10.				
11.				
12.				
13.				
14.				
15.				
16.				
17.				
18.				
19.				
20.				
21.				
22.				
23.				
24.				
25.				
26.				
27.				
28.				
29.				
30.				
31.				

PARENT

DAILY

TELEPHONE

REPORT

Youth I.D. _____

Week of _____
(Sunday)

thru

_____
(Saturday)

CONTINGENCY SYSTEM

_____

_____

Site: _____

CALLERS

_____

_____

_____

PLEASE CIRCLE...

CONTACT:			
Male	Female	Respite	Other

RELIABILITY	
YES	NO

PHASE:			
			FOLLOW
PRE	RX	POST	UP

#	BEHAVIOR	SUN	MON	TUE	WED	THU	FRI	SAT
1	Alcohol							
2	Arguing							
3	Back-talking							
4	Bed-wetting							
5	Boisterousness							
6	Competitiveness							
7	Complaining							
8	Crying							
9	Daydreaming							
10	Defiance							
11	Depression/Sadness							
12	Destructiveness							
13	Encopresis							
14	Fearfulness							
15	Fighting							
16	Hitting others							
17	Hyperactiveness							
18	Inappropriate sexual behavior							
19	Irresponsibility							
20	Irritability							
21	Jealousy							
22	Lying							
23	Marijuana/Drugs							
24	Negativism							
25	Nervousness (jittery)							
26	Not minding							
27	Pant-wetting (enuresis)							
28	Pouting							
29	Restraining/Holding							
30	Runaway							
31	School problems							
32	Self-destructiveness							
33	Short attention span							
34	Skipping meals							
35	Sluggishness							
36	Staying out late							
37	Stealing							
38	Swearing and/or obscenities							
39	Tantrums							
40	Teasing/Provoking							
41	Time-Out							
42	Truancy							
43	Whining						.	
44	Yelling							
45	# POSITIVE INTERACTIONS							
46	# NEGATIVE INTERACTIONS							
47	TOTAL POINTS							
48	MEDS TAKEN							

Adapted from: Chamberlain, P., & Reid, J.B. (1987). Parent observation & report of child symptom. Behavioral Assessment, Vol. 9, pp. 97-109. Reprinted with permission.

BOYS TOWN
TREATMENT FOSTER FAMILY SERVICES
CONTACT LOG

Consultant _____   Youth _____

BT Treatment Parents _____

Code: BTTP- BT Treatment Parent   CW - Caseworker   S - School Personnel
     OA - Outside Agency   BTS - Boys Town Staff   BF - Biological Family
     PO - Probation Officer

Date/ Time	Code	Content

BOYS TOWN TREATMENT FOSTER FAMILY SERVICES
APPOINTMENT RECORD
(Medical, Dental, and Mental Health)

Youth: _____   BT Treatment Parents: _____

Date of App't	Location and Phone Number	Person Providing Services	Reason Taken	Treatment Provided	Follow-Up Treatment	MA Card Accepted Y/N

Boys Town Treatment Parent interaction with service Provider:

Boys Town Treatment Parent interaction with service Provider:

Boys Town Treatment Parent interaction with service Provider:

Boys Town Treatment Parent interaction with service Provider:

Boys Town Treatment Parent interaction with service Provider:

Boys Town Treatment Parent interaction with service Provider:

Boys Town Treatment Parent interaction with service Provider:

Boys Town Treatment Parent interaction with service Provider:

Boys Town Treatment Parent interaction with service Provider:

MORNING REPORT

PROGRAM: RSF / TFFS / ESS

YOUTH/FT: _____ DATE: _____

___ 1. NEW YOUTH/FAMILY	___ 83. SUBSTANCE ABUSE TRMT INPATIENT*
___ 2. READMIT	___ 89. SCHOOL REFERRAL
___ 3. SCHOOL TRANSFER	___ 90. SUSPENSION IN-SCHOOL
___ 4. TRANSFER OUT OF HOME	___ 91. SUSPENSION OUT-OF-SCHOOL
___ 5. TRANSFER INTO HOME	___ 92. EXPELLED - HOMEBOUND
___ 6. FPS TEMPORARY REMOVAL	___ 93. EXPELLED - ALTERNATIVE PLACEMENT
___ 7. FPS PERMANENT REMOVAL	___ 94. EXPELLED
___ 8. FPS REUNIFICATION	___ 100. COMMUNITY COUNCIL
___ 9. DEPARTURE	___ 101. HOMEWARD BOUND
___ 15. APPROVED ABSENCE*	___ 102. PRE-SEPARATION MEETING
___ 16. BTUSA SCHOOL ABSENCE	___ 103. EXECUTIVE DIRECTOR MEETING
___ 17. ABSENT OVER LEAVE*	___ 104. SHELTER BEHAVIOR CONTRACT
___ 18. BOL/UNREPORTED WHEREABOUTS	___ 105. SHELTER MEDIATION CONTRACT
___ 19. RUNAWAY/AWOL	___ 106. SHELTER PLANNING CONFERENCE
___ 25. INJURY	___ 107. SITE DIRECTOR MEETING
___ 26. OUTPATIENT MEDICAL CARE	___ 108. INDIVIDUALIZED EDUCATION PRGM MEETING
___ 27. HOSPITAL*	___ 112. FAMILY/AGENCY CONTACT
___ 28. PREGNANCY	___ 113. VISITORS AND GUESTS
___ 34. MENTAL HEALTH SERVICE	___ 119. CHILD PROTECTIVE SERVICES
___ 35. PSYCHOTROPIC MEDICATION	___ 120. POLICE CONTACT - POSITIVE
___ 36. SAY GROUP*	___ 121. POLICE CONTACT - NEGATIVE
___ 37. PSYCHIATRIC HOSPITAL*	___ 122. COURT APPEARANCE
___ 38. EATING DISORDER	___ 123. DETENTION/JAIL*
___ 44. OUT OF INST CONTROL (SCHOOL)	___ 129. DEATH IN FAMILY
___ 45. OUT OF INST CONTROL (NONSCHOOL)	___ 130. DEATH OF A FRIEND
___ 46. RESTRAINING YOUTH	___ 136. AFTERCARE
___ 52. VERBAL/SYMBOLIC AGGRESSION	___ 137. CRUELTY OF ANIMALS
___ 53. PHYSICAL AGGRESSION	___ 138. FIRESETTING OR FIREPLAY
___ 54. PHYSICAL ASSAULT-PERPETRATOR	___ 139. GANG BEHAVIORS
___ 55. PHYSICAL ASSAULT-VICTIM	___ 140. JOB-RELATED ACTIVITIES
___ 56. SEXUAL EXPLOITIVE BEHAVIOR	___ 141. NOTEWORTHY INAPPROPRIATE BEHAVIOR
___ 57. SEX ASSAULT-PERPETRATOR	___ 142. PEER REPORT
___ 58. SEXUAL ASSAULT-VICTIM	___ 143. POSITIVE INCIDENT
___ 64. INAPP. SEXUAL BEHAVIOR/PDA	___ 144. POSSESSION OF A WEAPON
___ 65. SEXUAL MISCONDUCT/HETERO ACTIVITY	___ 145. PRIOR TO ADMISSION
___ 66. HOMOSEXUAL ACTIVITY/NONPHYSICAL	___ 146. PROPERTY DAMAGE
___ 67. HOMOSEXUAL ACTIVITY/PHYSICAL	___ 147. SATANISM
___ 73. SELF-DESTRUCTIVE BEHAVIOR	___ 148. STRUCTURED RECREATIONAL ACTIVITY
___ 74. SUICIDE IDEATION	___ 149. THEFT - PERPETRATOR
___ 75. SUICIDE ATTEMPT	___ 150. THEFT - VICTIM
___ 81. SUBSTANCE ABUSE/ALCOHOL/CHEMICAL	___ 151. YOUTH RIGHTS
___ 82. SUBSTANCE ABUSE TRMT OUTPATIENT	___ No event codes for this incident

* INCIDENT CODE HAS MANDATORY BEGIN/END DATES

_____ M / T / W / TH / F / S / SU , ____ / ____ / ____ _____

MET WITH _____ FOR THEIR WEEKLY SCHEDULED THERAPY
APPOINTMENT, THE SESSION WENT WELL.

ANY ADDITIONAL INFORMATION CAN BE WRITTEN ON THE BACK

222

MORNING REPORT NARRATIVE

BOYS TOWN
TREATMENT FOSTER FAMILY SERVICES
INCIDENT - POST CRISIS REPORT

Name of Youth: _____ Age: _____

BT Treatment Parents: _____ Address: _____

Date of Placement: _____ Date of Incident: _____ Date of Report: _____

Time of Incident: _____ Location of Incident: _____

Person Making Report: _____ Others Involved: _____

Type of Incident (check all which are appropriate)

MEDICAL

1. *Illness/Injury to Youth*

___ assaulted by peer
___ self-inflicted
___ BTP/Staff involved or inflicted
___ contagious disease
___ other

2. ___ *Emergency Hospitalization*
3. *Medication Problem*
___ Neglected to administer
___ Other _____
4. ___ *Injury of Treatment Parent*
5. *Abuse of Alcohol or Drugs*
___ suspicion
___ known
___ self-admitted
___ medically documented
___ dispensing to others

SOCIAL/LEGAL

6. ___ *Legal Problems*
7. *Police Involvement*
___ illegal actions
___ questioning
___ status offense
8. *Youth AWOL*
___ less than 1 hr.
___ 1-5 hours
___ more than 5 hours
___ has not been located
___ whereabouts known
___ child has returned
9. *Verbal/Physical Aggression*
Against:
___ BTP/staff
___ peers
___ other
10. *Property Damage*
___ 0-$10.00
___ $10-$50.00
___ $50.00+

OTHER

11. *Sexual Experimentation*
or Assault With:
___ BTP
___ staff
___ youth
___ others
12.___ *Possible Violation of*
Youth Rights
13. *Suicide*
___ verbal threat
___ physical gesture
___ physical attempt
(attach Lethal. Assessment)
14. *Allegation by Child Against:*
___ BTP/Staff
___ youth
___ others
___ physical (slapping)
___ sexual
___ other (swearing, ridiculing)

I. Has youth previously engaged in this behavior?   Yes _____   No _____

II. Describe facts preceding the incident (i.e. restrictions, ongoing activity, upcoming events, behavior of others).

_____

_____

_____

III. Describe any measures taken to prevent incident.

_____

_____

_____

IV. Describe the incident (i.e. why, what, where, when, and outcome).

_____

_____

_____

_____

_____

_____

V. Describe who was notified of the incident, when, and the response.

Name/Position	Date/Time Notified	Response
1.		
2.		
3.		
4.		
5.		

VI. * Consultant: Actions Taken and Follow-up Plan (i.e. future interventions).

_____

_____

_____

_____

_____

Boys Town Treatment Parents	Consultant	Program Director

VII. Final Status of Report: _____ No further discussion needed _____ Additional discussion/investigation required (specify): _____

* To be filled in by Consultant

BOYS TOWN
TREATMENT FOSTER FAMILY SERVICES

MONTHLY CLOTHING LOG

Youth: _____   BT Treatment Parent: _____

Month: _____

DATE OF PURCHASE	ITEM	STORE	AMOUNT	REMAINING BALANCE

ALLOWANCE LOG

DAY/DATE	AMOUNT	ITEM	STORE

BOYS TOWN TREATMENT FOSTER FAMILY SERVICES TREATMENT PARENT REIMBURSEMENT FOR THE MONTH OF _____

TREATMENT PARENT(S): _____   BLANKET ORDER: _____   COST CODE: _____

1	2	3	4	5	6	7	8	9	10	11	12	13	14	15	16	17	18	19	20	21	22	23	24	25	26	27	28	29	30	31

P=YOUTH IS PRESENT   HP=YOUTH IS IN HOSPITAL   A=YOUTH ON RESPITE   R=YOUTH ON RUNAWAY
X=ADDITIONAL YOUTH ON RESPITE   HV=YOUTH ON HOME VISIT   *=OTHER PLEASE SPECIFY

FOSTER CHILDREN	# OF DAYS RESPITE	# OF DAYS PROVIDING CARE	RATE OF REIMBURSEMENT	TOTAL BOYS TOWN REIMBURSEMENT
1. _____	_____	_____	_____	_____
2. _____	_____	_____	_____	_____
3. _____	_____	_____	_____	_____

(Use additional form if necessary)   *TOTAL CHILD CARE REIMBURSEMENT* _____

RECORD OF NONREIMBURSABLE RECEIPTS: **REIMBURSABLE RECEIPTS** (If Applicable):

Clothing Receipts: _____   Telephone Receipts: _____
Medical Receipts: _____   Transportation Receipts: _____
Child Care Receipts: _____   Child Care Receipts: _____
Other: _____   **TOTAL REIMBURSEMENT W/RECEIPTS:** _____

MILEAGE:

DATE	DISTANCE	PURPOSE OF TRAVEL	DATE	DISTANCE	PURPOSE OF TRAVEL
_____	_____	_____	_____	_____	_____
_____	_____	_____	_____	_____	_____

(Use additional form if necessary)   **TOTAL REIMBURSEMENT FOR MILEAGE:** _____
                                           GRAND TOTAL: _____

I, _____ (BOYS TOWN TREATMENT PARENT) HEREBY CERTIFY ALL EXPENSES HEREIN CLAIMED FOR REIMBURSEMENT TO BE STATED ACCURATELY TO THE BEST OF MY KNOWLEDGE.

_____   _____
CONSULTANT   DATE

_____   _____
COORDINATOR   DATE

BOYS TOWN
TREATMENT FOSTER FAMILY SERVICES
RESPITE INFORMATION SHEET

Youth _____ Age _____ Date of Birth _____

Name of Consultant and Phone Number _____

Reason for Respite _____

_____

Special Needs or Circumstances of Youth (medication, diet, biological family contact, etc.):

Effective Reinforcers:

Effective Consequences:

Describe any unusual characteristics of Treatment Plan:

Daily Allowance: _____

Date Respite Begins: _____ Date Respite Ended: _____

Time to drop off: _____ Time returned: _____

_____   _____
Boys Town Treatment Parent   Respite Parent

BOYS TOWN
TREATMENT FOSTER FAMILY SERVICES
RESPITE CHECKLIST

_____ State/Other Medical Insurance Card

_____ Consent Form

_____ Parent/Youth Book

_____ Medications

_____ Daily Behavior Cards

_____ Toothbrush

_____ Other Hygiene Items

_____ Play Clothes and Shoes

_____ Dress Clothes and Shoes

_____ Sleepwear

_____ Coat

_____ Suitcase or Tote

III. Documentation Completed by Consultants

BOYS TOWN
TREATMENT FOSTER FAMILY SERVICES
TREATMENT PLAN

YOUTH _____ SYSTEM _____ DATE _____

PROBLEM AT ADMISSION _____

TARGET BEHAVIOR (#____) _____

BASELINE: FREQUENCY OF PROBLEM BEHAVIOR _____ PER WEEK (AVERAGE)

PROBLEM DEFINITION: (Who, What, Where, When, Specific Behavior)

_____

_____

_____

_____

_____

_____

GOAL: Frequency of Problem Behavior _____ per week

GOAL: % of Teaching to Alternative Behavior _____ per week (80%)

STRATEGY: (Preventive Teaching, Spontaneous Teaching, Family Meeting, Relationship Development, Problem-Solving)

_____

_____

_____

_____

_____

_____

_____

_____

_____

_____

_____

_____

_____

| _____ | _____ | _____ |
| YOUTH | BOYS TOWN TREATMENT PARENTS | CONSULTANT |

BOYS TOWN
TREATMENT FOSTER FAMILY SERVICES
TREATMENT PLAN REVIEW

NAME _____ SYSTEM _____ MONTH REVIEWED _____

TARGET BEHAVIOR: (#_____) _____

GOAL: FREQUENCY OF PROBLEM BEHAVIOR _____ PER WEEK (AVERAGE)

PROGRESS: FREQUENCY OF PROBLEM BEHAVIOR _____ PER WEEK (AVERAGE)

NOTES: (UPDATE)

_____
_____
_____
_____
_____
_____

ACHIEVED: % of Teaching to Alternative Behavior _____ per week (average)

REVISED GOAL: % of Teaching to Alternative Behavior _____ per week (80%)

REVISED STRATEGY: (Preventive Teaching, Spontaneous Teaching, Family Meeting, Relationship Development, Problem-Solving)

_____
_____
_____
_____
_____
_____
_____
_____
_____
_____

_____   _____   _____
        YOUTH   BOYS TOWN TREATMENT PARENTS   CONSULTANT

BOYS TOWN
TREATMENT FOSTER FAMILY SERVICES
CONSULTATION/OBSERVATION FEEDBACK

Boys Town Treatment Parents: _____

Consultation/Observation Date: _____

Parenting Strengths/Progress Areas: _____

_____

_____

_____

_____

_____

Examples Observed: _____

_____

_____

Target Areas: _____

_____

_____

_____

_____

_____

_____

Examples Observed: _____

_____

_____

Suggestions/Follow-Up: _____

_____

_____

_____

_____   _____
Consultant Signature   Date

BOYS TOWN
TREATMENT FOSTER FAMILY SERVICES
WEEKLY CONSULTATION AGENDA

Youth: _____ Date: _____

Treatment Parents: _____ Consultant: _____

Agenda Prompts:

____ School	____ Medical/Dental	____ Mental Health	____ Behavior
____ Logs	____ PDRs	____ Daily Summaries	____ Treatment Plan Review
____ Morning Events	____ Incident Reports	____ Biological Family Contact	____ Evaluation
____ On-Call Coverage	____ Respite	____ Skill Review	____ Inservice Training
____ Reimbursement	____ Fire Drills	____ Licensure	____ Observation Feedback

Notes:

Follow-Up:

_____**Consultant:**

_____**Treatment Parents:**

236

BOYS TOWN
TREATMENT FOSTER FAMILY SERVICES
TEACHING/TREATMENT PROGRESS REPORT

Legal Name _____   Date _____

Nickname _____   Report Period _____ to _____

Boys Town I.D. Number _____   SS# _____

Birth Date _____ Age _____   Sex _____ Grade _____

BT Treatment Parents _____   Religious Preference _____

Address _____

_____

REASON FOR PLACEMENT

HEALTH STATUS

Ht. _____ Wt. _____

Date of last physical _____ Physician _____

Physician/Clinic address _____

Date of last dental visit _____ Dentist _____

Dentist's address _____

EDUCATIONAL/VOCATIONAL STATUS

School _____ Grade _____

Type of Classroom/Setting _____

BIOLOGICAL PARENT/LEGAL GUARDIAN/AGENCY INFORMATION

Status Changes:

Contacts:

PREPLACEMENT/PLACEMENT ADJUSTMENT

Preplacement Behaviors:

Referral Behaviors:

Other Behaviors of Concern:

Behavioral Strengths:

Behavioral Improvements:

238

TEACHING/TREATMENT PLAN

Placement Status:

Current Treatment Goals:

Behavior Goals:

How We Will Teach:

What Will Be Taught:

Overall Summary:

_____   _____
Boys Town Treatment Parent   *Date*

_____   _____
Youth   *Date*

_____   _____
Consultant   *Date*

_____   _____
Program Director   *Date*

Appendix D

SKILLS FOR CHILDREN AND TEENS

1. Following Instructions

2. Accepting Criticism

3. Accepting "No" Answers

4. Staying Calm

5. Disagreeing with Others

6. Asking for Help

7. Asking Permission

8. Getting Along with Others

9. Apologizing

10. Conversation Skills

11. Giving Compliments

12. Accepting Compliments

13. Listening to Others

14. Telling the Truth

15. Introducing Yourself

16. Setting Appropriate Personal Boundaries

The steps to each of these skills, reasons to give a child for why the skills are important, and helpful hints on how a child should carry them out are presented on the following pages.

Following Instructions

When you are given an instruction, you should:

1. Look at the person who is talking.

2. Show that you understand ("I understand," "Okay," or "I'll do it"). Make sure you wait until the person is done talking before you do what is asked. It is usually best to answer, but sometimes nodding your head will be enough to show the person that you understand.

3. Do what is asked in the best way that you can.

4. Let the person know that you have finished.

Reason:

It is important to do what is asked because it shows your ability to cooperate and it saves time. Following instructions will help you in school, in the home, and with adults and friends.

Helpful Hints:

- After finding out exactly what has been asked, start the task immediately.

- If you have any doubts that doing what is asked will result in some type of negative consequence for you, or you don't understand, ask a trusted adult.

- Do what is asked as pleasantly as possible.

- Check back as soon as you finish. This increases the chances that you will get credit for doing a job well. It also means that somebody else doesn't have time to mess it up before you check back.

Accepting Criticism

When others tell you how they think you can improve, they give you criticism. When you accept criticism, you should:

1. Look at the person. Don't give negative facial expressions.

2. Remain calm and quiet while the person is talking.

3. Show that you understand ("Okay," or "I understand").

4. Try to correct the problem. If you are asked to do something different, do it. If you are asked to stop doing something, stop it. If you can't give a positive response, at least give one that will not get you into trouble ("Okay," "I understand," or "Thanks").

Reason:

Being able to accept criticism shows maturity and prevents having problems with people in authority. If you can control yourself and listen to what others have to say about how you can improve, it will result in fewer problems for you. And, the criticism may really help you!

Helpful Hints:

- It is most important that you stay calm. Take a deep breath if necessary.

- Giving criticism back, becoming angry, or making negative facial expressions will only get you into more trouble.

- When you respond to the person who is giving you criticism, use a pleasant voice tone as much as possible. You will receive criticism for the rest of your life – all people do. The way you handle it determines how you are treated by others.

- Most criticism is designed to help you; however, sometimes it is hard to accept. If you don't agree with the criticism, ask your Treatment Parent or another trusted adult.

- Always ask questions if you don't understand (but don't play games by asking questions when you really do understand it and are just being stubborn). Give yourself a chance to improve!

Accepting "No" Answers

1. Look at the person.

2. Say "Okay."

3. Calmly ask for a reason if you really don't understand.

4. If you disagree, bring it up later.

Reason:

You will be told "No" many times in your life. Getting angry and upset only leads to more problems. If you are able to appropriately accept a "No" answer, people will view you as cooperative and mature.

Helpful Hints:

- Don't stare, make faces, or look away. If you are upset, control your emotions. Try to relax and stay calm. Listening carefully will help you understand what the other person is saying.

- Answer right away and speak clearly. Take a deep breath if you feel upset.

- Don't ask for a reason every time or you will be viewed as a complainer. People will think you are serious about wanting to know a reason if you ask for one calmly. Don't keep asking for reasons after you receive one. Use what you learn in these situations in the future.

- Take some time to plan how you are going to approach the person who told you "No." Plan in advance what you are going to say. Accept the answer, even if it is still "No." Be sure to thank the person for listening. At least you had the opportunity to share your opinion.

Staying Calm

When people feel angry or upset, it's hard to stay calm. When we feel like "blowing up," we sometimes make poor choices. And when we make poor choices, we usually regret it later. If you feel that you are going to lose self-control, you should:

1. Take a deep breath.

2. Relax your muscles.

3. Tell yourself to "Be calm," or count to 10.

4. Share your feelings. After you are relaxed, tell someone you trust what is bothering you.

5. Try to solve the situation that made you upset.

Reason:

It is important to stay calm since worse things always seem to happen if you lose your temper. If you can stay calm, other people will depend on you more often. They will see you as mature and able to handle even the worst situations. Teachers and employers will respect you and look upon you as someone who can keep "cool."

Helpful Hints:

- You might try to talk yourself into the idea that "blowing up" is the only thing to do, or that the other person or thing "deserves it." Forget it. It doesn't work that way. And, you're setting yourself up to get more or worse consequences. Be calm.

- After you have calmed down, pat yourself on the back. Even adults have a hard time with self-control. If you can control yourself, you will have accomplished something that many adults are still struggling with. Give yourself some praise! You have done the right thing.

Disagreeing with Others

When you don't agree with another person's opinion or decision, you should:

1. Remain calm. Getting upset will only make matters worse.

2. Look at the person. This shows that you have confidence.

3. Begin with a positive or neutral statement. "I know you are trying to be fair but...."

4. Explain why you disagree with the decision. Keep your voice tone controlled. Be brief and clear.

5. Listen as the other person explains his or her side of the story.

6. Calmly accept whatever decision is made.

7. Thank the person for listening, regardless of the outcome.

Reason:

It is important to disagree in a calm manner because it increases the chances that the other person will listen. This may be the only opportunity you have to get the decision changed. You have a right to express your opinions. But you lose that right if you become upset or aggressive. If the other person feels that you are going to lose self-control, you won't have a good chance of getting your views across.

Helpful Hints:

- You're not going to win every time. Some decisions will not change. However, learning how to disagree calmly may help change some of them.

- Don't try to change everything. People will view you as a pest.

- If you are calm and specific when you disagree, people will respect you for the mature way you handle situations. It pays off in the long run!

Asking for Help

When you need help with something, you should:

1. Decide what the problem is.

2. Ask to speak to the person most likely to help you.

3. Look at the person, clearly describe what you need help with, and ask the person for help in a pleasant voice tone.

4. Thank the person for helping you.

Reason:

It is important to ask for help from others because it is the best way to solve problems you can't figure out. Asking for help in a pleasant manner makes it more likely that someone will help you.

Helpful Hints:

- It's nice to figure out things by yourself. Sometimes, this isn't possible. Asking someone who has more experience, or has had more success with a similar problem, is a way to learn how to solve the problem the next time.

- Sometimes, people become frustrated when they can't figure something out. Sometimes, they even get mad. Learn to ask for help before you get to this point and you will have more successes than failures.

- Always tell the person who is helping you how much you appreciate the help. It might be nice to offer your help the next time that person needs something.

Asking Permission

When you need to get permission from someone else, you should:

1. Look at the other person.

2. Be specific when you ask permission. The other person should know exactly what you are requesting.

3. Be sure to ask rather than demand. "May I please...?"

4. Give reasons if necessary.

5. Accept the decision.

Reason:

It is important to ask permission whenever you want to do something or use something that another person is responsible for. Asking permission shows your respect for others and their property, and increases the chances that your request will be granted.

Helpful Hints:

- If something doesn't belong to you, it's always wise to ask permission to use it. It doesn't matter if it is a sack of potato chips or someone's bike; ask permission!

- Sometimes you won't get what you want. But if you have asked permission politely and correctly, it is more likely that you may get what you want the next time.

- It may help you to remember how you would feel if someone used something of yours without asking first. Besides feeling like that person was not polite or respectful of your property, something could get broken or lost.

Getting Along with Others

To be successful in dealing with people, you should:

1. Listen to what the other person says.

2. Say something positive if you agree with what that person said. If you don't agree, say something that won't result in an argument. Use a calm voice tone.

3. Show interest in what the other person has to say. Try to understand his or her point of view.

Reason:

It is important to get along with others because you will be working and dealing with other people for most of your life. If you can get along with others, it is more likely that you will be successful in whatever you do. Getting along with others shows sensitivity and respect. If you can get along with others, it is more likely that they will behave the same way. In other words, treat others the way you want to be treated!

Helpful Hints:

- Sometimes it is not easy to get along with others. If someone does something that you do not like, or says something negative, you may feel like behaving the same way. Don't! Stop yourself from saying things that can hurt others' feelings. Teasing, cussing, and insults will only make matters worse. It is better to ignore others' negative behavior than to act like them.

- Getting along with others takes some effort. It is hard to understand why some people act the way they do. Try to put yourself in their place and maybe it will be easier to understand.

- If you find that you don't like someone's behavior, it is better to say nothing rather than something negative.

Apologizing

When you have done something that hurts another person's feelings or results in negative consequences for another person, you should:

1. Look at the person. It shows confidence.

2. Say what you are sorry about. "I'm sorry I said that" or "I'm sorry, I didn't listen to what you said."

3. Make a follow-up statement if the person says something to you. "Is there any way I can make it up to you?" or "It won't happen again."

4. Thank the person for listening. (Even if the person did not accept your apology!)

Reason:

It is important to apologize because it shows that you are sensitive to the feelings of others. It increases the chances that other people will be sensitive to your feelings in return. Apologizing also shows that you are responsible enough to admit to making a mistake.

Helpful Hints:

- It is easy to avoid making apologies; it takes guts to be mature enough to do it. Convince yourself that making an apology is the best thing to do and then do it!

- If the other person is upset with you, the response you receive may not be very pleasant at that time. Be prepared to take whatever the other person says. Be confident that you are doing the right thing.

- When people look back on your apology, they will think that you were able to realize what you had done wrong. They will think more positively of you in the future.

- An apology won't erase what you did wrong. But it may help change a person's opinion of you in the long run.

Conversation Skills

When you are talking with other people, you should:

1. Look at the other person.

2. Answer any questions asked of you, and give complete answers. Just saying "Yes" or "No" does not give the other person any information that can keep the conversation going.

3. Avoid negative statements. Talking about past trouble you were in, bragging, name-calling, cussing, or making other negative statements gives a bad impression.

4. Use appropriate grammar. Slang can be used with friends, but don't use it when guests are present.

5. Start or add to conversation by asking questions, talking about new or exciting events, or asking the other person what he or she thinks about something.

Reason:

It is important to have good conversation skills because you can tell others what you think about something and find out how they feel. Good conversation skills make guests feel more comfortable and make visits with you more enjoyable. Conversation skills also help you when you apply for a job or meet new people.

Helpful Hints:

- Always include the other person's ideas in the conversation. If you don't, it won't be a conversation!

- Smile and show interest in what the other person has to say, even if you don't agree.

- Keep up on current events so that you have a wide range of things to talk about. People who can talk about what's happening and are good at conversation usually are well-liked and admired by other people.

Giving Compliments

When you want to say something nice about someone, you should:

1. Look at the other person.

2. Give the compliment. Tell him or her exactly what you liked.

3. Make a follow-up statement. If the person says "Thanks," say "You're welcome" in return.

Reason:

Giving compliments to others shows that you notice the accomplishments of someone else. It shows friendliness; people like being around someone who is pleasant and can say nice things. It also shows that you have confidence in your ability to talk to others.

Helpful Hints:

- Think of the exact words you want to use before you give the compliment. It will make you feel more confident and less likely to fumble around for words.

- Mean what you say. People can tell the difference between real and phony.

- Don't overdo it. A couple of sentences will do. "You did a good job at..." or "You really did well in...."

- It is nice to smile and be enthusiastic when you give compliments. It makes the other person feel that you really mean it.

Accepting Compliments

Whenever someone says something nice to you, you should:

1. Look at the other person.

2. Listen to what the other person is saying.

3. Don't interrupt.

4. Say "Thanks," or something that shows you appreciate what was said.

Reason:

Being able to accept compliments shows that you can politely receive another person's opinion about something you have done. It also increases the chance that you will receive future compliments.

Helpful Hints:

- Many times it is easy to feel uncomfortable when you receive a compliment. For example, someone could give you a compliment on a sweater you are wearing, and you might say, "You mean this old rag?" Statements like that make it less likely that the other person will give you compliments in the future. Don't reject what the other person is saying.

- People give compliments for a variety of reasons. Don't waste a lot of time wondering why someone gave you a compliment. Just appreciate the fact that someone took the time to say something nice to you!

Listening to Others

When others are speaking, you should:

1. Look at the person who is talking.

2. Sit or stand quietly.

3. Wait until the person is through talking. Don't interrupt, it will seem like you are complaining.

4. Show that you understand. Say "Okay," "Thanks," "I see," etc., or ask the person to explain if you don't understand.

Reason:

It is important to listen because it shows pleasantness and cooperation. It increases the chances that people will listen to you. And, it increases the chances that you will do the correct thing since you understand.

Helpful Hints:

- If you are having trouble listening, think of how you would feel if other people didn't listen to you.

- Try to remember everything the person said. Write it down if you think you might forget.

- People who listen well do better on jobs and tasks, and in school.

- Don't show any negative facial expressions. Continue looking at the other person, and nod your head or occasionally say something to let the other person know you are still listening.

Telling the Truth

When you have done something, whether it's good or bad, you need to tell the truth. Telling the truth makes other people trust you. If they can believe what you say, you will be trusted in more situations. Sometimes, a person will ask you questions about your involvement in a situation. To tell the truth you should:

1. Look at the person.

2. Say exactly what happened if asked to supply information.

3. Answer any other questions. This can include what you did or did not do, or what someone else did or did not do.

4. Don't leave out important facts.

5. Admit to mistakes or errors if you made them.

Reason:

It is important to tell the truth because people are more likely to give you a second chance if they have been able to trust you in the past. We all make mistakes, but trying to avoid telling the truth will lead to more problems. If you get a reputation as a liar, it will be hard for people to believe what you say. Plus, when you tell the truth, you should feel confident that you have done the right thing.

Helpful Hints:

- Telling the truth is hard. Many times, it will seem that lying is the easiest way out of a situation. But when people find out that you have lied, the consequences are much worse.

- Lying is the opposite of telling the truth. Lying is similar to stealing or cheating; all will result in negative consequences for you.

Introducing Yourself

When you introduce yourself to others, you should:

1. **Stand up straight**. If you were sitting down or doing something else, stop immediately and greet the person.

2. **Look at the other person.**

3. **Offer your hand and shake hands firmly.** (Don't wait!)

4. **As you are shaking hands, say your name clearly and loudly enough to be heard easily**. This shows the other person that you are confident.

5. **Make a friendly statement**. "Nice to meet you."

Reason:

It is important to introduce yourself because it shows your ability to meet new people confidently. It makes others feel more comfortable and you make a good first impression. Being able to introduce yourself will be helpful on job interviews and is a pleasant way to "break the ice."

Helpful Hints:

- Being pleasant is very important when introducing yourself. If you are gruff or your voice is harsh, people won't get a good impression of you. Smile when giving your name to the other person.

- Introductions are the first step in conversation. If you start out on the right foot, it is more likely that you will have a pleasant conversation. Make your first impression a good impression.

- If the other person does not give his or her name, say "And your name is?"

- After you have met a person once, you will have to choose how to reintroduce yourself. If there is a long time in between, or if the person has forgotten who you are, then you should follow the same steps as above. If the time in between is short, you may choose just to say, "Hi, in case you forgot, I'm _____."

- Try to remember the other person's name. Other people will be impressed when you take enough time to remember them.

Setting Appropriate Personal Boundaries

Note: This skill is presented in a different way because it includes information for Treatment Parents rather than just steps to a social skill.

Children show inappropriate boundaries with others by hugging people without permission, making sexual comments that embarrass or harass other people, not respecting the privacy of others, or initiating sexual contact with children or animals. If a child demonstrates difficulty respecting the personal boundaries of others, Treatment Parents should teach the following:

1. **Apologizing**. It is important for children to apologize when they have offended another person. This helps the child re-establish relationships by showing sensitivity to others' feelings.

2. **Asking Permission**. Learning this skill will help children learn how to appropriately negotiate personal boundaries with others. For example, the Treatment Parents can help the child practice knocking on a closed door and asking permission to enter. The child also could practice asking a person for a hug, rather than touching others without their permission.

3. **Reporting Whereabouts**. The child should be rewarded for checking in with adults when asked to do so. This helps ensure that the child is engaged in appropriate behaviors and is taking responsibility for being where he or she should be.

4. **Keeping Hands and Feet to Self**. This skill ensures that children are not violating others' boundaries by touching them in an inappropriate manner.

5. **Following House Rules**. Each Treatment Family should have basic house rules posted so that new children can easily find them. (See Chapter 23 for more information.) This helps children remember the basic rules for respecting the personal boundaries of others. Treatment Parents are encouraged to add or modify rules as they learn what is needed in their home.

6. **Talking About Feelings**. It is very important for children to learn how to describe their feelings and share them with adults. Many children who enter Treatment Foster Family Services do not know how to describe their feelings. When they learn to do this, they are less likely to act out feelings (need for affection, attention, or friendship) and they are more able to talk about them.

7. **Sex Education**. Most children who have been sexually abused have not received appropriate sex education. They know what has happened to them, but they may be very confused about how their bodies actually work. It is important for them to have accurate information so they can take better care of their bodies or ask for help when they aren't feeling well. If Treatment Parents teach sex education, it should be in the child's Treatment Plan and the child's legal guardian should be aware of it.

Helpful Hints:

- Monitoring is extremely important. All the teaching in the world cannot replace the Treatment Parents' job of closely monitoring the foster child. Children do not learn the complex skill of "Setting Appropriate Personal Boundaries" overnight, so Treatment Parents should not assume that role-playing skills will immediately enable the child to engage in new behaviors. Some children do not consistently use these skills for months or years. In the meantime, it is the Treatment Parents' responsibility to monitor all children to ensure their safety in the home. Monitoring will be more effective if it is done on an unpredictable schedule.

- Encourage age-appropriate play activities. Some children who have been sexually abused have been encouraged to fulfill the social and sexual expectations of adults. It is very important that children have opportunities to "learn to play" rather than having to worry about engaging in adult activities and roles. Many children can gradually reduce behaviors that have sexual themes as they become more interested in age-appropriate play.

- Be a good role model. Treatment Parents can more effectively teach children appropriate boundaries when they model them in their own lives.

Appendix E

POSITIVE CONSEQUENCES
THAT COST NO MONEY

Stay up late

Stay out late (supervised)

Have a friend over

Pick the TV program

Extra TV (or video game) time

One less chore

Pick a movie (Treatment Parents must approve)

Mom or Dad read a story at night

Stay up late reading

Permission for a special event

Dinner in the family room

Extra time on the computer

Extra phone time

Plan the menu

Messy room for a day

Leave the radio on at night

Go over to a friend's house

Sit at the head of the table

Pick an outing

Shorter study period

Decide where to go for dinner

Trip to the library, zoo, pet store, park, etc.

Play game with Mom or Dad

Special snacks

Sleep in late

Pick the breakfast cereal

Bike ride or fishing trip with Treatment Parents

Indoor picnic

Appendix F

TIME-IN AND TIME-OUT WITH FOSTER CHILDREN

What is time-in?

Time-in is the positive time you spend with your foster child. In order for time-out to be effective, you must first have time-in. You can establish this relationship in many different ways, but the best way to start is by using Effective Praise. (See Chapter 12 for more details.) When you maintain a high level of praise and positive interactions with your foster child, it helps to make time-out more effective. Your foster child will find it reinforcing to be around you and will miss those interactions.

What is time-out?

Time-out is a way of disciplining your foster child for misbehavior without raising your hand or your voice. Time-out involves removing your foster child from the good things in life, for a small amount of time, immediately after a misbehavior. Time-out for children is similar to penalties used for hockey players. When a hockey player has misbehaved on the ice, he is required to go into the penalty area for two minutes. The referee does not scream at, threaten, or hit the player. He merely blows the whistle and points to the penalty area. During the penalty time, the player is not allowed to play, only watch. Time-out bothers hockey players because they would rather play hockey than watch. Time-out can be effective for foster children because they would rather be doing something fun than sitting quietly alone.

When should I use time-out?

Your Consultant will work with you to decide when to use time-out. In general, time-out is used for aggressive behavior, and for repeatedly not following instructions. It's important that you do not use time-out for every problem behavior. For minor behaviors, the child should earn a consequence, such as loss of a privilege. For more serious behaviors, you may use time-out.

You may use time-out as a consequence in the Corrective Teaching sequence. Immediately following a problem behavior, tell your foster child what he or she did and send the child to time-out. For example, you might say, "Hitting is not okay. Go to time-out." Say this calmly and only once. Do not reason with or give long explanations to your foster child. Remember, you will teach to the behavior in a little while, but first you want to give your foster child a chance to calm down. In rare instances, your foster child may refuse to go to time-out, or may be too upset to do so (e.g. laying on the floor kicking and screaming). Before you physically assist her, be sure to discuss the situation with your Consultant.

Where should the time-out area be?

Again, this will be decided by you and your Consultant. If possible, it's best to use the same place every time. It might be a chair in the kitchen, a step, or the couch. Make sure the area is well-lit and free from any dangerous objects. Also, make sure your foster child cannot watch TV or play with toys during time-out. The main purpose of time-out is for your foster child to be alone and quiet with no outside reinforcement.

How long should time-out last?

The upper limit should be one quiet minute for every year of your foster child's age. The amount of time your foster child spends in time-out will depend not only on the child's age, but also on his or her developmental level. Frequently, children in treatment foster care are not at the same developmental level as other children their age. With this in mind, it may not be appropriate for a seven-year-old child to be in time-out for a full seven minutes. This may be too long for him. Your Consultant will help decide how long your foster child's time-out should be. Initially, the child may only be in time-out for a few minutes with the goal of working up to the full seven minutes.

Keep in mind that children do not like time-out, and they can be very public with their opinions. So, although your goal may be to get a child to sit quietly for three minutes, it may take some time to achieve this goal. This is especially true in the beginning when children don't know the rules and still can't believe you are doing this to them. For some reason, the calmer you remain, the more upset they are likely to become. This is all part of the process. Discipline works best when administered calmly.

So, do not begin the time-out until your foster child is calm and quiet. If your foster son is crying, throwing a tantrum, swearing, or doing any of the other wonderful behaviors kids do, it doesn't count toward the required time. If you start the time-out because he is quiet but he starts to cry or tantrum, wait until he is quiet and start the time over again. Do not let him out of time-out until he has calmed down. The child must remain seated and quiet to get out of time-out.

What counts as quiet time?

Generally, quiet time occurs when your foster child is not angry or mad. You must decide when your foster child is calm and quiet. Some children get perfectly still and quiet while in time-out. Other children find it hard to sit still and not talk. Fidgeting and "happy talk" should usually count as calm and quiet. If, for example, your foster daughter sings or talks softly to herself, that counts as quiet time. If she is arguing or talking back, that does not count as quiet time.

What if your foster child leaves the time-out area before time is up?

Prior to using time-out with your foster child, you and your Consultant will have developed a plan for what to do when this happens. Calmly tell the child to go back to the time-out chair. If he doesn't respond, let him know what the consequence will be. For example, he may lose one or all of his privileges until he completes his time-out. Provide him with a short reason why it's important to finish his time-out; for example, "The quicker you finish time-out, the quicker you'll be able to do what you want to do."

What if my foster child misbehaves during time-out?

Say nothing and ignore everything that is not dangerous to the child, to yourself, or to the furniture. Most negative behavior during time-out is an attempt to get you to react and say something, anything. So expect the unexpected. Your foster child may whine, cry, complain, throw things, or make a big mess. He may make many unkind comments about you, your spouse, or your children. These types of comments are frustrating and may be hard to ignore. But remember, he is saying them to get a reaction out of you. Remaining calm and not responding is the best way to handle it. Don't worry. He will like you again when his time is up.

What do I do when time is up?

When the time-out period is over, ask your foster child, "Are you ready to get up?" Your foster child must answer "Yes" in some way (or nod yes) before he or she may get up. Go back and finish Corrective Teaching. Tell the child what you want him or her to do, and practice.

What do I do when my foster child is out of time-out?

When the time-out is over, be sure to take the opportunity to praise good behavior. Now is the time to reward your foster children for the kinds of behaviors you want them to have. So "catch 'em being good!"

Should I explain the rules of time-out to my foster child?

Before using time-out, explain the rules to your foster child through Preventive Teaching. At a time when your foster child is not misbehaving, explain what time-out is, which problem behaviors time-out will be used for, and how long time-out will last. Practice time-outs with your foster child before using the procedure. While practicing, remind him or her that you are "pretending" this time. The child probably still will have difficulty when you do your first real time-outs but you'll be reassured that you've done your part to explain the process.

Summary

1. Choose a time-out area.
2. Explain time-out.
3. Use time-out every time the problem behavior occurs.
4. Be specific and brief when you explain why your foster child must go to time-out.
5. Do not talk to or look at your foster child during time-out.
6. If your foster child gets up from the time-out before the time is up, do some teaching and provide reasons.
7. Your foster child must be calm and quiet to get up from time-out.
8. Your child must politely answer "Yes" when you ask, "Would you like to get up?"
9. If you wanted your foster child to follow an instruction, give him or her another chance after time-out is over.
10. Catch 'em being good.

GLOSSARY

Active Listening   Verbally reflecting back the feelings that have been expressed through the actions and words of another person. Examples are, "You have tears in your eyes" or "If I understand what you just said, you are feeling very frustrated right now." **(Chapter 20)**

Antecedents   The events or conditions observed in the environment before a behavior occurs. For example, asking for a snack would be the antecedent to opening a bag of cookies. Antecedents help determine whether a behavior is appropriate or inappropriate and what skill to teach. **(Chapter 7)**

Applied Consequences   Consequences that are deliberately arranged and given in response to behavior. In the Boys Town program, applied consequences take the form of "tokens" (for example, stars, stickers, poker chips, or points) that children earn for appropriate (positive) behavior and lose for inappropriate (negative) behavior. **(Chapter 17)**

Appropriate Teaching   Teaching that provides a specific, consistent, concrete, positive, interactive, and informative approach to changing problem behavior. Appropriate Teaching helps build self-esteem, teaches foster children to get along well with others, and gives them the skills to make their own decisions. **(Chapter 5)**

Assessment System   The time immediately following placement of a foster child in a Treatment Home when Treatment Parents observe the foster child's behavior in detail in order to obtain an initial overview of the child's social and behavior skills. Only natural and logical consequences are used during this time. **(Chapter 18)**

Attachment   An affectionate bond between two individuals that endures through space and time and serves to join them emotionally (Klaus & Kennell, 1976). **(Chapter 22)**

Behavior   Anything a person does that can be observed and measured. **(Chapter 6)**

Bribery   Giving a reward for inappropriate behavior. Giving a foster child a candy bar to stop him from crying in the grocery story checkout lane is an example of a bribe. **(Chapter 10)**

Certifications   The evaluation process that determines whether Treatment Parents are providing appropriate treatment to the child in their home and are professionally working with the treatment team. Treatment Parent evaluations consist of a six-month review, twelve-month certification, then annual certification evaluations. **(Chapters 1, 2)**

Child Protective Services   (also referred to as CPS) A state-funded agency whose primary function is to help children who may be physically or sexually abused, or neglected. The agency coordinates its services with law enforcement, county attorneys, and community agencies. In some states, workers may assist with investigating claims of abuse and neglect. Families may voluntarily agree to accept Child Protective Services assistance or they may be ordered by the court to accept these services. **(Chapter 2)**

Child Rights Rights that are dictated by law and/or policy regardless of the child's behavior. Examples of Child Rights are three good meals a day, the right to sleep in one's own bed, the right to treatment, the right to respect, etc. **(Chapter 2)**

Child Rights Violation Inquiries (also known as Fact-Finding Inquiries) Investigations into suspected inappropriate practices reported by a foster child or another consumer, or observed by program staff or another Treatment Parent. All claims against the Treatment Parent are investigated regardless of their perceived validity or seriousness. **(Chapter 2)**

Child Sexual Abuse Any form of touching, kissing, fondling, touching of the genitals of either the victim or the perpetrator, or anal/genital intercourse between an adult and a child, (or between an older child and one who is at least three years younger) in which the child victim is being used for the sexual stimulation and/or gratification of the older person (Finklehor, 1979). (See also Incest.) **(Chapter 24)**

Clinical Psychologist An individual who has completed a four-year undergraduate degree program, four to five years of graduate training in clinical psychology, and a one-year internship. Psychologists perform a variety of activities, including psychotherapy, psychological assessment, and teaching. A clinical psychologist cannot prescribe medication. **(Chapter 3)**

Closed-Ended Question A question that prompts a simple, short answer. An example would be a question that can be answered with a "Yes" or "No" response. **(Chapter 20)**

Consequence An event or object that follows a behavior and affects whether the behavior will increase or decrease in frequency in the future. For example, a paycheck is a consequence of going to work; a stomachache is the consequence of eating too much. **(Chapters 2, 7, 9)**

Consultant A Treatment Parent's immediate supervisor. The Consultant works closely with the Treatment Parents and other professionals, writes the foster child's Treatment Plan with input from the Treatment Parents, and helps to monitor the child's progress. The Consultant is on call 24 hours a day, seven days a week. In other agencies, this person may be referred to as the caseworker. **(Chapter 1)**

Consultation Meetings Meetings between the Consultant and Treatment Parents that are held every week at first. The frequency of the meetings may be decreased over time, with a minimum of a meeting every other week. **(Chapters 1, 2)**

Consumers Interested persons from outside the treatment foster care program who are members of the child's treatment team. Teachers, caseworkers, probation officers, and family members are examples of consumers. Consumers are asked to give their written opinion at least once a year about the care and treatment the foster child is receiving. **(Chapter 2)**

Contingency Commonly called "Grandma's rule," because grandmothers used it long before it ever showed up in a book. It means that one activity (a privilege your child likes) is available to your child after he or she finishes an activity that you want done. For example, "You can watch TV after you have finished your homework." **(Chapter 9)**

Coordinator   The person responsible for overseeing Treatment Foster Family Services at that particular site. Responsibilities include supervising the Consultants, working closely with agencies that refer children to treatment foster care, Treatment Parent recruitment, monitoring the budget, and all other aspects of the program to make sure it runs smoothly. In other agencies, this person may be referred to as a unit manager or supervisor. **(Chapter 1)**

Corporal Punishment   Physical punishment of the foster child. Examples include hitting, punching, pushing, or physically harming a child. Corporal punishment is never allowed in Treatment Foster Family Services, and is a Child Rights violation. **(Chapter 2)**

Corrective Teaching   A five-step teaching process that combines clear messages with consequences and practice to help Treatment Parents change a child's problem behavior. The steps include: Stop the problem behavior; Give a consequence; Describe what you want/label the skill; Give a reason; and Practice what you want. **(Chapters 11, 15)**

Crisis Situations   An unstable or crucial time when unpredictable or rapid change can occur. Examples include suicide threats or gestures, serious illness, or a lost child. **(Chapter 1)**

Daily Medication Log   Documentation of the foster child's medically prescribed medications or diets and when they are to be given to the child. **(Appendix C)**

Documentation   Writing down and keeping a record of events in a professional manner. Treatment Parents document phone calls, crisis events, or significant child misbehaviors to help the Consultant evaluate what happened and what should be done to help the child and Treatment Parents. **(Chapter 3)**

Effective Praise   A teaching technique for praising a child for a positive behavior. The steps of Effective Praise are: Show your approval by smiling, or giving the child a pat on the back or a brief praise statement; Describe what the child did that you liked by giving a clear, specific description of the behavior; and Give a reason by telling how the behavior helps the child, or why that behavior is appreciated by others. **(Chapters 2, 12)**

Empathy Statements   Words and phrases that show an understanding of what another person might be feeling. For example, "You must be feeling very disappointed right now." **(Chapter 15)**

Feedback   Information about the effects of one's behavior on other people and on the environment. Feedback can be positive, such as, "You look very nice today." Or it can be given to correct a problem, such as, "Next time you give him an instruction, it would helpful to smile and speak more slowly." **(Chapter 3)**

Five-Second Rule   A rule that requires other children to clear an area when a child is becoming uncooperative. Other children who are present have five seconds to leave the area and go to a pre-arranged area. This protects them from aggressive behaviors of the uncooperative child. It also helps reduce distractions and eliminates an "audience." **(Chapter 16)**

Give a Reason   A step in Effective Praise where the Treatment Parent explains to the foster child how his or her own behavior helps him or her, or why the foster child's behavior is appreciated by others. This also is a step in Corrective Teaching where the Treatment Parent explains why a new skill or appropriate behavior should be used in place of an inappropriate behavior. **(Chapter 12)**

Grooming Process   A term used to describe how an abuser sets the stage for sexual abuse to occur. Very often, abusers do not need to resort to violence to gain sexual contact with a child. In most cases of sexual abuse of children, coercion or tricking is the main way the abuser convinces the child to allow a sexual relationship to develop. The abuser starts by encouraging the child to trust him or her. This is done by giving the child presents of candy, food, money and clothing, or by spending time with the child and assuring the child of the "rightness" of what they are doing (Christiansen & Blake, 1990). **(Chapter 24)**

High Tolerance Level   Having a high threshold for inappropriate behavior, meaning consequences are not given to the foster child unless behavior occurs repeatedly or is severe. An example would be allowing a child to repeatedly hit the dog before finally giving a consequence. (See also Low Tolerance Level.) **(Chapter 9)**

House Rules   Rules family members use to ensure each other's privacy and safety, settle disputes, and describe individual roles. An example would be knocking before opening a closed door. **(Chapters 13, 24)**

Inappropriate Punishment   Punishment that is harsh, unreasonable, violent, or harmful. Examples include yelling, belittling, ridiculing, or isolating the foster child. **(Chapter 5)**

Incest   A form of child sexual abuse in which the perpetrator or abuser is a relative who involves a family member in sexual activity that meets the definition of child sexual abuse. The abuser might be a parent, stepparent, grandparent, older brother or sister, or an uncle or aunt. (See also Child Sexual Abuse.) **(Chapter 24)**

Individualized Treatment   Refers to the fact that each foster child has his or her own Treatment Plan to meet his or her needs. Treatment Plans describe the target areas in which the child will receive teaching and education, as well as the necessary psychological or medical services required to meet the foster child's needs. **(Chapters 1, 2)**

In-Home Training   Training for the Treatment Parents that is provided by the Consultant. This includes reviewing skills learned in Preservice Training, developing skills that are needed in order to work with the foster child, and providing new information to keep the Treatment Parents up to date. **(Chapter 3)**

Inservice Training   Training that is held monthly or bimonthly for Treatment Parents to address their needs. Such training is required by Boys Town, and also may be necessary to meet state requirements for continuing education. **(Chapter 2)**

Less-Restrictive Environment A setting in which fewer restrictions are placed on a child's actions than in the child's previous placement or residence. For example, if a child had been in a locked hospital ward, a less-restrictive environment would include foster care, the child's own home, or a group emergency shelter. **(Chapter 1)**

Life Book A book with photographs and other momentos that tell the story of the foster child's life. It is similar to the types of family albums that many families own. Life Books have a story printed in them which describes the pictures, explains why children experienced certain family changes, the reasons they were placed outside of their home, who they lived with, where they went to school, and who their caseworkers were. **(Chapter 23)**

Low Tolerance Level Having a low threshold for inappropriate behavior, meaning that consequences are given as soon as a behavior begins and before it becomes severe. An example would be giving a foster child a consequence the first time he hits the dog. (See also High Tolerance Level.) **(Chapter 9)**

More-Restrictive Environment A setting in which more restrictions are placed on a child's actions than in the child's previous placement or residence. For example, if a child lived at home, more-restrictive environments would include jail or detention facilities, psychiatric wards, residential treatment centers, or group emergency shelters. **(Chapter 2)**

Morning Event Reports Incidents that typically are reported to Consultants by Treatment Parents on a daily basis. Treatment Parents report individual events or a series of related events that involved a child or Treatment Parent during the previous 24 hours. Examples include significant positive or negative child behavior, family or agency contact, or participation in mental health services. **(Chapter 16, Appendix C)**

Motivation System A system designed to reinforce positive/appropriate behavior with a meaningful reward. An example is a Treatment Parent giving a foster child a candy bar for cooperating instead of whining or crying when he is told "No" to other things. **(Chapter 3, 17)**

Natural Consequences Consequences that are not given but instead occur naturally as the typical or expected results of behavior. For example, the natural consequence of not getting up on time is being late to school or work. **(Chapter 17)**

Negative Consequences Consequences that people don't like and want to avoid. Negative consequences encourage people to change their actions so that they won't receive more negative consequences. Behavior that is followed by a negative consequence is less likely to occur again (or will not occur as frequently). For example, losing a sweet snack is the negative consequence for refusing to help clean the kitchen. (See also Punishment, Response Cost.) **(Chapter 11)**

Negative Reinforcement The removal of something negative, which increases appropriate behavior. An example is when a Treatment Parent "nags" the foster child about doing the dishes until the child follows instructions and does the dishes. Taking away the nagging is the child's reward for doing the dishes. **(Chapter 17)**

Ongoing Behavior   Any behavior occurring during teaching that interferes with the teaching. An example of ongoing behavior is a child who refuses to stop talking, sit down, or look at you when you are giving her instructions. **(Chapters 2, 16)**

Open-Ended Questions   A question that requires more than just a one-word or simple answer, and that encourages a person to share information. For example, "Tell me about the argument you had at school with your classmate." **(Chapter 20)**

Passive Listening   Listening to another person or child without speaking, but behaving in such a way that the speaker knows the listener is paying attention. Examples of attentive behaviors include nodding one's head, smiling, or saying "Yes" or "Uh-huh" while the other person is speaking. **(Chapter 20)**

Passive Restraint   Using the least possible force to prevent a foster child from harming himself or herself, or others. Treatment Parents should use passive restraint **ONLY** after receiving training and permission to do so from the Consultant. **(Chapter 2)**

Permanency Plan   A written plan that describes what an agency or court believes is the best plan for finding a permanent home for a child. **(Chapter 23)**

Placement Meeting   A meeting of the entire treatment team that occurs after the Treatment Family and the foster child have decided that they want to live together and before the child actually moves in with the Treatment Parents. Meeting for the first time, the treatment team discusses the child's needs and how those needs can be met. **(Chapter 23)**

Positive Consequences   (also known as Reinforcers or Rewards) Consequences that people like and are willing to work to get. For example, reading an extra bedtime story would be a positive consequence for a child who gets ready for bed on time. Behavior that is followed by a positive consequence is more likely to occur again. **(Chapter 10)**

Positive Correction   Giving a foster child an opportunity to earn back some consequences by practicing the appropriate behavior. An example is taking away one hour of TV time because your two foster children were arguing. After you finish, both of the children apologize and say they will work together to do the dishes. If they cooperate, you could give back 15 to 20 minutes of the TV time you took away. **(Chapter 15)**

Positive Reinforcement   The application of something positive, which increases appropriate behavior. For example, a foster child earns a cookie or Effective Praise for making her bed; the child then makes her bed the next day. **(Chapter 17)**

Preplacement Process   The entire process of selecting and matching a foster child with Treatment Parents. **(Chapter 23)**

Preplacement Visits   Visits between the foster child and the Treatment Family to help everyone decide if the family and child are right for each other. **(Chapter 23)**

Preservice Training   Training provided to Treatment Parents before a child is placed in their home. This training includes instruction in the use of the Boys Town Family Home Model of changing children's behavior, Policies and Procedures, Creating a Safe Environment, Being Sensitive to Cultural Differences, etc. **(Chapters 1, 2, 3)**

Preventive Prompt   A Treatment Parent's comment that helps the foster child remember important skills to use. A preventive prompt usually is given just before a child needs to use a skill. For example, a Treatment Parent might give this prompt to a child who is about to enter a juvenile courtroom: "Remember when you meet the judge, to look her in the eye and say 'Hello.'" **(Chapter 13)**

Preventive Teaching   Teaching the foster child what he or she will need to know for a future situation and practicing it in advance. The steps include: Describe what you would like (before the child can do what you want, he or she must know what it is that you expect); Give a reason (children benefit from knowing why they should act a certain way); and Practice (knowing what to do and how to do it are two different things; any new skill needs to be practiced). **(Chapter 13)**

Privilege   A special activity, object, or favor granted to the foster child. Privileges may include extra TV time, sweet snacks, later bedtimes, etc. **(Chapters 2, 11, 17)**

Professionalism   The ability to perform in an occupation that requires a high level of training and proficiency. Professionals also agree to abide by ethical and technical standards. **(Chapter 3)**

Psychiatrist   An individual who has completed a four-year undergraduate degree program, four years of medical school training, a one-year internship, and three years of residency in psychiatry. Psychiatrists are more likely to be involved with treating hospitalized patients, and can prescribe medication. **(Chapter 3)**

Punishment   (a type of Negative Consequence) Applying something negative following a behavior in order to discourage that behavior from happening in the future. Punishment can be physical (spanking) or meaningless extra work (scrubbing the floor with a toothbrush). In Boys Town Treatment Foster Family Services, overcorrection, spanking, and other forms of physical punishment are **not** allowed. **(Chapters 5, 17)**

Reimbursement   Monthly payment to the Treatment Parents that covers the cost of providing for a child's basic care and special needs. **(Appendix C)**

Reinforcer   (also known as a Positive Consequence or Reward) Any event or object that follows a behavior and increases the probability that the behavior will occur in the future. For example, a good report card is a reinforcer for doing homework. **(Chapter 10)**

Respite   Temporary relief from the emotional and physical demands of being a Treatment Parent; the foster child stays in an approved respite provider's home during this time. **(Chapter 3)**

Response Cost (a type of Negative Consequence) Removing a privilege following a behavior, which decreases the probability that the behavior will occur in the future. For example, not allowing a child to ride his bike for two days can be a response cost for riding the bike too far from home. **(Chapter 17)**

Reunification The foster child returning to live with his or her own family after placement outside the home is completed. **(Chapter 21)**

Reward (also known as a Positive Consequence or Reinforcer) A type of consequence that is given after a behavior in order to increase the frequency of that behavior in the future. **(Chapter 9, 10)**

Role Model An individual whose behavior is closely watched and used as an example of appropriate behavior. Treatment Parents must be good role models for foster children. **(Chapter 3)**

Role-Plays Practicing a new skill by acting out a situation. For example, "Sara, let's practice the steps of "Accepting 'No' Answers." **(Chapter 13)**

Safe Environment An environment that is free of abuse and one in which the foster child can grow spiritually, emotionally, intellectually, and physically. Also, a safe environment respects the rights of foster children and uses the most positive, least-restrictive practices in caring for children. **(Chapter 2)**

School Note A clear, easy-to-use method that allows each foster child's teacher to provide regular feedback on social and academic behavior. A variety of school notes can be used to give a child feedback on behavior and inform the Treatment Parents of the child's progress. **(Chapter 17)**

Separation The foster child being apart from his or her primary caregivers (e.g. own family, relatives, former foster parents, etc.) with whom an attachment has been established. **(Chapter 22)**

Shaping Praising or reinforcing attempts or approximations by the foster child to use a new skill that is being taught. For example, if a foster child is not used to making her bed, you would enthusiastically praise her for pulling the covers up the bed. **(Chapter 10)**

Site Director The person responsible for making sure that all Boys Town programs (e.g. Treatment Foster Family Services, Emergency Shelter Services, Common Sense Parenting, etc.) in the same city are running smoothly and working together to help children and families. In other agencies, this person may be referred to as the agency director. **(Chapter 1)**

Social Worker An individual who has completed a four-year undergraduate degree program in the social sciences, plus one to two years in graduate training in social work. A social worker may conduct psychotherapy, and/or may work with individuals who need help getting services. **(Chapter 3)**

SODAS A five-step problem-solving method for foster children that uses the following steps: Situation, Options, Disadvantages, Advantages, and Solution. **(Chapter 19)**

Target Areas (also known as Target Behaviors or Behavioral Goals) Skills listed in the Treatment Plan that a foster child needs to learn or improve on with the help of the Treatment Parents and Consultant. These skills can include "following instructions," "accepting criticism," "improving self-esteem," "appropriately expressing feelings," etc. **(Chapter 1, 23)**

Testing Limits (also known as Limit-Testing) When children engage in inappropriate behavior to determine how much of that behavior the Treatment Parents will allow. **(Chapter 15)**

Time-In The positive time Treatment Parents spend with their foster children. In order for time-out to be effective, you must first have time-in. When you maintain a high level of praise and positive interactions with your foster child, it helps to make time-out more effective since the foster child will miss the positive interactions. **(Appendix F)**

Time-Out A way of disciplining young children without raising your hand or your voice. Time-out involves removing the child from "the good things in life," for a small amount of time, immediately after a misbehavior. **(Chapter 2 and Appendix F)**

Token Economy A Motivation System in which applied consequences take the form of tokens (e.g. stars, stickers, poker chips, or points) that foster children earn for appropriate (positive) behavior and lose for inappropriate (negative) behavior. As an applied consequence, tokens are effective only because they can be exchanged for a wide variety of privileges such as snacks, TV time, free time, allowance, etc. **(Chapter 17)**

Tolerances The amount of inappropriate behavior that a Treatment Parent will allow before doing Corrective Teaching or giving a consequence. (See also High Tolerance Level, Low Tolerance Level.) **(Chapter 9)**

Treatment Providing appropriate medical, psychological, social, educational, and spiritual care to the foster child. **(Chapter 1)**

Treatment Foster Family Services (also known as TFFS) The Boys Town program that serves children who require specialized services due to emotional disturbances, delinquent behavior, abuse, or neglect. These children cannot be cared for by their families, but can be safely cared for by specially trained and supported Treatment Families. Such children are at "high risk" to sent to more-restrictive settings due to their needs. Other agencies may call this therapeutic foster care, treatment foster care, or specialized foster care. **(Chapter 1)**

Treatment Parent An individual who has received extensive training in the Boys Town Treatment Foster Family Services program and who has a high level of commitment to work with children. A Treatment Parent must be willing to be a good role model, to have appropriate tolerances, and to be open-minded and willing to learn. Other programs may refer to these individuals as professional parents, therapeutic parents, foster parents, etc. **(Chapters 1, 3)**

Treatment Plan (also known as Goals or Strategies) A written description of the treatment strategies and services that will be used with a foster child in order to meet his or her individual needs. Treatment planning is an ongoing process where Consultants and Treatment Parents create or update ways to change a child's behavior or attitudes. The steps to the Treatment Planning process are: Identify the Problem, Target Specific Skills, Develop a Specific Plan, Carry Out the Plan, and Review the Plan. **(Chapter 1, 18)**

Treatment Team In the Boys Town program, a network of people, including the Coordinator, Consultant, Treatment Parents, the child's parents, mental health professionals, school personnel, caseworkers, and other Treatment Foster Family Services staff, working together to help the child reach his or her treatment goals. **(Chapter 1)**

Uncooperative or Defiant Behavior Refusing to follow instructions. Behaviors could include yelling, cursing, destroying property, or refusing to talk. **(Chapter 16)**

Youth Consumer A questionnaire administered to the foster child at least twice a year that asks whether or not he or she has been mistreated by the Treatment Parents or others. Each foster child also is asked to express his or her opinions on the pleasantness and supportiveness of the Treatment Parents and others. **(Chapter 2)**

REFERENCES

Bagley, C., & Ramsey, R. (1986). Sexual abuse in children: Psychological outcomes and implications for social work. **Social Work in Human Sexuality, 4,** 33-48.

Bagley, C., Wood, M., & Young, L. (1994). Victim to abuser: Mental health and behavioral sequels of child sexual abuse in a community survey of young adult males. **Child Abuse and Neglect, 18**(8), 683-697.

Bayless, L., & Love, L. (Eds.) (1990). **Assessing attachment, separation and loss.** Atlanta, GA: Child Welfare Institute.

Bedlington, M.M. (1983). The relationship between staff teaching and measures of youth delinquency and satisfaction: A correlational component analysis (doctoral dissertation, University of Kansas). **Dissertation Abstracts International, 44**, 4B.

Bourguignon, J.P., & Watson, K.W. (1987). **After adoption: A manual for professionals working with adoptive families.** Springfield, IL: Illinois Department of Children and Family Services.

Bowlby, J. (1973). **Attachment and loss, Volume 11. Separation: Anxiety and anger.** New York: Basic Books.

Cartledge, G., & Milburn, J.F. (Eds.) (1980). **Teaching social skills to children.** New York: Pergamon Press.

Chamberlain, P., & Reid, J.B. (1987). Parent observation and report of child symptom. **Behavioral Assessment, 9**, 97-109.

Christiansen, J., & Blake, R. (1990). The grooming process in father-daughter incest. In A.L. Horton, B.L. Johnson, L.M. Roundy, & D. Williams (Eds.), **The incest perpetrator: A family member no one wants to treat** (pp. 88-99). Newbury Park, NJ: Sage Publication.

Collins, L., & Collins, R., (1989). **The SAY book: A manual for helpers.** Boys Town, NE: Boys Town Press.

Combs, M.L., & Slaby, D.A. (1977). Social skills training with children. In B.B. Lahey & A.E. Kazdin (Eds.), **Advances in clinical child psychology** (pp. 161-201). New York: Plenum Press.

Fahlberg, V. (1991). **A child's journey through placement.** Indianapolis, IN: Perspectives Press.

Finkelhor, D. (1979). **Sexually victimized children.** New York: Free Press.

Finkelhor, D. (1984). **Child sexual abuse: New theory and research.** New York: Free Press.

Finkelhor, D. (1986). **A sourcebook on child sexual abuse.** Beverly Hills, CA: Sage Publication, Inc.

Gove, P.B. (Ed.) (1986). **Webster's third international dictionary** (unabridged). Spring-field, MA: Merriam-Webster Inc.

Gresham, F.M. (1981). Assessment of children's social skills. **Journal of School Psychology, 19**(2), 120-133.

James, B., & Nasjleti, M. (1983). **Treating sexually abused children and their families.** Palo Alto, CA: Consulting Psychologists Press, Inc.

Jenkins, S., & Sauber, M. (1966). **Paths to child placement.** New York: The Community Council of Greater New York.

Kadushin, A. (1983). **The social work interview.** New York: Columbia University Press.

Klaus, M.H., & Kennell, J.H. (1976). **Maternal-infant bonding.** St. Louis, MO: C.V. Mosby Company.

Kubler-Ross, E. (1975). **Death: The final stage of growth.** Englewood Cliffs, NJ: Prentice-Hall, Inc.

MacFarlane, K., & Waterman, T. (1986). **Sexual abuse of young children: Evaluation and treatment.** New York: Guilford Press.

Mott, M.A., Authier, K., Shannon, K.K., Arneil, J.M., & Daly, D. (1995). **Treatment foster family services: Development, implementation, and outcome of a national multisite program.** Unpublished manuscript.

Patterson, C.H. (1985). **The therapeutic relationship: Foundations for an eclectic psychotherapy.** Monterey, CA: Brooks/Cole Publishing Company.

Patterson, G.R. (1976). **Living with children: New methods for parents and teachers.** Champaign, IL: Research Press.

Russell, D.E.H. (1986). **The secret trauma: Incest in the lives of girls and women.** New York: Basic Books.

Saccuzzo, D.P., & Kaplan, R.M. (1984). **Clinical psychology.** Boston: Allyn & Bacon.

Sgroi, S.M. (1978). **Sexual assault of children and adolescents.** Lexington, MA: Lexington Books.

Sgroi, S.M. (1982). **Handbook of clinical intervention in child sexual abuse.** Lexington, MA: D.C. Heath.

Steinberg, Z., & Knitzer, J. (1992). Classrooms for emotionally and behaviorally disturbed students: Facing the challenge. **Behavioral Disorders, 17**(2), 145-156.

Stephens, T.M. (1978). **Social skills in the classroom.** Columbus, OH: Ohio State University.

Stovall, B. (1981). **Child sexual abuse.** Ypsilanti, MI: Social Work Department, Eastern Michigan University.

INDEX

V

values, 180
venereal diseases, 169
Violation Inquiries, Child Rights, 19
violence, 167
visitation schedule, 160
visitation, guidelines, 15
vocational choices, 182-183
vocational services, 160
voice tone, 44

W

warnings, 60-61
Waterman, T., 165, 286
Watson, K.W., 150, 285
Weekly Consultation Agenda, 236
Wegner, Father Nicholas, 1
what, 44
when, 44
where, 40
whereabouts, reporting, 259
who, 44
Wood, M., 166, 285
work, adding, 68
work, right not to be given meaningless, 12
wrestling, 174
written documentation, 12-13
    guidelines, 13

Y

Young, L., 166, 285
Youth Consumers, 8